Prima's Official Strategy Guide

Michael Searle

PRIMA GAMES
A DIVISION OF RANDOM HOUSE, INC.

3000 LAVA RIDGE COURT
ROSEVILLE, CA 95661
(916) 787-7000
WWW.PRIMAGAMES.COM

Associate Product Manager: Jill Hinckley
Project Editor: Michelle Trujillo
Editorial Assistant: Matt Sumpter

ISBN: 0-7615-3510-1
Library of Congress Catalog Card Number: 2002114013
Printed in the United States of America

02 03 04 05 BB 10 9 8 7 6 5 4 3 2 1

Contents

chapter 1

Master the Galaxy!

An emperor needs more than new clothes to rule the universe. In *Master of Orion III*, you must broaden your playing skills or you're paste. Gone are the days of building the biggest cannon and blasting your opponent to smithereens. To conquer the galaxy *MOO-style*, you will be called upon to master research, finance, domestic duties, espionage, and diplomacy, as well as the ever-present military.

Who will rule the galaxy? You or one of the 15 other alien powers?

You start with just one planet in a remote corner of the galaxy—but that will all change soon enough.

Imagine the vastness of space, all the unseen worlds floating around shimmering stars, all a space lane away. Like early Earth pioneers, you start with a small group of ships and navigate the frontiers of uncharted space. Colonize the most hospitable worlds and work toward a productive economy . . . if you don't get attacked by other alien powers. Then you need to build your scouts, troop transports, and world-class destroyers to fight back the invaders.

Humans might be the most natural race for you to play; however, you have fifteen other strange and interesting choices. The cyborg-like Cynoid and Meklar run governments with the efficiency of machines. The reptilian Sakkra and Grendarl house the best militaries and will drive the weak into the nearest black hole. The nature-loving Eoladi and Imsaeis live in the swirling atmospheres of gas giants and are expert bioharvesters. In contrast to the mentally superior but physically disabled Psilon, the crystalline Silicoid are the toughest race and actually eat a planet's minerals as food. The Ithkul, bioengineered killer parasites, hate all species and look to enslave everyone as they themselves were once enslaved.

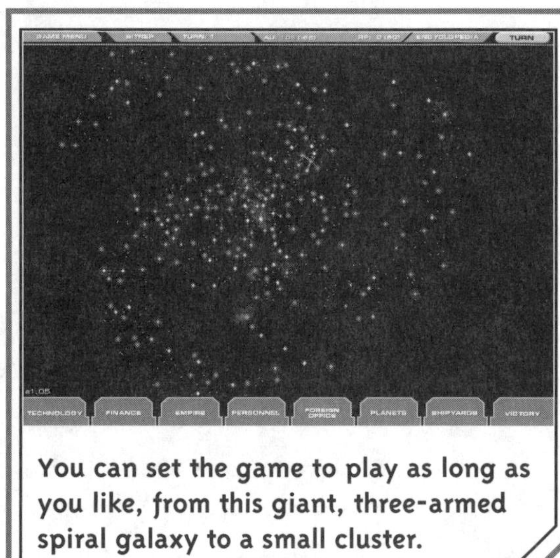
You can set the game to play as long as you like, from this giant, three-armed spiral galaxy to a small cluster.

With its rich history and intense game play, *Master of Orion III* can offer you a million hours of entertainment. Balance military and finances and diplomacy in an intricate strategy game of galactic supremacy. It's the perfect game on those long trips into deep space.

Where To Go

Chapters in this guide follow the game's layout, so you can read up on whatever piques your curiosity or the area in which you need the most help. Start out by reading the Alien Races and Planets sections—these are the building blocks for a successful civilization. The Technology, Finance, Empire Options, Personnel, Foreign Office, Military, and Victory Conditions sections outline the main menus on *MOO*'s galactic map. Master them all and you'll be ready to run for president in our own country.

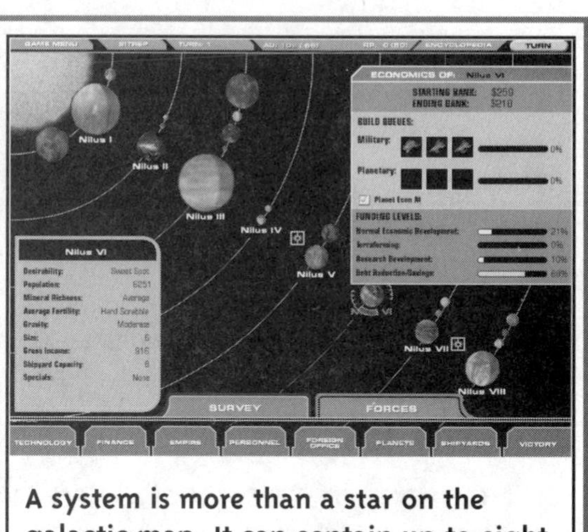

A system is more than a star on the galactic map. It can contain up to eight planets with independent civilizations and special treasures on each.

Once you have the basics under control, flip to the Managing Your Homeworld section. Here you'll get a step-by-step tutorial for the first ten turns of building the most important planet in your empire. The Exploration, Combat, and Dealing with Emergencies sections offer more advanced strategies for expanding and maintaining your empire. The second half of the book details scenarios for winning with each of the game's 16 different races.

So what are you waiting for? Fire up your stardrive engines!

Alien Races

Which Cybernetik race is more proficient at research, the Meklar or the Cynoid? Can humans become the best diplomats in the galaxy? Will your race begin the game as a member of the Orion Senate? The mysteries of the universe aren't as cryptic as you might think. With a little analysis, you'll know your Sakkra from your Grendarl, and you'll figure out that Imsaeis are superior to Humans on the diplomatic front.

Alien Race Skills

Race	Bioharvesting	Mining	Manufacturing	Research	Trade	Environmental	Economics	Accuracy
Human	Average	Average	Average	Good	Average	Poor	Investors	Average
Evon	Average	Average	Average	Average	Good	Superior	Monetarists	Good
Psilon	Poor	Poor	Average	Superior	Good	Average	Specie	Average
Meklar	Poor	Average	Good	Good	Poor	Poor	Barter	Superior
Cynoid	Poor	Superior	Superior	Good	Superior	Poor	Monetarists	Good
Sakkra	Poor	Average	Good	Good	Poor	Poor	Specie	Superior
Raas	Good	Average	Superior	Average	Good	Poor	Specie	Good
Grendarl	Average	Average	Good	Average	Good	Poor	Barter	Good
Trilarian	Good	Average	Good	Superior	Average	Good	Monetarists	Average
Nommo	Superior	Average	Good	Superior	Good	Average	Monetarists	Poor
Imsaeis	Superior	Good	Poor	Poor	Average	Superior	Specie	Poor
Eoladi	Superior	Poor	Poor	Good	Average	Superior	Specie	Average
Silicoid	Good	Superior	Average	Poor	Poor	Superior	Monetarists	Poor
Klackon	Good	Superior	Average	Poor	Poor	Average	Barter	Average
Tachidi	Poor	Superior	Good	Average	Average	Average	Barter	Average
Ithkul	Superior	Average	Superior	Good	Poor	Good	Specie	Good

Alien Race Skills *(continued)*

Race	Reflexes	Toughness	Diplomacy	Government Type	Orion Senate	Citizenship	Cunning	Creativity
Human	Average	Poor	Average	Representative	Random	Liberty	Dangerous	Normal
Evon	Good	Average	Poor	Representative	Random	Loyalty	Dangerous	Adaptive
Psilon	Poor	Poor	Superior	Representative	Random	Association	Quick	Original
Meklar	Average	Good	Good	Absolutist	Random	Duty	Dangerous	Original
Cynoid	Good	Good	Poor	Absolutist	Random	Association	Quick	Adaptive
Sakkra	Average	Superior	Poor	Absolutist	Random	Loyalty	Quick	Normal
Raas	Good	Poor	Good	Absolutist	Random	Association	Sharp	Normal
Grendarl	Good	Superior	Poor	Absolutist	Random	Duty	Sharp	Imitative
Trilarian	Average	Poor	Good	Absolutist	Random	Loyalty	Slow	Adaptive
Nommo	Poor	Poor	Superior	Absolutist	Random	Liberty	Sharp	Original
Imsaeis	Poor	Poor	Superior	Absolutist	Random	Loyalty	Slow	Adaptive
Eoladi	Poor	Poor	Good	Absolutist	Random	Loyalty	Slow	Original
Silicoid	Poor	Superior	Poor	Collectivist	Random	Association	Slow	Adaptive
Klackon	Good	Poor	Average	Collectivist	Random	Loyalty	Slow	Imitative
Tachidi	Poor	Superior	Poor	Collectivist	Random	Duty	Slow	Normal
Ithkul	Superior	Superior	Poor	Absolutist	No	Liberty	Quick	Normal

Non-Player Character Races

Species	Race
Metashifters	Darloks
Non-Corporeal	Brye Ehts
Protoplasmic	Ajadar
Plant	Audrieh
Fungal	Phaigour
Avian	Alkari
Gargantua	Rhea
Bulrathi	Bulrathi
Mrrshan	Mrrshan
Elerians	Elerians
Gnolam	Gnolam

Depending on how many players you set at the game's beginning, you could have several neighbors immediately.

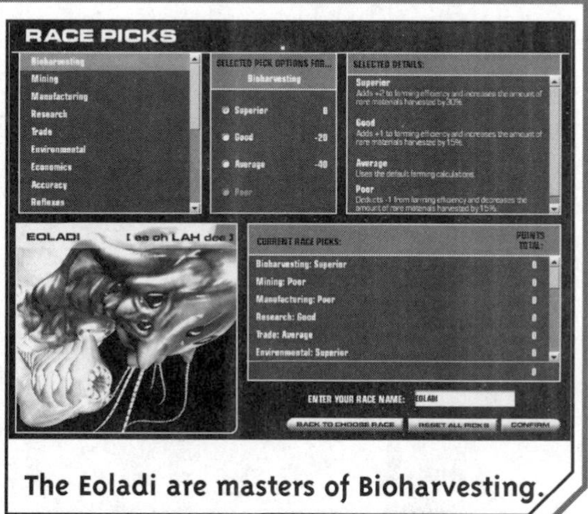

The Eoladi are masters of Bioharvesting.

Race Traits

Not all alien DNA make-ups are the same. Two dozen different traits form an alien race in *Master of Orion III.* Bioharvesting rates how well you gather the food for your population, Citizenship can reduce unrest during the game, while Creativity influences the effectiveness of your technological advances. Let's take a look at the primary traits so you can decide which alien race will run your homeworld.

Bioharvesting

Everyone has to eat. Even the solid crystal Silicoids require some form of sustenance to keep going. Bioharvesting represents your race's ability to build farms, manage them through good and bad times, and eventually harvest crops.

There are four ratings in Bioharvesting: superior, good, average, and poor. As you can imagine, a superior rating is the best and adds +2 to farming efficiency and increases the amount of rare materials harvested by 30 percent. A good rating nets +1 to farming efficiency and bumps up harvested rare materials by 15 percent. Average, of course, uses the default farming calculations. At the bottom of the barrel, a poor rating nets -1 from farming efficiency and decreases the amount of rare materials harvested by 15 percent.

Mining

To create most of your society's goods, mine your planet for resources. Mining reflects your ability to gather these resources from different terrains and environments. If you want your race to concentrate on industry, it all starts with Mining.

As with all traits, Mining has four ratings: superior, good, average, and poor. Similar to Bioharvesting, superior Mining nets +2 to efficiency and increases rare materials found by 30 percent. A good rating throws +1 toward efficiency and adds 15 percent to rare materials mined. Average keeps the default values, while poor nets -1 from efficiency and decreases the rare materials mined by 15 percent.

Manufacturing

If you enjoy driving in your car, swimming in your pool, or putting on a warm coat in the winter, you appreciate the benefits of manufacturing. Whether you're creating goods for recreational use or as barter to make money off other races, Manufacturing is one of the key stats in the game.

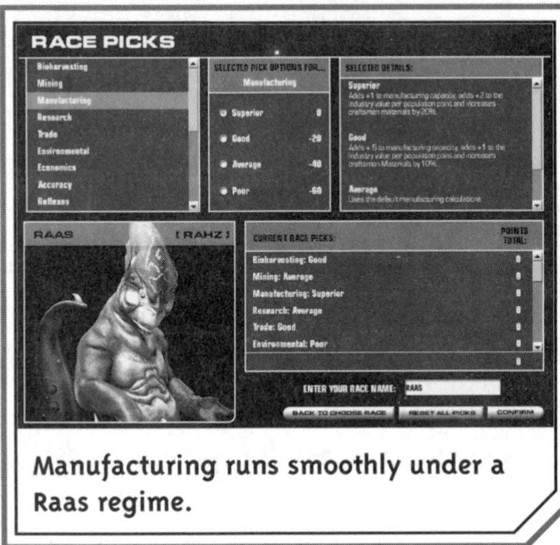

Manufacturing runs smoothly under a Raas regime.

It's the same rating range here—superior, good, average, and poor. Superior adds +1 to Manufacturing capacity, increases craftsman materials by 20 percent and nets +2 to the industry value per population point. Each planet has an industry value that measures the operating potential of the planet's industry based on factory and population output. A good rating works half as effectively; average gives you no bonuses whatsoever. Poor nets -0.5 from Manufacturing capacity, nets -1 from industry values, and decreases craftsman materials by 10 percent.

Research

Scientists research to find the next big technological achievement. It could be discovery of a new mathematics equation, perfection of a deadly laser, or the next leap in behavioral studies. Research unlocks the secrets in your technology tree, which can then be transformed into practical advancements for your race.

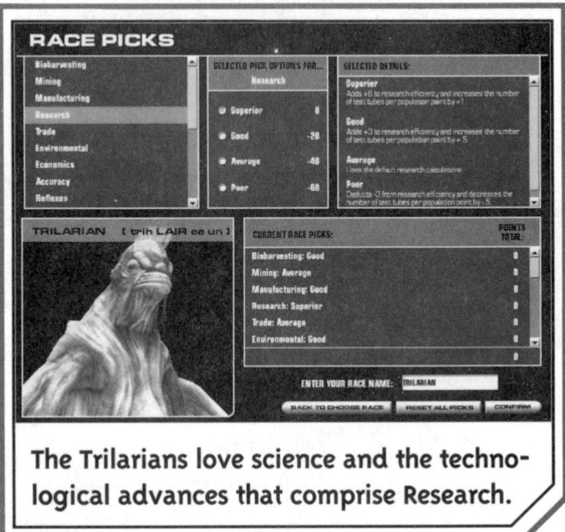

The Trilarians love science and the technological advances that comprise Research.

A superior rating in Research adds six points to efficiency and increases the number of test tubes per population point by +1. Each planet has a test tube value that measures the potential of the planet's scientific community based on research centers and population output. A good rating contributes +3 to efficiency and increases test tubes by .5 per population point. Average uses default calculations, and poor doesn't help your cause—you lose -3 from efficiency and drop test tubes by .5 per population point.

TIP

Manufacturing and Research help your society advance. The most important trait, however, is Trade. You can generate enormous income from working with the other alien races.

Trade

You can make serious cash through trade routes. Most trading happens between alien races, though you can also network space ports to pump up revenue. When dealing with other alien races in the Foreign Office, Trade is *the* most important trait. Alien races can give you an economic boost, secure military information, and swap technology, but only if you negotiate well, tapping into your Diplomacy trait, *and* your Trade skill is high enough to make it all worthwhile.

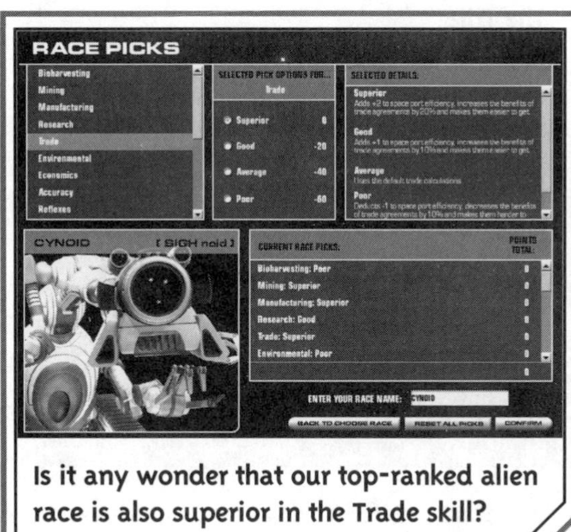

Is it any wonder that our top-ranked alien race is also superior in the Trade skill?

A superior trader adds +2 to space port efficiency, beefs up the benefits of trade agreements by 20 percent, and makes them easier to obtain. Good donates +1 to space ports, increases trade agreements by 10 percent, and helps you negotiate them. Average is middle-of-the-road—no bonuses. Poor cuts space port efficiency by one, decreases the benefits of trade agreements by 10 percent, and makes them harder to get.

Environmental

If you're in tune with your world's ecology—cultivate national parks, don't violate the waterways with chemicals, that sort of thing—your Environmental trait will be high. Environmental represents your race's ability to effectively terraform the planet into a paradise and its ability to deal with the negative consequences of pollution.

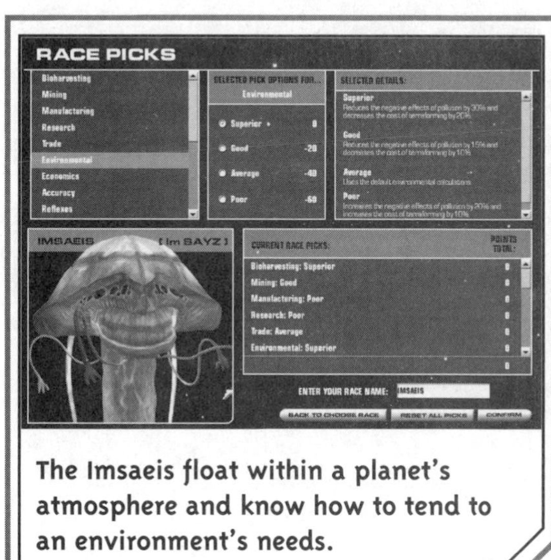

The Imsaeis float within a planet's atmosphere and know how to tend to an environment's needs.

A superior rating reduces pollution's negative effect by 30 percent and decreases the cost of terraforming by 20 percent. Good does half that—reduces pollution by 15 percent and lessens terraforming by 10 percent. Average does nothing for you, while a poor rating increases pollution by 20 percent and increases the terraforming cost by 10 percent.

Economics

What type of economic system does your race employ? Economics answers that question with four different possibilities: investors, monetarists, specie, and barter. For those who like to track Wall Street every morning, Economics should be tops on your list.

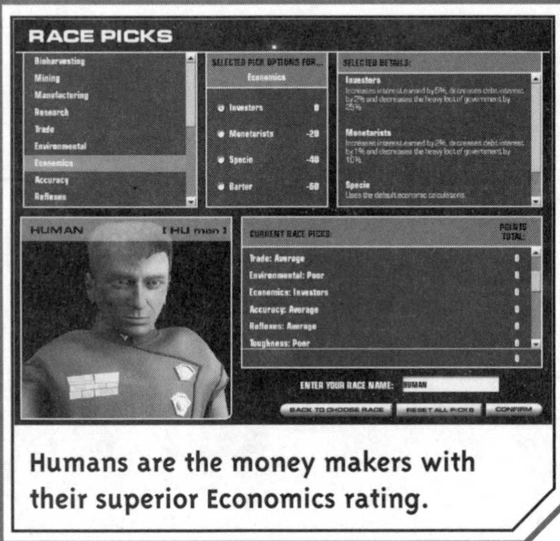

Humans are the money makers with their superior Economics rating.

Investors sit atop the economic pyramid. They increase interest earned by five percent, decrease debt earned by two percent, and reduce the heavy foot of government by 25 percent. Each planet has a "heavy foot of government" stat that tracks government oppression and contributes to unrest. Coming in second, monetarists increase interest earned by two percent, reduce debt interest by one percent, and decrease the heavy foot of government by ten percent. Specie use default economic values. Finally, races employing a barter system decrease interest earned by one percent, increase debt interest by one percent, and contribute to the heavy foot of government by five percent.

Accuracy

Looking to conquer galaxies with your military? You want your Accuracy to be the best it can. Accuracy gives bonuses or minuses to combat. If you curse each time an infantry unit misses in a crucial battle, your Accuracy might be too low.

It's a rather simple formula for Accuracy. Superior increases ground combat ability by +2, good shoots it up +1, average is the status quo, and poor delivers a -1 penalty. These modifiers stack with Reflexes and Toughness.

Reflexes

Ships don't have reflexes, people do. Reflexes apply to your ground forces and represent combat initiative. If you want to get the drop on your opponent and attack first, shoot for a high Reflexes value.

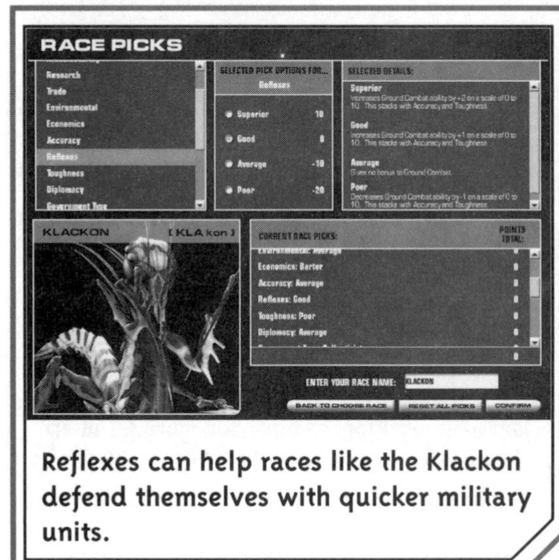

Reflexes can help races like the Klackon defend themselves with quicker military units.

Reflexes works off the same scale as Accuracy. Superior increases ground combat ability by +2, good bumps it up +1, average is the status quo, and poor delivers a -1 penalty. These modifiers stack with Accuracy and Toughness.

Toughness

Another ground force bonus, Toughness helps when you're getting shelled. Tougher units will last longer in combat, which might make all the difference in a close match.

Toughness works off the same scale as the other combat traits. Superior beefs up ground combat ability by +2, good increases it by +1, average is the status quo, and poor delivers a -1 penalty. These modifiers stack with Accuracy and Reflexes.

> **TIP**
>
> **The combat stats—Accuracy, Reflexes, Toughness—offer cumulative military bonuses. The most formidable forces have superior values in all three.**

Diplomacy

Second only to Trade, the Diplomacy trait might make or break you when dealing with other alien races. In some ways, it might be more important, since you can't even strike a deal if you don't negotiate the correct way. Fortunately, negotiations don't entirely rely on your Diplomacy skill, though it helps to influence foreign powers.

A superior rating greatly increases other races' favorable attitudes toward you by modifying their initial reactions to your race. Good slightly increases a race's favorable

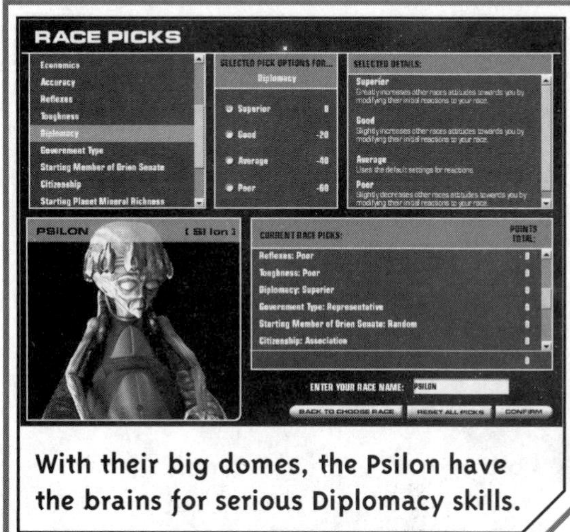

With their big domes, the Psilon have the brains for serious Diplomacy skills.

attitude toward you. Average means the race has no opinion of you to start. Poor slightly decreases the race's initial attitude toward you.

Government Type

Choosing a government can affect every facet of your society. Don't let that early decision consume you. Once the game begins, you can switch your government type. Sure, it causes initial unrest, but once you control the unrest, you gain the benefits of the new government you want without worrying about the choice up front. If you'd like to start with the best government, choose Collectivist over Representative, Absolutist, and Transitional.

Starting Member of Orion Senate

There are only three possibilities for the Orion Senate category. Either you're on the Senate, not on the Senate, or there's a random chance of starting out as a member of the Senate. Senate members can vote on laws that will change the course of the game, such as diplomatic sanctions and declarations of war.

Most races will start with a random chance at the Orion Senate. If you want to ensure you're a member, you have to pay extra.

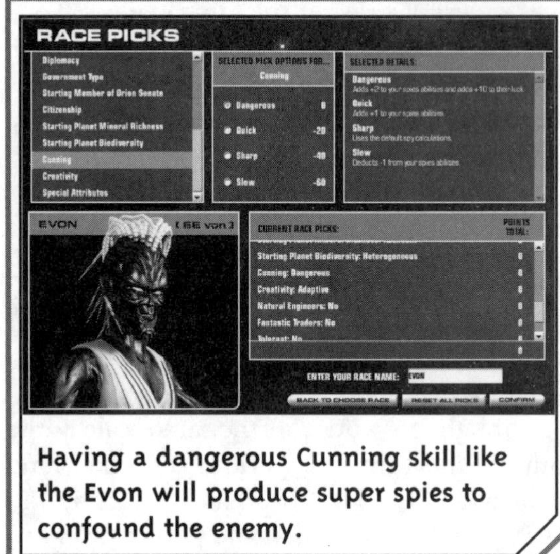

Having a dangerous Cunning skill like the Evon will produce super spies to confound the enemy.

Every race except the Ithkul begins with a random chance at the Orion Senate; the Ithkul never start on the Senate.

Citizenship

How patriotic are you? Citizenship categorizes the general state of your population in terms of loyalty toward the current government. A weak Citizenship rating can cause unrest problems throughout your empire, leading to production delays and possibly revolt.

Loyalty, the best Citizenship rating, deducts 15 points from the unrest total each turn. Duty deducts seven points. Association neither increases nor decreases unrest. Liberty adds five points to the unrest factors on all your planets.

Cunning

The chief trait for your empire's espionage campaign is Cunning. Depending on how many spies you plan to crank out into enemy territory, Cunning can be important or negligible.

The top rating, dangerous, adds +2 to all your spy abilities—Cloak, Dagger, and Loyalty—and +10 to a spy's Luck. Cloak represents the spy's ability to escape detection, Dagger signifies his chance to destroy enemy targets, Loyalty embodies the chance that the spy will not betray you to the enemy, and Luck stands for how long the spy can survive out in the field. A quick rating adds +1 to Cloak, Dagger, and Loyalty. Sharp remains the default, and slow deducts one point each from Cloak, Dagger, and Loyalty.

Creativity

Creativity has nothing to do with the arts. In *Master of Orion III*, Creativity ties into technology overruns, which can hinder technology research and cost a lot of money to fix. The greater your sense of Creativity, the quicker you can adapt to the changes affecting your technology.

An original rating decreases the chance of having a technological overrun by 10 percent and increases the odds that the overrun is beneficial by 10 percent if it occurs. Adaptive decreases the chance of a technological overrun by five percent and improves the odds that it's beneficial by five percent. Normal is normal. Imitative increases the chance of having a technological overrun by five percent and decreases the odds that the overrun is beneficial by five percent.

Ranking the Races

Every race offers something. Depending on your game style, you may want to play a race that runs a good economy all by itself or a race that cranks out military. Still, it's nice to know what you're getting into. Here's a guide to the best races based on the power of raw stats and race versatility.

#1 Cynoid

Think of them as ATMs. Cynoids accept currency in all sorts of trades, hold on to it for interest, and then exploit it in every possible way. They love to barter in an effort to improve the lot of their citizens, thus making them more productive and, ultimately, more taxable.

If they were better diplomats, the Cynoid would steal the title of "trade master" away from the Psilon. Their excellent trade practices, along with their uncanny ability to strip a planet clean of raw materials, place this cyborg race tops on the list.

Strengths

They can mine a planet and turn it into a fleet of spaceships before you can finish a sandwich. With a superior skill in both Mining and Manufacturing, settle these robots on a mineral-rich planet and you're gold. Cynoids follow this specialty up with excellent principles in Trade, Economics, and Research. They aren't slouches in combat, scoring a well in each category.

What do the Cynoid do well? Everything. They can make money like nobody else.

Weaknesses

It's a double whammy on the nature side of things. Poor ratings in both Bioharvesting and Environmental almost doom a planet's ecosystem before you even start. You must pay extra care to terraforming and pump more than the usual amount of funds into balancing your farmlands, or you'll easily "starve" the population.

Diplomatic Tendencies

Machines usually don't have emotion, so your best approach when bargaining with the Cynoid is to state each request simply. They respond to formality and civil meetings. Don't make outrageous demands on them, be patient, and they will share many things at their disposal with you. Since they start out with a big advantage over everyone else, you want to initiate positive talk as soon as you spot them in the galaxy.

TIP

The Cynoid and Ithkul rule the other races. Consider them superpowers to the other sovereign nations.

#2 Ithkul

Genetically engineered as parasites to destroy the other races in the Orion Sector, the Ithkul made some unexpected evolutionary leaps and took matters into their own "hands." Thinking for themselves, the sole harvester race in the game absorbed knowledge and philosophy from their enlightened hosts and leapfrogged their civilization to suddenly overtake the others. Borrowing a little bit from everywhere, the Ithkul choose to lean toward self-sufficiency rather than rely on cooperation or conquest of the other races.

The Ithkul are loaded. They have the highest overall stats, they arguably have the best military, and their economy can rival the Cynoids'. One glaring weakness keeps them off the top spot—trade.

The Ithkul "consume" other living creatures in addition to their bioharvesting activities (they get 10 Food for each Population Point they consume). Planets with Ithkul and another race will notice a larger than normal number of your population points disappearing. Harvesters are not nice; that's why everyone hates and fears them. Unfortunately, playing nice with them often isn't sufficient. They're prone to declare war at any time, and don't pay a lot of attention to diplomatic offers, though they've been known to stay nice for a while if the price is high enough.

Strengths

Superior Bioharvesting gathers the goods, and then superior Manufacturing makes you more money than you can imagine. Good Research supplements the economic advances. A super-powerful military force—with only Accuracy falling below perfect level—can pummel any force that decides the Ithkul are their enemy.

The Ithkul also have two special attributes: Tolerant and Antaran Background. Tolerant reduces the negative effects of pollution by 50 percent and that drives Bioharvesting into the stratosphere. Antaran Background increases your chance of discovering Antaran technology—one of the game's victory conditions—by 20 percent. If you can't win through the normal channels, the Ithkul have the best opportunity to find the five Antaran Xs.

Weaknesses

First, they have a poor rating in the most important trait, Trade. That hurts when you want to work with the other races. Second, they have a poor rating in Diplomacy. That kills when you want to work with the other races. With all the Ithkul have going for them, they won't be able to rely on the support of the other powers.

Diplomatic Tendencies

You might have to play nice with the Ithkul, especially if they're an immediate neighbor and you don't want to get attacked early. They are self-reliant, but you may be able to pull a fast one—who's to say they know anything about a good deal with a poor Diplomacy and Trade rating?

#3 Nommo

Calamari, anyone? The squid-like Nommo protect their soft bodies with a manufactured shell that conveys status, capability, and class. They are delusional and think they are descended directly from the "Old One," the Antaran scientist who seeded the first world. As "children of the god," they have declared jihads in the name of divine right.

The Nommo are an elite race with superior Diplomacy.

When playing the Nommo, you've got the goods . . . well, most of them anyway. Superior Diplomacy puts them in an elite class—only the Imsaeis and Psilon can make the same claim—and upper-echelon Bioharvesting and Research skills contribute to the "backbone" of your economy. Just don't anger any of your neighbors.

Strengths

Your important categories are covered in a big way. Superior Bioharvesting, Diplomacy, and Research can win you games outright. Backed by good ratings in Economics, Manufacturing, and Trade, your empire will soar once you exploit the alien relationships around you. That's where it gets tricky . . .

Weaknesses

The Nommo military is lacking. The Nommo combat division can't even launch a rocket into space straight. Even the peace-loving Trilarians are stronger than them.

The problems don't end there. Unrest gives you headaches as early as turn one. Pump extra funds into unrest control or your population will turn on you quickly. With unrest high, if a foreign power decides to come for you, your sudden climb in military spending might cause a revolt and finish you before you start.

#4 Raas

They rose from slaves to a hot spot on the race list. Considered the best slave stock among their species, the Raas fought oppression at the hands of their fellow Saurians and broke away to form their own clans. The most industrious of the Saurians, the Raas have steadily excelled in everything they pursued—government, industry, religious institutions, even interstellar conquest.

They are stacked in all the right traits. Talk about well balanced: They only have one combat weakness and maintain an average skill or better in all other applications except for the lone poor in Environmental. Other than the three races above, the Raas are hands and tail above the rest.

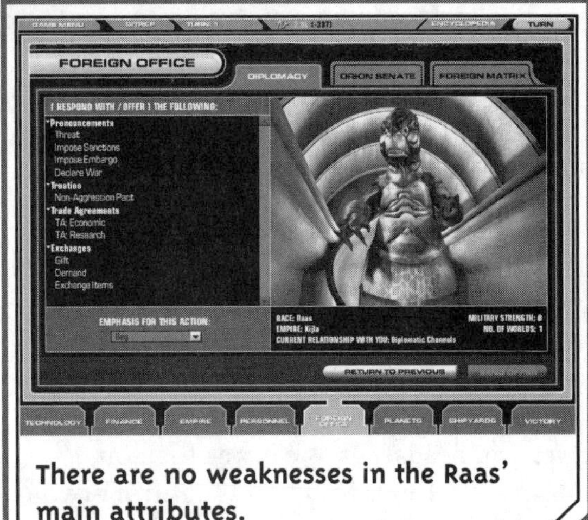

There are no weaknesses in the Raas' main attributes.

Strengths

Look no further than Manufacturing for the Raas' most productive resource skill. Their Mining suffers a bit at an average rating, but once the raw materials come in, the Raas crank up the productivity. Bioharvesting ranks high, but it drops a bit from the carelessness the Raas show to their environment. Trade and Diplomacy both rank good, so they can usually receive exactly what they want from foreign nations.

Weaknesses

If you search long enough you can find a small weakness—average in Mining and only an Association level for Citizenship. They're ranked poor in Toughness; however, a good rating in both Accuracy and Reflexes more than balances out their combat stats. Environmental also brings down their overall Bioharvesting effectiveness.

Diplomatic Tendencies

They're a civilized race, and they listen to reason. As long as you keep negotiations open and respond with politeness, even in the face of some of their arrogant outbursts, you will make friends with the Raas and profit from their initial strength.

> **NOTE**
>
> **Trilarians and Nommo get bonuses for being aquatic. Similar to the floating species, these folks get bonuses when there's lots of water. Frozen worlds or hot ones aren't much use to these folks, so they are at a disadvantage there.**

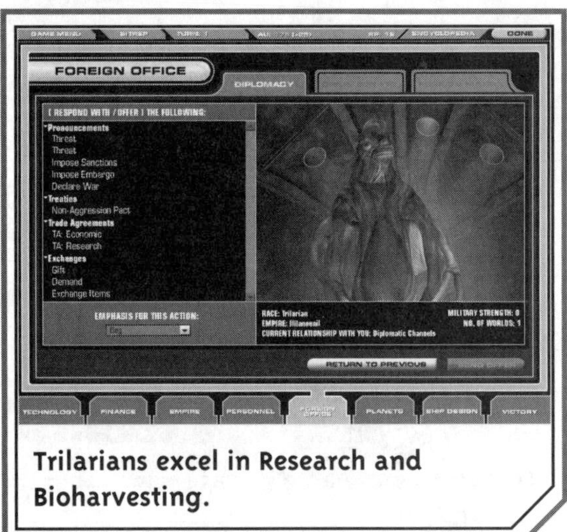

Trilarians excel in Research and Bioharvesting.

#5 Trilarian

The sole remnant of the once-proud Ichthytosian Empire, the Trilarians cling to the ghosts of the past and desperately strive to rebuild their ancestors' glory. Pacifists at heart, the Trilarians focus not on military conquest but on the "finer" pastimes—art, architecture, and philosophy. Their peaceful society would rather be left alone to revive their Renaissance period.

Don't be fooled by the Trilarians' peaceful ways. They aren't pushovers. They may not beat you through military; given a chance, though, they'll beat you in every other arena.

Strengths

Trilarians excel in technological pursuits. A superior Research and adaptive Creativity grant them speedy advancements and resiliency to setbacks. As you would expect from a thoughtful society absorbed in the fine arts, unrest is low and Citizenship is very loyal.

Besides Research, the Trilarians have mastered Bioharvesting and turn around a healthy profit off Manufacturing. Despite the appearance of military weakness, Trilarians employ good diplomats and frequently convince other alien powers that their goals are the same.

Weaknesses

Trilarians avoid combat, and rightly so—they don't have the combat skills to back up large-scale conflicts. An average Trading trait can become a hindrance in longer games where treaties with several foreign powers may develop.

Diplomatic Tendencies

Always treat Trilarians politely. They listen to reason in a conversation, and may be intrigued by a military alliance given their usual lack of defense. If you lose patience with them, they might be difficult to sway back to your side.

#6 Evon

Mysterious and mystical, the Evon are the most secretive of the Orion Sector. Little is known about their societies, other than they are wrapped in ritual and ceremony. The truth is that the Evon believe themselves far superior to all other races and try not to be bothered by alien nonsense.

When playing the Evon, think of your race as "Joe Average." They don't do anything great, but don't have many inherent

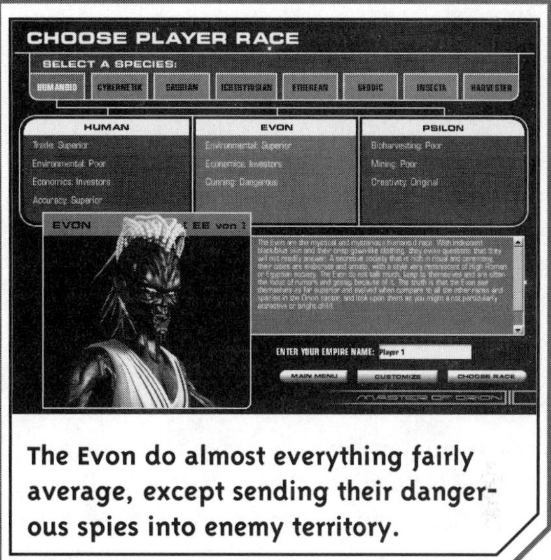

The Evon do almost everything fairly average, except sending their dangerous spies into enemy territory.

weaknesses either. Your personal preferences will guide them in a particular direction more than any trait.

Strengths

Their average Bioharvesting is brought up to a higher level by their superior Environmental skill. Though not perfect, they are competent in Trade, Economics, and Cunning. Once they have their hooks in you, their monetarist trait turns trade surplus into profit. In a close battle, the Evon's dangerous Cunning can send killer spies into alien territory and throw the enemy into chaos.

Weaknesses

They only have one poor rating: Diplomacy. Don't engage in too many treaties, and the other races won't take advantage of you. On the other hand, most of their main traits are rated average. If you don't want a run-of-the-mill economy, serious exploration has to augment the consistent, if unspectacular, industry contributions.

Diplomatic Tendencies

Don't demand anything from the Evon. When talking trade, remember that the Evon believe they are above you on the evolutionary ladder. Begging and humble replies play to their egos. Avoid the hard line with them, and you'll come away with an agreement.

#7 Psilon

The ultimate researchers favor their minds over their bodies. Psilons have developed their mental prowess at the expense of their physical capabilities. They are responsible for many discoveries used in the Orion Sector, but require mechanical assistance—their patented hover-chairs—to move around.

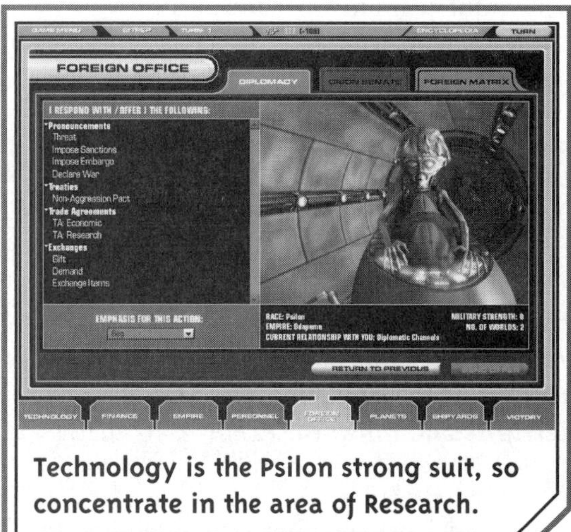

Technology is the Psilon strong suit, so concentrate in the area of Research.

Thinking of winning through technology? The ol' chromedomes are your race. They can quickly get you a plasma projector or an anionic energy warhead, but don't expect your crops to grow or your mines to spit out ore.

Strengths

Superior Research and original thinking are an elite combination. Psilons can crank out advances, and then when technology falls prey to an overrun, they can turn the defeat into a bonus success. Without interference from other races, the Psilons churn out weaponry upgrades and mathematical equations better than anyone. They are also a shrewd lot. If they can't outgun the other powers in technology, a superior Diplomacy enables them to manipulate their neighbors into bargains that aid the Psilon cause.

Weaknesses

Resources are hard to come by with poor Bioharvesting and Mining. Weak in combat, Psilons find it difficult to defend themselves militarily and rely on a quick Cunning to compensate in the espionage arena.

Diplomatic Tendencies

Don't trust the Psilon. They are master manipulators and use you to further their goals. You should enter into an alliance with them if you think it will benefit your race, but don't beg or plead or they'll "hover" all over you.

TIP

Besides the big two, Cynoid and Ithkul, the Grendarl and Sakkra are the only other military powerhouses.

#8 Grendarl

The Grendarl enjoy supreme comfort, but they're not soft. Their high level of military training and "death before dishonor" mantra makes them a dangerous threat to any race that doesn't take them seriously. A strict code of sacred ethics guides their clan structure, and most Grendarl will do anything to be accepted into a clan, including destroying foreign interlopers.

Fighting isn't a problem with the military-inclined Grendarl.

If your goal is to make as much money as possible and rule the universe, the Grendarl aren't the race to raise you to your pedestal. Average in most of the traits that count, their weaker scores barely raise them above the pass/fail mark.

Strengths

A good Trade skill is a plus and helps generate extra revenue. Unfortunately, a poor Diplomacy rating severely hamstrings you. A good rating in Manufacturing can balance things out —if you gather enough resources. All that combat training pays off with good Accuracy, good Reflexes, and superior Toughness. Fighting isn't a problem.

Weaknesses

An average rating in nearly everything is a handicap. As the Grendarl, you'll have too many holes to fill while balancing your economy; more often than not, you'll want to give up and dig your own grave. When the raw materials finally flood in, your production can help overcome shortages.

Diplomatic Tendencies

The Grendarl like to kick butt around the galaxy, and they don't have time for trade talk nonsense. At least that's the way it seems; the Grendarl take forever to respond to your communications. Despite their slow, cautious ways, the Grendarl develop quickly militarily and can be good allies. Be reasonable and polite with their ambassadors and you may cultivate a strong ally.

#9 Sakkra

Killing is second nature to the Sakkra. Filled with bitterness and resentment over their species' treatment by other races, this aggressive warrior race hates everyone and destroys everything in their way. Tread lightly or they might be the last race you see.

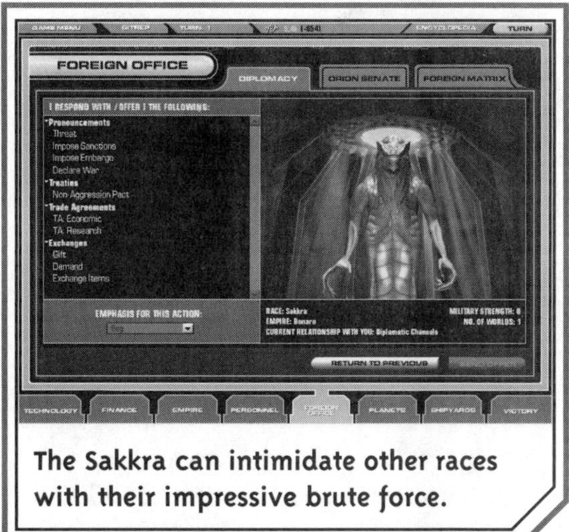

The Sakkra can intimidate other races with their impressive brute force.

If you like combat, you'll love the Sakkra. They fight better than anyone, except maybe the Ithkul and Grendarl; balance their economy for them, and you can stomp through the galaxy and intimidate civilization after civilization.

Strengths

Besides their impressive Accuracy, Reflexes, and Toughness combat skills, the Sakkra generate capital by capturing planets and transforming them into cash farms. Good Manufacturing and Research increase the efficiency of the captured worlds, while the high Loyalty rating ensures unrest won't get you down.

Weaknesses

The Achilles' heel of the Sakkra lies in their inability to get along with other races. Poor ratings in Diplomacy and Trade shut out many of the lucrative possibilities that dealing with other races grants you. Expect to mostly go it alone when controlling the Sakkra, as it will be difficult to consistently rally reliable allies to your cause. Bioharvesting is the pits, so concentrate on seizing mineral-rich worlds to keep your economy alive.

Diplomatic Tendencies

The Sakkra are an angry people, so don't expect politeness and good manners to get you anywhere. The Sakkra respect a forceful approach. Demand they accept your trades and insult them at every opportunity. Treat them like your worst enemy and you'll get along fine.

#10 Meklar

Super industrious, the Meklar excel in computer technology and have the ability to become one with any machine. With massive computers at their disposal, their wealth of knowledge transforms into power, and gives them cutting-edge surveillance of other races.

Use the Meklar's high Research rating to exploit technologies and improve your galactic position.

If you decide to play the Meklar, prepare for a middle-of-the-road experience. The Meklar's positives and negatives generally balance each other out.

Strengths

They have a superior rating in Accuracy and Cunning, but that's it. Fortunately, the Meklar claim good ratings in Manufacturing, Research, and Diplomacy (probably because they know everything about everyone). It might be a bumpy ride, but you can exploit Manufacturing and Research to get ahead of the other races if you're careful.

Weaknesses

The inorganic Meklar don't interact well with their organic environment. Judged poor in Bioharvesting and Environmental, the Meklar rely on Mining to gather their resources—unfortunately, Mining ranks only average. They need help from other races, but with a poor Trade value it's harder for them to score agreements, and when they do, the Meklar lose 10 percent off the profits.

Diplomatic Tendencies

Speak like a machine and you'll connect with the Meklar. Declare your trade agreements loudly, so they won't misinterpret them. A cold tone is deemed warm by the machines. Advise your diplomats to give them the cold shoulder whenever possible.

> **TIP**
>
> **Your first race should probably be Human. You are, after all, familiar with their strengths and weaknesses. Soon you'll discover there are better choices.**

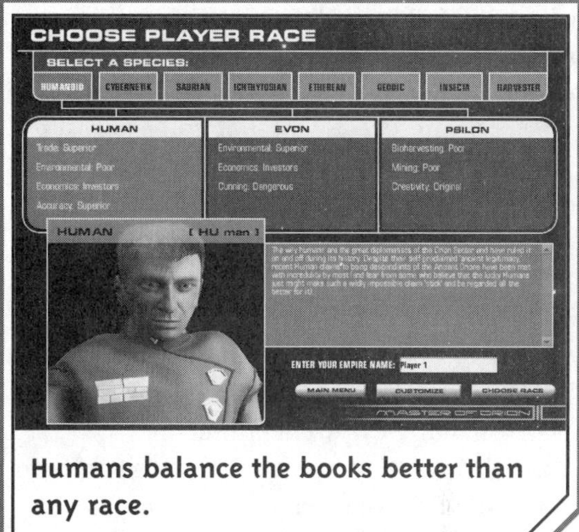

Humans balance the books better than any race.

#11 Human

Like a dynasty team in professional sports, Humans have ruled the Orion Sector on and off for long periods of time. Their self-proclaimed "ancient legitimacy," that they're descendants of the Ancient Orions, fuels their drive for the throne, though most of the other races view such a claim with skepticism and annoyance.

You probably know how to play these guys already. Most games use humans as the default, keeping all their stats as the norm, and adjusting other races around them. *Master of Orion III* gives Humans these same basic tools. You can learn with them, and then move on to the race that best fits your style.

Strengths

They are the master investors. With a top-notch ranking in Economics, backed by a good rating in Research, Humans are a whirlwind of industrial activity. They can quickly turn a bargain with another race into instant profit or sudden technology advance.

Learn how to abuse your average resource ratings—Bioharvesting, Mining, Manufacturing, and Trade—and Humans can control planetary economics better than anyone else.

When the going gets rough, Humans won't fall down. With a dangerous Cunning, Human spies can infiltrate any alien power and slow down potential threats. If a hostile race engages, Human military forces have a chance to beat it back. In terms of military effectiveness, they rank about middle-of-the-road.

Weaknesses

The biggest Human downside is dealing with unrest. There's a price to pay for the freedom in Human government—liberty allows people to occasionally stir up trouble. Expect to devote extra income to quelling unrest early in the game. Humans also aren't known for their awareness of nature. Human industry throws pollution into the environment and harms whatever planet they decide to colonize.

Diplomatic Tendencies

Humans are a wily lot. Some are true to their word, others can't be trusted; as a whole, they're unpredictable. Still, if you approach them with reasonable offers and maintain a polite attitude, you'll establish good temporary alliances.

#12 Eoladi

You never know what to expect with the Eoladi. Each Eoladi has an individual code of ethics, making every encounter unpredictable. Often the same situations can have different conclusions if new Eoladi are involved. Great society builders and competent leaders, the Eoladi have advanced their civilization to the point where they believe it is their duty to share personal and social improvements with others.

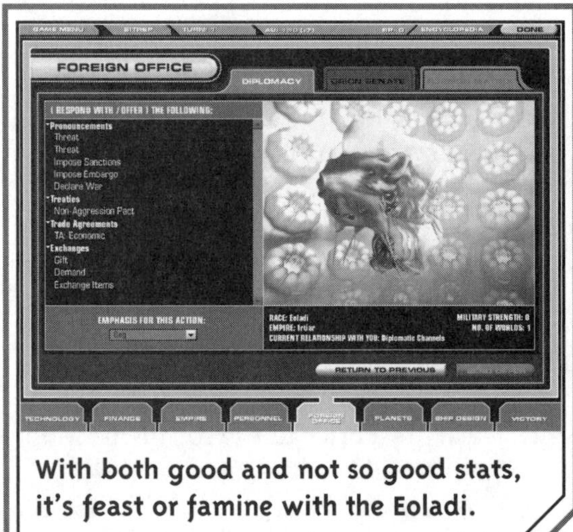

With both good and not so good stats, it's feast or famine with the Eoladi.

It's feast or famine when tackling the Eoladi. Some key stats are good, some are poor, with very few in between. Quickly learn your strengths, and protect your weaknesses, to advance the Eoladi to the ultimate level.

Strengths

They only have one set of superior traits, Bioharvesting and Environmental. The Eoladi thrive off the land, with superior Environmental skills increasing the surplus. Research contributes to the military effort, while good Diplomacy helps raise their Trade status above average. Citizenship and Creativity also rank the highest in their categories.

Weaknesses

Eoladi suffer with five poor traits. Mining carts out rubble instead of gems. Manufacturing creates lemons, not hotrods. Eoladi combat Reflexes and Toughness wouldn't last against a flock of penguins. Their spy intelligence has more double agents than dedicated clock-punchers. You'll have your hands full with emergencies if you choose the Eoladi.

Diplomatic Tendencies

Your default approach to a race you don't know anything about should be reasonable, polite offers. It works with the Eoladi, who respect a trade that mutually benefits both races. Don't insult them, and they walk away from the negotiation table.

#13 Tachidi

Call them "gentle giants," and never forget their strength can kill. These adolescent insectoids are full of curiosity and energy. On numerous occasions, chance encounters with other races have turned deadly because they don't know their own strength.

They lack the discipline to be as productive as their insectoid brothers, the Klackon; however, their raw skills in Mining and superior Toughness in combat give them an edge on the popularity chart.

The Tachidi pull rocks out of the ground and smelt ore into good money.

Strengths

The Tachidi are good at pulling rocks out of the ground; and their entire production line depends on it. A good Manufacturing trait helps bump up the Mining to a respectable industry. In combat, the Tachidi aren't fast or accurate, but they are tough enough to take a few to the head and keep coming.

Weaknesses

Other than Mining, their industry leaves a lot to be desired. Average Research drops them behind most races. To increase your stress, poor Bioharvesting and barter-level Economics hamper your other efforts at a reasonable society.

Diplomatic Tendencies

Treat them like children. Declare any trade offer as if it's the only choice and you know best. The Tachidi might debate it for a while, they might even disagree and cancel the first couple of agreements. Stick with them. Eventually, if you're persistent, they'll listen to your advice.

#14 Imsaeis

They watch what everyone is doing. The Imsaeis are the great observers of the Orion Sector, and their ability to gain acceptance through humility and listening to other races has produced a flood of information into their empire. The Imsaeis frequently know more than they let on, and always appear to be in control of events.

Loyal citizens allow the Imsaeis the luxury to leave government alone and concentrate on finances.

Despite their savvy diplomacy with the great powers in the Orion Sector, the Imsaeis aren't as in control of things as they like others to think. Weak across the board, the Imsaeis battle efficiency within their empire to keep up with the Orion space race.

Strengths

Few races interact with other races better than the Imsaeis. They know what to say to gain an advantage; unfortunately, their Trade and Manufacturing departments cannot exploit those advantages to the fullest. If they avoid conflict with their neighbors, the

NOTE

The Imsaeis and Eoladi both get "flier" adjustments because they live in the atmospheres of gas giant planets, which a lot of space available for growth, depending on the atmospheric density (airless worlds are a hindrance to them).

Imsaeis can rise to become a powerhouse. As an added bonus, their loyal citizens give them no unrest problems and superior Bioharvesting grants an influx of cash.

Weaknesses

They gather intelligence well, but with a low Cunning rating, the Imsaeis spy network doesn't produce many James Bonds. Poor ratings in two key traits, both Manufacturing and Research, make for a slow developing race. The Imsaeis don't look like they can fight, and that evaluation is correct. All three combat skills rank at the bottom, so unless you like taking a beating, avoid military conflicts with the other powers.

Diplomatic Tendencies

The Imsaeis are hard to figure out. They love to negotiate, so it's easy to set up agreements at first. However, don't let their friendly nature walk all over you. Be forceful and declare all treaties. If they know from the outset that you mean business, they will offer trades that work for both powers.

#15 Silicoid

Stick the Silicoid on any planet and it doesn't bother them. Run your factories until you've got a dark cloud cover —who cares, they're not affected by pollution. The only known crystalline life form in the Orion Sector, the Silicoid can take punishment; however, their bodies are restrictive in terms of movement and reproduction. Being the most alien of all the races, they are the least understood.

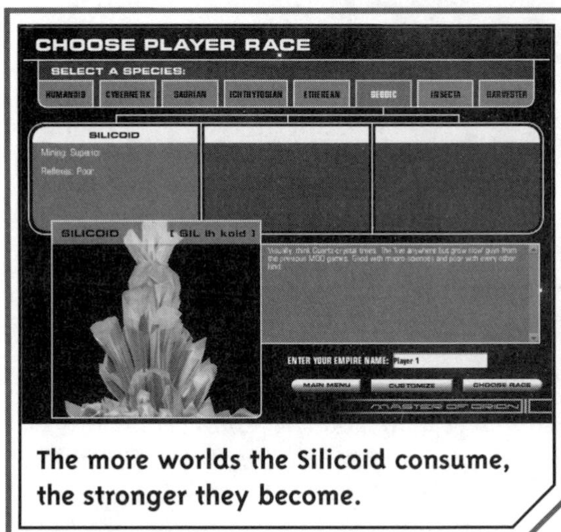

The more worlds the Silicoid consume, the stronger they become.

They eat minerals, so don't be fooled by the Silicoid's superior Mining—they aren't turning it into profit. The luxury of dropping them on any planet doesn't reap any rewards, because they have a weak economy and science division.

Strengths

Mining can be strong. Bioharvesting, due to superior Environmental control, does well on most planets. An average Manufacturing is the best the rest of the culture has to offer, and that doesn't stack up well against 14 of the other races.

Weaknesses

They're pretty to look at, but not to work with. Their industry is slow to start, and it gets killed by the Silicoid's poor Diplomacy, Trade, and Research traits. It's hard to get momentum going, and it takes an enormous amount of hands-on control to balance the Silicoid empire.

Diplomatic Tendencies

Crystals like to be treated very formally. Clearly state all your proposals and instruct your diplomats to abide by all formal customs. Respect those rules and the Silicoid will respect you.

#16 Klackon

A hive-like nature allows the Klackon to adapt to the changing universe around them—when one Klackon learns of a change, the rest of the colony will soon. Because of their collective way of thinking, the Klackon are better at adapting new technologies than researching new ones. They compensate for their lack of Creativity through diligence and hard work.

It's hard to imagine a race worse than the Klackon . . . and that's because there isn't.

To play the Klackon, you have to be a glutton for punishment. Concentrate on Mining, and hope you discover some planets with rare gems. All their other "skills" are miserable.

The Klackons get a "subterranean" bonus, which means they can fit more population points per region than other races. They have a huge advantage in their population growth rate (40% above normal); they multiply like crazy.

Strengths

You will be able to gather raw materials. Mining ranks superior and Bioharvesting clocks in at good. That's stable enough to generate an early economy, but it will take a lot of coaxing to use your average Manufacturing to earn big money. A hive society earns high Citizenship points, so you'll hardly worry about unrest.

Weaknesses

An average Diplomacy rating saves your Trade industry from total disaster. A poor Research rating doesn't add a thing to your progress, and you don't have much to offer in the way of exchange to ask for technology from the other races. You go first in most fights; so destroy the enemy swiftly or your forces could get decimated.

Diplomatic Tendencies

For the "uni-mind" that is a hive, the Klackon are an argumentative lot. They like to disagree with your trade offers and alliance proposals. Don't be dissuaded. Argue back, and respond to any offers with cool indifference. This is the emotive preference for the Klackon, and you will connect with them quicker with an icy, combative attitude.

CAUTION

Only play the Klackon if you enjoy a challenge.

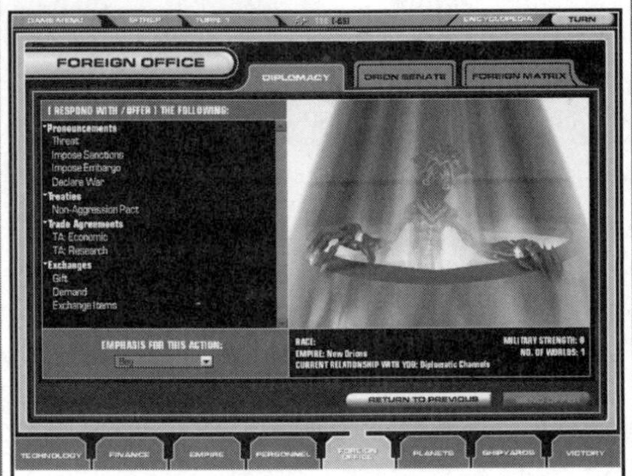

You can't play the New Orions, though you will meet them inside the game. They don't favor military, but they do stock up on technology and political voting power.

The Sakkra are usually better than the Humans. You can change that when you customize your own race.

Creating Your Own Race

Sixteen different aliens offer many choices for your starting race. Even so, after you play the game a bunch of times, you might want to customize your own super power. As with every facet of *Master of Orion III*, you can take this in a dozen directions, whatever style you like to play. Want to build the ultimate spy network? Tired of a military that has the pounding force of a sponge? Choose "customize" under the "Race Picks" menu to bring a new race to the Orion Sector.

Human Error

Let's face it, humans are far down on the evolutionary ladder in the competitive Orion galaxy. That's no reason to give up on good ol' flesh-and-blood humanoids, though. You just have to build a better—or actually, more specialized—*homo sapiens*.

Go ahead and build your "ultimate race." With your first try, you probably had the point total up to 150 over the limit. Much as you may want to play a broken race like that, the designers have balanced stats so you can't stack up without penalties. Based on your chosen race's base stats, no matter how much you add, you'll have to subtract that same amount to continue. Exercise caution by choosing one or two preferences to work into your race.

Trading Places

How about we build a master trader? Our goal will be to strike up offers with the other alien powers and arrange agreements for economic boosts or alliances for defense. Some of our other governmental operations might suffer, but that's the price you pay to specialize your race.

The two key stats for a master trader are Diplomacy and Trade. You want to get other powers to listen to you, then you want an economic boost from a successful trade.

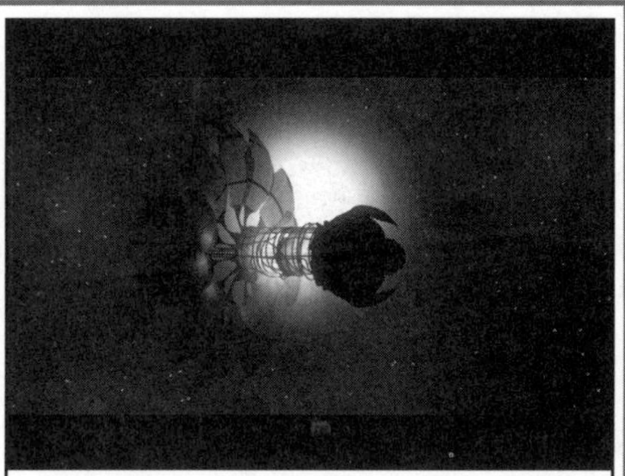

To build a master trader, a Human must bump up his Diplomacy and Trade traits.

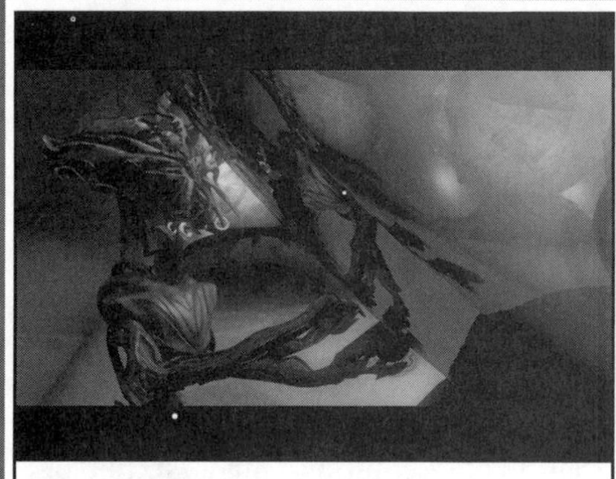

Bioengineer a new race at the Race Picks screen.

Unfortunately, Humans start out average in both these stats, so it'll take some points to make them expert traders. Spend 40 points to jump up Trade two spots to superior level.

Do the same for Diplomacy by raising it to superior for 20 points. We're 60 points in the hole, but have our two primary stats in order.

NEXT GENERATION HUMAN

You can customize your own races. Try this new human species on for size. They specialize in Trade and hope to generate a huge cash flow through their agreements with other foreign powers.

- **Bioharvesting:** Average
- **Mining:** Average
- **Manufacturing:** Good (+20)
- **Research:** Average (-10)
- **Trade:** Superior (+40)
- **Environmental:** Poor
- **Economics:** Specie (-20)
- **Accuracy:** Average
- **Reflexes:** Average
- **Toughness:** Poor
- **Diplomacy:** Superior (+20)
- **Government Type:** Representative
- **Starting Member of Orion Senate:** Random
- **Citizenship:** Liberty
- **Starting Planet Mineral Richness:** Poor (-10)
- **Starting Planet Biodiversity:** Similar (-10)
- **Cunning:** Slow (-30)
- **Creativity:** Imitative (-10)
- **Natural Engineers:** No
- **Fantastic Traders:** Yes (+10)
- **Tolerant:** No
- **Empathic:** No
- **Antaran Background:** No

Special Attributes

Only the Silicoid and Ithkul races start with special attributes. These can be powerful traits that the 14 other races don't enjoy. Natural Engineers add +.5 to the manufacturing capacity of your planets. Fantastic Traders increase trade agreements by 15 percent. Tolerant reduces the negative effects of pollution by 50 percent. Empathic increases all areas of diplomacy for your race. Finally, Antaran Background increases your chances of discovering Antaran technology—a game-winning victory condition—by 20 percent.

Only the Silicoid and Ithkul begin with special race attributes.

Much as we'd like Empathic for our new Human, we can only afford so much. A definite is Fantastic Traders. For 10 extra points, we gain a 35-percent increase with trade agreements (when you factor in our superior Trade skill, too). Every successful deal you make with your allies brings in a third more revenue.

Homemade Improvements

We're not done shopping yet. Your economy can't be all about trades. What happens if the other races snub you? With average Bioharvesting and Mining, we're behind most of the other races in terms of planetary economies. To give us a boost, let's raise our Manufacturing from average to good. Those 20 points will make up for themselves when we have a dozen planets churning out lucrative production.

Build up your Manufacturing trait to take advantage of your industry DEAs.

Balancing the Biological Budget

If you count up our upgrades, we're down 90 points. It's tough to go higher than that without crippling too many major areas. Now it's time to trim traits and hope we don't do too much damage.

Starting Planet Biodiversity can be set to similar to save 10 points. It's better to be heterogeneous, but you'll be living on more than one planet soon enough. The same is true with your Starting Planet Mineral Richness. Decrease it to poor for the extra points, and suffer through the slow beginning. Shave off ten more by dropping your Creativity to imitative. In the technology arena, overruns are annoying—they cost you extra time and money—but eventually you work through them. You need points from somewhere, so deal with the inconvenience.

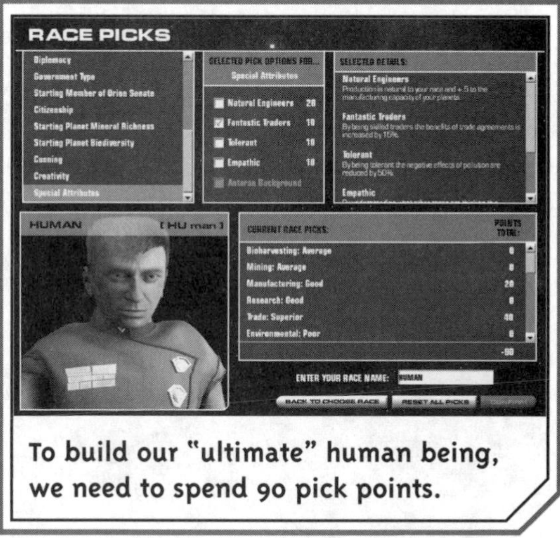

To build our "ultimate" human being, we need to spend 90 pick points.

It gets tougher now. You still have to make up 60 points, with few categories left to do it in. Humans are usually the best at espionage, but not our new race. We're going from first to worst. Drop Cunning from dangerous to slow, and save 30 points. Yes, we would rather have expert spies that undermine our enemies, but this is one of the sacrifices we must make.

The last two cuts are the hardest. Research drops from good to average. One of the keys to victory lies in research. We're worse now, but still average. Our technology advances will move slow; however, with our expert trading, we might be able to exchange technology with our allies and overcome this limitation. Even more difficult to chop is Economics. We plummet from investors to specie, gaining 20 points and losing a lot of potential interest on our money. The plan is to generate constant revenue through trade and spend money to make money. If it's not sitting in the bank, our lower Economics score won't hurt us as much.

We have to shave many traits down a notch to balance our pick points and play our customized race.

Military Agenda

That balances us to zero, but we haven't thought about our three military stats—Accuracy, Reflexes, and Toughness. With average, average, and poor ratings in the three categories, we score a combined -1 penalty to our military efforts. Not something we want, so we didn't choose to reduce these traits when building our new human. We also didn't have any left over points, so we couldn't increase their efficiency. By cutting our espionage budget to shreds, we've left ourselves open to attack.

After you pay for your new traits, your customized race can journey out into the galaxy.

Or have we?

We're not complete military wimps and can still beat several of the other races one-on-one. Our real plan is to use our superior negotiation skills to set up full alliances or defensive alliances with several neighbors. Should we get attacked, we will then have a "big brother" watching out for us. Our allies' space fleets will do our fighting for us.

Our new Human race isn't very good in combat, so we'll rely on our allies' help.

The Complete Package

Our new Humans can meet and greet with the best of them, so quickly explore the galaxy and strike up diplomatic talks with every new race you find. Work on generating revenue through trade and building alliances, before making your move in the galaxy. Hang with the top of the pack until your finances spit out more military than the rest can handle, or join the Orion Senate and negotiate your way into better position. Given time, your new master merchants should be able to copyright planets on either end of the great spiral.

Visit as many alien cities as you can with a trading race so you can strike up profitable negotiations.

chapter 3

Planets

Without planets, there would be no life, save for some microbes imbedded in comets floating around the vastness of space. Planets are the lifeblood for organic activity. In *Master of Orion III*, planets are the driving force behind the game interaction.

Planets are the jewels in your crown. If you run your empire correctly, people will be dedicating statues to you in no time.

Early on in the game, you'll find yourself spending much more time in the Planets section than anywhere else. To balance a world economy, there are a ton of tweaks on the individual planet menus, and chances are you'll be consumed until you get them right. Once you master planetary economies, the road to domination will be smooth.

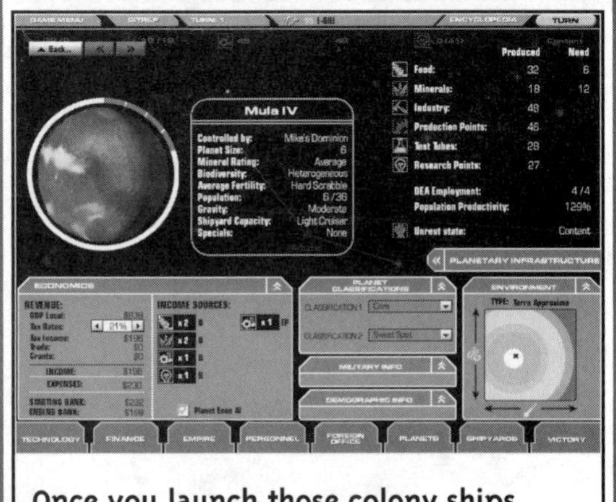

Once you launch those colony ships, you'll spend most of your game time at the Planet screen.

Home Sweet Home

In the beginning, there was one—one planet, that is. Early on, your empire is manageable, and that's the time you want to put in to fine-tuning your world-building skills. For the first ten or so turns, you want to watch your home planet closely to see where it excels and where it has trouble.

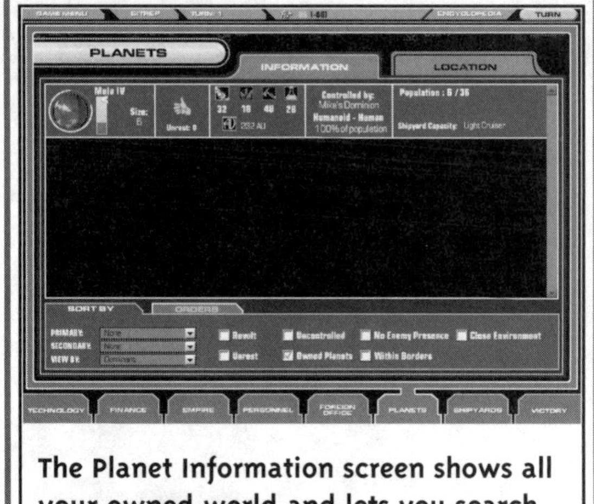

The Planet Information screen shows all your owned world and lets you search for new ones to conquer.

On the Planet Information screen, you'll see your planet icon on the left. This gives you the planet's environmental statistics and size. We'll talk about this more during the "Planet Scanning" section.

Unrest

Next, you'll see an unrest indicator. It starts out green with the thumbs-up symbol. Make sure it stays green and that the number doesn't rise too high—depending on various factors, in general, you want to keep the unrest number in the single digits or mid-teens. Once it hits the yellow open-hand symbol, it's a warning that things are going to

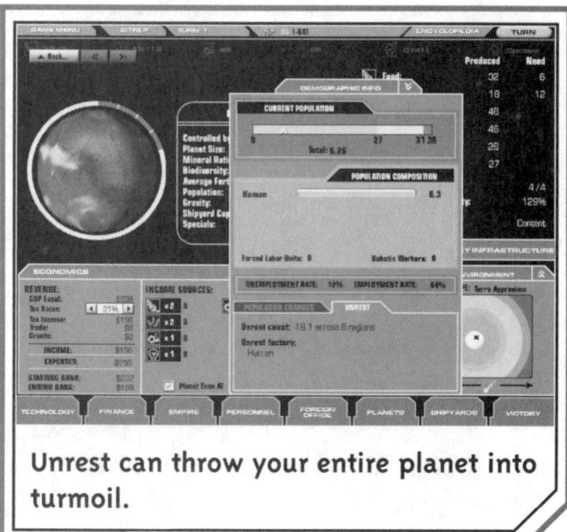

Unrest can throw your entire planet into turmoil.

get ugly. You need to immediately devote resources at this point. Should it hit the red fist symbol, your planet is in revolt. The population will begin destroying buildings and economic centers, and within a turn or two, you'll lose control of the planet.

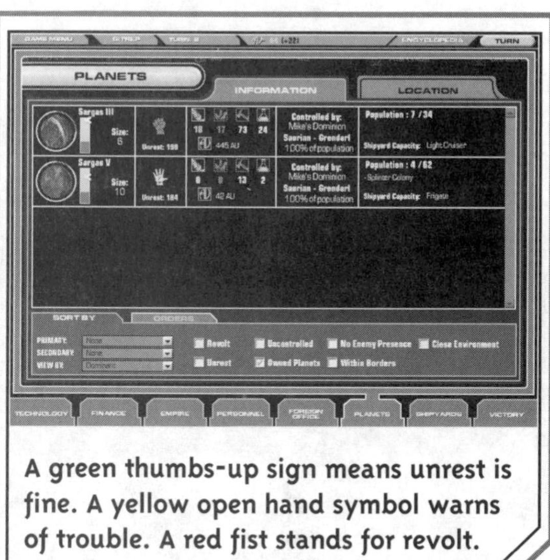

A green thumbs-up sign means unrest is fine. A yellow open hand symbol warns of trouble. A red fist stands for revolt.

CAUTION

Unrest can undermine your planet's economy early. Balance your tax rate and make your population happy so they work hard for you.

How do you stop unrest? Keep your people happy. Under the Demographic menu, there is an unrest tab that shows the unrest count and displays the unrest factors. Usually, the cause is high taxes, but it can be other things like starvation or overcrowding. You need to check this and adjust your numbers to reduce the unrest factors.

Lowering taxes can reduce the unrest level in a hurry.

Taxes are a simple matter. Assuming you've set your empire taxes appropriately, each planet has a specific tax rate under the Economics menu. Click the tax rate down one or two percentage points and monitor the unrest next turn. If it's gotten significantly better, you've done your job and you can leave the planet alone for a while. If it's still high, you may be gouging the populace too much and need to reduce the taxes even more.

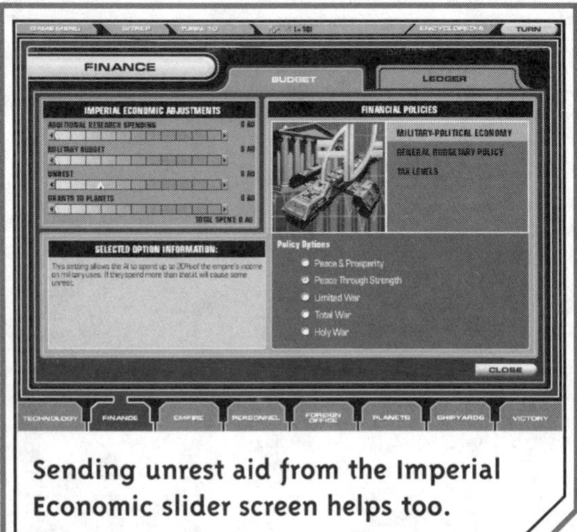
Sending unrest aid from the Imperial Economic slider screen helps too.

Another easy fix is the Imperial Economic Adjustments menu under the finance section. One of your four choices is "unrest," and you can spend as many AUs (Antaran Units) as you need to reduce the unrest. Money spent from the Imperial Economic Adjustments screen are AUs taken directly out of the net profit and flooded back into that particular area. In effect, you can "buy off" your unrest problems with worldwide celebrations, minor planetary improvements, and even well-placed political bribes.

Alternatively, you can try setting up a recreation DEA. Go under the planetary infrastructure tab and add one to a region that will support it. A recreation DEA will significantly reduce unrest, plus it has the added benefit of generating extra money from tourism if there's a space port in the same region. Both of the recreational benefits

Recreation always makes people happy and will soothe unrest.

have an outreach effect—they extend to adjacent solar systems and help to keep those worlds happy and profitable.

Primary Statistics

To the right of the unrest box are your planet's main stats: food, minerals, industry, production points, test tubes, and research points. A quick glance at them each turn will tell you if your society is headed in the direction you need it to head.

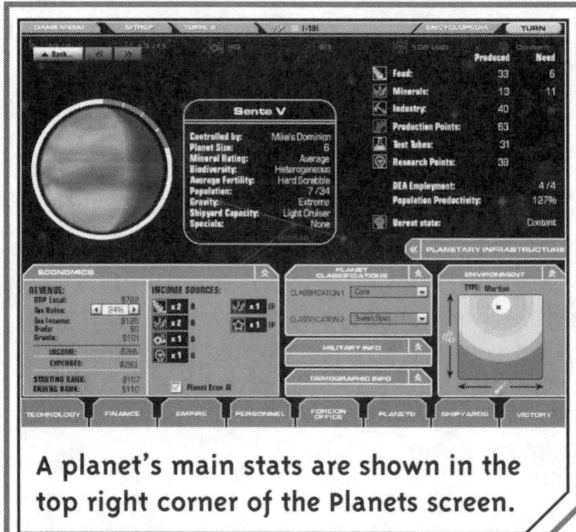
A planet's main stats are shown in the top right corner of the Planets screen.

Food represents the output of your Bioharvesting DEAs. Most populations consume one food per population point. Should you drop below this level, your population growth will significantly decrease and unrest will climb. Drop below 50 percent of the population's requirements, and they begin to die off. Watch the "Produced" and "Consumed" columns so your civilization doesn't eat itself out of a home. If you run into difficulties, increase your terraforming so that your planet's efficiency improves, and build another farming DEA if your viceroy (the AI-controlled planetary leader) hasn't gotten around to it yet.

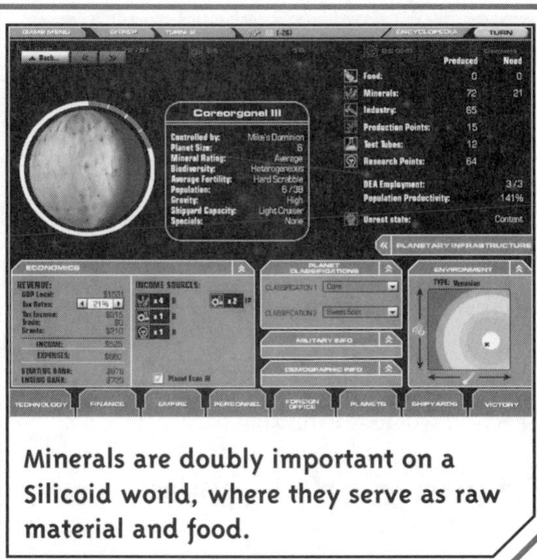

Minerals are doubly important on a Silicoid world, where they serve as raw material and food.

Minerals stand for the output of your Mining and follow the same trend as your food stat. Usually the margin of "Produced" and "Consumed" will be closer with minerals, but you can bump up your normal economic development slider to help out or design another Mining DEA to help with output. Note that the factory consumption rate (mineral amount needed per 10 industry) can be reduced over time through Research achievements.

Industry creates production points, which are used to build your infrastructure.

Industry, the output of factories and the general population, determines the final cost of production points. If a planet has 100 industry, then the first 100 production points would be one AU per point. Additional production points would kick industry into overdrive, taxing the whole system, and would increase the cost of each of those points beyond 100. Avoid this if possible—you're just wasting money—or fund various Research projects to cut down on production spending.

TIP

For races relying on Manufacturing, monitor a planet's industry carefully. If you prefer Research, watch your test tubes.

Production points determine how much funded Manufacturing the planet is performing that turn. The more buildings, DEAs, and money you want to make off industry, the higher this value should be.

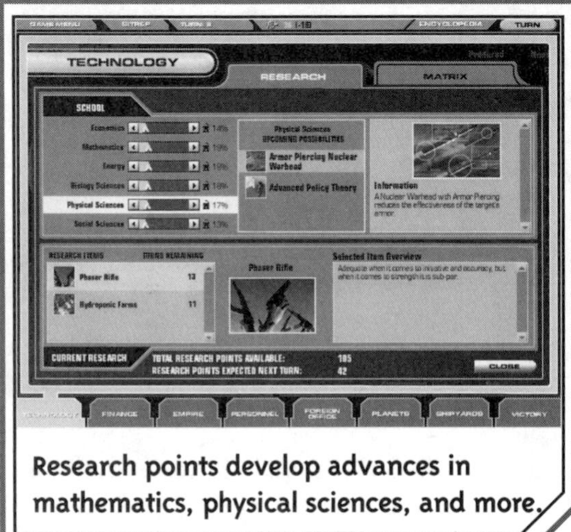

Research points develop advances in mathematics, physical sciences, and more.

On the Research side of things, test tubes show the output of your population and scientific DEAs. Think of it as the research potential for the planet. Much like industry works for production points, test tubes work for research points.

Following the same pattern, Research points determine how much funded research the planet is conducting that turn. Keep this value high and you'll be cranking out new toys each turn, which helps other aspects of your society.

Below your four main stats lies the AU symbol. This value matches your "starting bank" value on the economics tab; it represents how much money the planet has at the beginning of the turn.

Use the "Univalue," which is displayed in the ring surrounding the planet on the Planet Screen and is a composite of a number of factors, to accurately represent the desirability of a particular world.

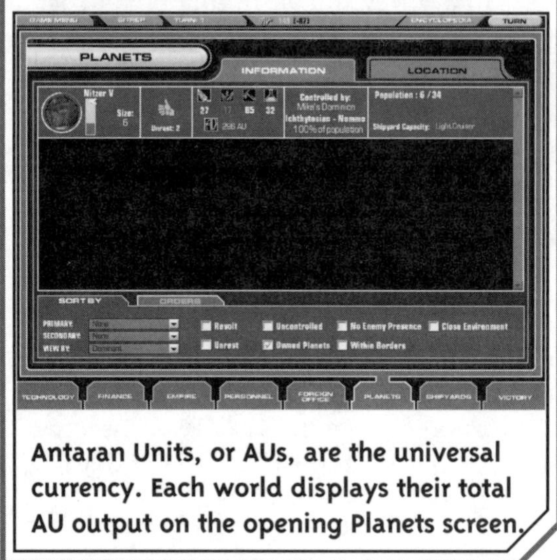

Antaran Units, or AUs, are the universal currency. Each world displays their total AU output on the opening Planets screen.

Planet Scanning

The game's about growing your empire, and the only way to do that is to colonize more planets. Consider exploration, smart exploration, your most important task. So, in the gigantic vastness of space, where do you start?

Stars and Types

Start with the galaxy map. Generally, you begin with a colony ship orbiting your homeworld and space lanes leading to two or three other systems. One of these new systems will be your target, but you need to know something about spectral analysis before you can choose the best route.

The color and size of a star will determine the solar system around it. Depending on your race's genetic makeup,

TIP

Before you head out to another system, click on your home system. Sometimes, you can find a second hospitable world right there and avoid wasted turns of space travel.

certain stars, and their respective planets, will have a better chance for an environment ideally suited for your beings. Planets with an environment closer to your "sweet spot" will generate greater revenue because you won't spend as much terraforming the planet to your home conditions. Generally, hot stars will host hot planets. Violet-white stars are the hottest, then blue-white, white, yellow-white, yellow, orange and red. While exploring, head toward the star colors closest to your race's starting colors.

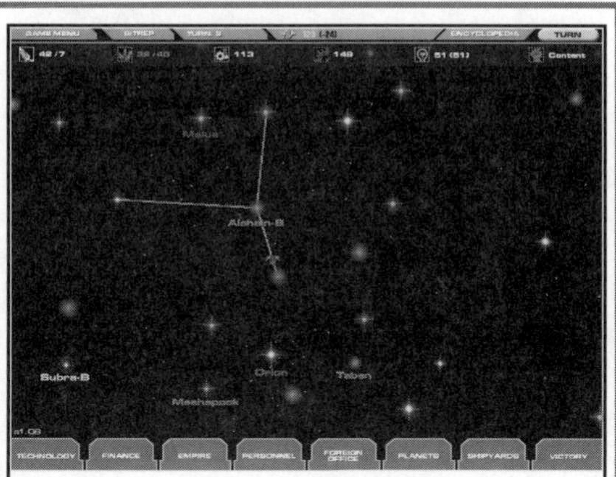

Head toward stars with the same color and size as your home system star for the best chances at "sweet spot" planets.

If you're playing Human, a yellow star or an orange dwarf will most likely hold the better planets. Forget about a violet-white star—all those planets will be inhospitable unless you have significant technological advancements *and* put in a lot of terraforming work to bring the planet's environment into better alignment for your race. It's not worth it.

Sorting It Out

To save yourself the hassle of clicking on each explored solar system and running through it planet by planet, you can use the "Sort By" tab to call up all the planetary info you need to make your decisions. Click off "Owned Planets" and click on "Uncontrolled"—this will call up all the non-colonized planets in your explored systems. Then click on "Close Environment" to further weed out the planets not hospitable to your race. You can even sort it by other race's preferences, so you can immediately spot which planets are prime real estate for an aggressive neighbor.

TIP

On the Planets menu, sort your recent discoveries by "Close Environment" and quickly determine which will readily support your race. Turn off the "Owned Planets" check box when searching for Close Environment planets; it's a quick and easy way of locating good worlds that happen to be in systems you've already explored.

Environmental Activist

Pay attention to the environment bar near the planet. The arrow will show you how close the planet's environment is to perfect. Red is bad. Your people will live in biodomes, a maximum of one population per region can exist, there's no farming until technological advancements permit it, and building maintenance increases by 100 percent. You don't want to be anywhere near this.

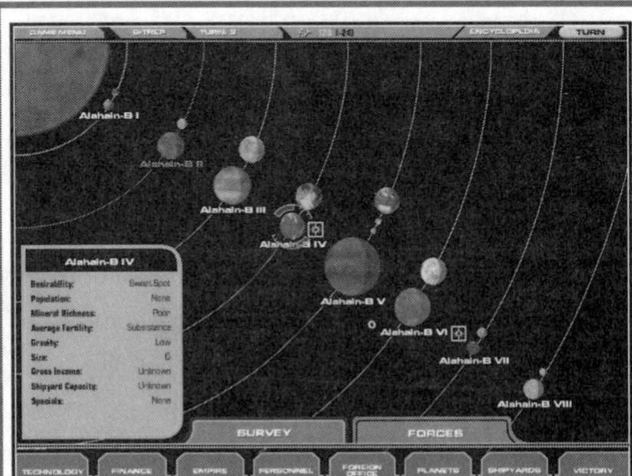

Look for "sweet spot" or "green" worlds that match your homeworld's environment. Stay away from "yellow" or "red" hostile worlds.

NOTE

You have to terraform a planet to Paradise once you reach a certain technology level that enables the transition (terraforming Achievements Atmospheric Processors and Bio-Engineered Life). You're pretty unlikely to run across such a world, but it can happen.

Yellow is a bit better, but you should avoid these worlds unless they have something exceptional. Your people can live in a yellow atmosphere if they wear a breathing apparatus. Maximum population is 40 to 50 percent of the equivalent-sized homeworld, there's no farming until achievements permit it, and building maintenance is increased by 50 percent.

NOTE

The presence of moons can affect the starting conditions and specifically the living space of planets.

Green worlds are fine. Maximum population might only be 70 to 85 percent of a homeworld-like planet, but everything else is normal. You'll build most of your colonies on green worlds.

"Sweet spot" worlds match your homeworld and shouldn't be passed up. If you're ever fortunate enough to run across a "Paradise," colonize it immediately. All regions on a paradise planet are perfectly terraformed and population can reach 120 percent of homeworld levels.

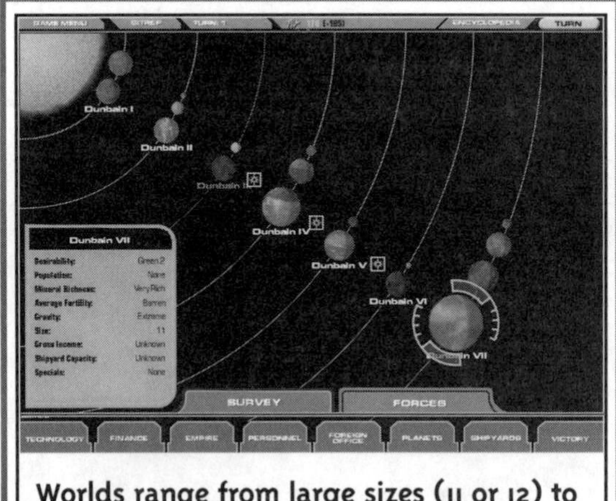

Worlds range from large sizes (11 or 12) to medium (6) and small (3 and below).

To the right of the environment bar, note the planet's size. Earth would be right in the middle at six, though sizes can range from 1–12. The size equals the number of regions on that planet. If you can score a larger planet, you will have more room to build DEAs and potentially make even larger profits.

TIP

When choosing a world for colonization, if your Bioharvesting is better than your Mining, you want to look at fertility first.

Either Ore

Most races will look at minerals next. Choose a world with either rich or very rich mineral content. If none exist, move on to the next system. Avoid very poor and poor mineral planets. Should you be lucky enough to stumble upon an ultra-rich mineral planet, set up camp. Rich mineral worlds produce almost twice as much as average worlds, very rich worlds churn out three times as much, and ultra-rich planets pump out four times as much. Planets surrounding younger stars generally have greater mineral richness.

Fertile Ground

Based on the habitability zone and the ecosystem density (how many animals and plants live there), fertility alters food production and population growth rate. Races with good or superior Bioharvesting values should look for fertile worlds to maximize their potential. Fertility ranges through six categories: lush, hard scrabble, subsistence, barren, hostile, and toxic. Higher density planets are more fertile.

Subsistence fertility is better than hostile or toxic soil.

Moons can be tiny or the size of medium planets.

Gravity of the Situation

Five gravity conditions exist: crushing, heavy, average, light, and nil. Each race has an ideal gravity, so be aware of yours and search out worlds with the same. At ideal gravity, your race receives 100 percent output from all DEAs. Depending on how far gravity diverges from your race's norm, your DEA output can be reduced by 25 to 50 percent.

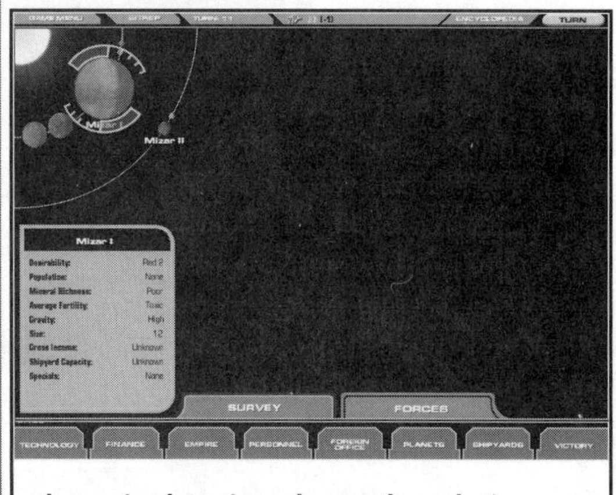

The univalue ring shows the relative development of the planet's civilization at a glance.

Full Moon Rising

You can't click on a moon and see what it offers. Moons contribute to a planet's value without being a direct target for your colonization. Planets with mineral-efficient moons have their mineral value adjusted higher. Bioharvest-efficient moons better a planet's food production. "Habitable" moons can't be colonized directly, but the additional living space increases the planet's maximum population allowance. Finally, moons with bonus DEA output increase the efficiency of Manufacturing on the home planet.

Univalue Ring

The funky circle spinning around planets you click on is called a "univalue ring." It shows the relative development of that planet by the civilization that controls it, based on economics, population size, and military defense. It's very useful for high-level planning. You can click through a new solar system and quickly gauge the best targets, or scan through your own to decide which planets need reinforcement.

Colonization

After you find the best planet, you have to colonize it. You have three options: send colony ship, send outpost ship, and set migration. Colony ships are usually the most fruitful choice, though outpost ships and migration can work in the correct situations.

Colony ships carry an entire mini-civilization inside their hulls; when they arrive at a planet, expect a full-fledged colony a few turns later. Under the "Orders" tab, you can select a planet and click on "Send Colony Ship." The next available colony ship will head off to that planet and—voila!—instant planetary economy.

CAUTION

Population point figures for Colony and Outpost ships apply to Green planets only. When colonizing Yellow or Red planets, fewer colonists will survive, so there will be less than a full Population Point on the planet when the ship lands. It will be treated as less than a full Colony until there's a full point there. Fortunately, it's possible to send more than one Colony (or Outpost) ship to a single planet at a time, so you can ensure that a full colony will be created by sending two ships to a Yellow world and four to a Red one. You can land as many settlers as you want on the turn when a full Colony is established, but not thereafter.

There are many different ways to colonize a planet. The easiest is to select the new planet at the solar system screen.

Colony ships hold four times as many pioneers as outpost ships.

TIP

Go with colony ships over outpost ships if you have the funds. Colony ships supply a full-blown colony, while outpost ships are only loaded with one-quarter the population needed to instantly colonize a new world.

Outpost ships are smaller versions of colony ships. They carry a one-quarter population point, which can grow into a starter colony (one full population point), though they grow *very* slowly. When they do finally create a colony, they generate a military DEA with it. Not really cost effective, outposts are helpful for colonizing red or yellow mineral-rich systems that have hostile environments. Outpost ships also "lay claim" to a system, so friendly races will leave the system alone.

Your last option for colonizing a world is to set a migration policy. This encourages your people to move to this planet. If you can get population high enough on your owned worlds, people will head for "greener pastures" on the migration world. It's not exactly reliable, but you don't have to pay for those expensive colony ships, either.

Running a Planet

Each planet elects a viceroy to run the planet for you. Not bad, considering there are a million items to keep track of in an empire and you rarely have time to micromanage each planet's DEAs. For the most part, you'll want to let the viceroy run things—they do a good job. Even if you make changes to a planet's management, your viceroy will gradually take control over the span of 10 to 20 turns and run it the way he thinks best.

Planetary viceroys run things for you when you're out of the office.

Economics

When you want to monitor a planet's economy, you'll access the economics tab often. Here you can check on the revenue, expenses, tax rates, build queues, funding level, and more. Your viceroy will adjust the rates for you, but you may disagree and want to tweak them yourself.

Adjust your planet's finances if you don't like the job the viceroy is doing.

Under revenue, your income and expenses are detailed out for you. GDP local stands for gross domestic product and represents the total amount of pre-tax AUs generated by the planet before trade. Tax income accounts for the amount of GDP retained for the planet's use. Trade shows the AUs generated through taxation on interplanetary and interstellar trade. Grants can be set under the Finance menu and equal the AUs given to the planet from the empire's bank.

Below revenue, expenses are calculated to show you how much the planet costs you to keep running. Production indicates the total AUs used by the build queues and funding levels. Maintenance rates show what has been built on the planet and the cost of buildings, ground forces, and the current terraforming level. Industry creates pollution, and the last expense represents the AUs needed to clean up pollution generated during the turn.

At the bottom of the money sheet, your starting bank shows the AUs you had at the start of the turn, while ending bank shows what remains in the bank after the turn's income is added and expenses are subtracted. If your ending bank is higher than your starting bank, you have a profitable planet.

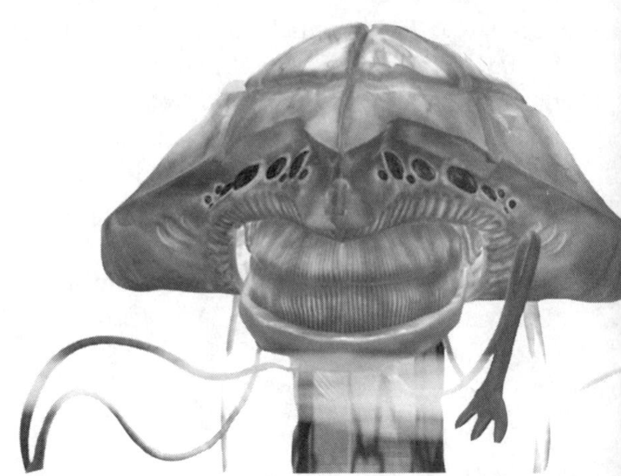

Construct military and planetary buildings in the Economics tab.

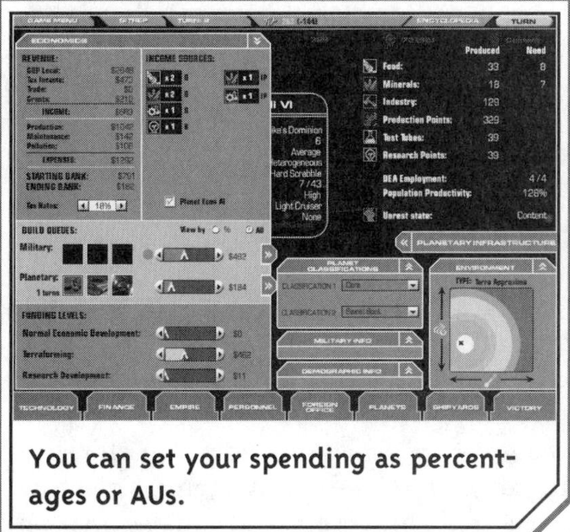

You can set your spending as percentages or AUs.

Build Queues

Military and planetary buildings are constructed in the Build Queues area. The tab displays three icons that show you what is being built. Items on the left are worked on first, followed by the middle item, and then the rightmost item. As an item is completed, a new one moves into place on the right-hand side. Planetary buildings work exactly the same way.

To the right of the icons, you can set the percentage of that turn's money to be spent on military. AUs allocated to military go toward each item in the queue, though an emphasis is placed on the leftmost item. Keep in mind that the sliders for military, planetary, and normal economic development all pull from the same industrial resources, so moving one affects the others. If you spend a lot on military, you won't be able to adjust economic development without paying a hefty price.

At any point during construction, you can click on the itemized build list to the far right of the military queue. This shows you exactly which three military units are under construction. Here you can delete the queued items and build new ones if you like. For example, you might not agree with your viceroy's decision to create a missile base and two infantry units. Maybe you want to go on a colonization spree. Under the itemized build list, delete the missile base and build a colony ship instead. Any cash spent on the missile base will be lost; however, you've gained precious time in building what you desire. If you don't want to destroy an item, but just want to delay its production, left-click on the item and drag it to the right side of the queue.

Funding Levels

Besides military funding, the three sliders at the bottom of the Economics tab will require most of your attention. Normal economic development, terraforming, and research development control how your money will be spent and, ultimately, what sort your planet will evolve into. If you want to tweak your economy, these three sliders, plus the military slider, should equal 100 percent to maximize your progress. Sinking less than 100 percent into the economy will save you money, but slow your growth.

Spend points on your funding levels and you'll see your expenses climb. The trick is to gain maximum benefit without overspending. As you move the slider, notice that it tends to go from green to yellow to shades of red. This represents your efficiency in production for each given area. The more you spend, the less efficient you become and the less you get for your extra spending. You really want to stay in the green, where spending efficiency is one for one, one AU for one production or research point. Slide into yellow (2:1) if you feel you must have the boost for that turn. Go higher if your homeworld is under attack and you need military, or when you have money to burn.

FUNDING EFFICIENCY

Green = 1:1 (maximum efficiency)
Yellow = 2:1
Bright Orange = 3:1
Dark Orange = 4:1
Bright Red = 6:1
Dark Red = 6:1–8.1(lowest efficiency)

TIP

Spend a lot when you're at 8:1 because it can't get any worse.

Normal economic development is the catchall for normal economic entities on the planet DEAs, building, etc. Notice that when you move this slider—and military and planetary for that matter—you pay extra money to pollution control. If your world lies in the "sweet spot" or high in the green, most of your efforts should go into economic development or research.

"Sweet spot" worlds like your homeworld don't need much terraforming help.

The terraforming slider helps convert your new world into a paradise for your subjects, and also turn it into an industry-efficient world. If you have the technological advancements to do so, it's generally a good idea to spend whatever leftover percentage points on terraforming to optimize your world.

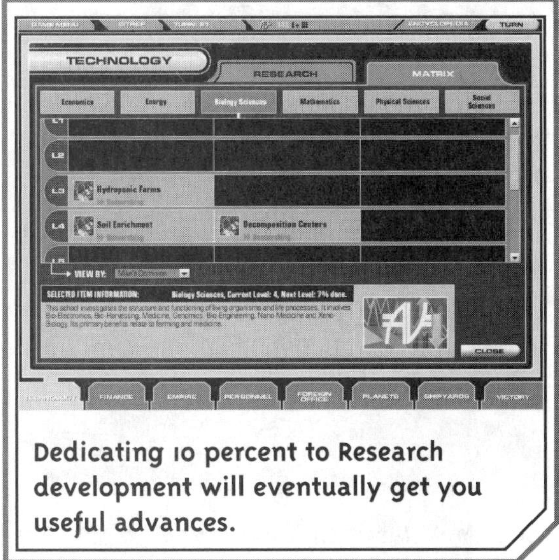

Dedicating 10 percent to Research development will eventually get you useful advances.

Each region on your planet can hold up to two different DEAs and one Spaceport DEA, or dominant economic activities.

Most worlds find it hard to spend on Research development, so don't be worried if you can only push this number up to 10 or 15 percent. That little boost should help generate Research points to fund advancements, which make it easier for your civilization in turns to come.

Planetary Infrastructure

Check out the income sources on the Economics tab first. This shows all your DEAs (dominant economic activities), including the built ones (marked with a B) and the "in progress" ones (marked with an IP). There are eight DEAs: Farming, Mining, Manufacturing, Research, Government, Military, Recreation, and Spaceport.

Under the Planetary Infrastructure tab, the top of the list shows your planetary structures. When you build a new defense installation or planetary supercomputer, it shows up here.

Below this, you can scroll down your various regions. Regions are characterized by terrain (mountain, broken, or plains), ecosystem density (amount of living material in the region), and fertility (as we mentioned before, this ranges from lush to toxic).

The region's terrain affects it the most. Plains are well suited for farming, but poorly suited for mining (except for the Silicoids, who farm in the mountains and mine the plains, and the Cybernetics, who see no effects); mountains are the inverse. Broken lies in the middle, average for both farming and mining. Each region can contain two DEAs and one space port.

Bioharvesting (farming), Mining, Industry, and Research DEAs are all self-explanatory: they increase the amount and efficiency of the designated category. A

Government DEA increases the efficiency of taxation, reduces unrest, and in the case of an empire seat, can spread its influence as far out as adjacent solar systems. Military DEAs increase the stacking limit of military buildings and orbitals around the planet and reduce unrest. Recreation DEAs can also reduce unrest and generate some funds from tourism if a space port inhabits the same region.

Speaking of space ports, they allow you trade between other space ports, even outside your home system. Late in the game, a Space Port DEA may be able to trade with another space port up to four space lanes away.

> **TIP**
>
> **Defend your Government DEAs with serious ground and space forces. If attackers destroy all Government DEAs, they gain control of a planet.**

Planet Classification

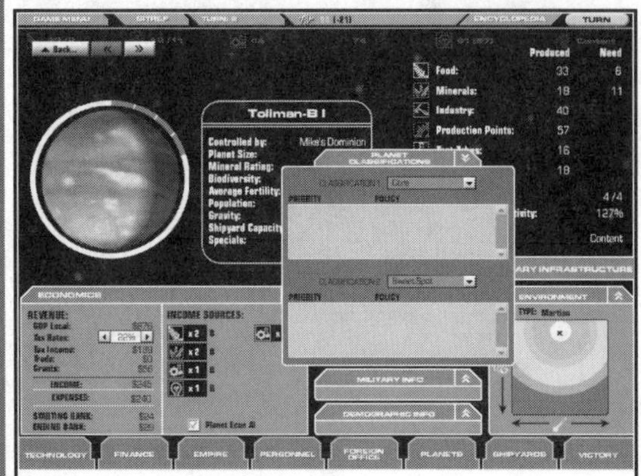

A planet classification lets you "tag" worlds you want to give group orders to, like an industry-rich world or one driven by Bioharvesting.

Think of this area as a notepad. You can designate a planet as a "Military Center" or "Mining Colony." Rather than fuzz through all of the planet's numbers, a glance at the planet classification can jog your memory for the planet's function. You can also tie this into development plans and have your viceroy customize the world based on this classification. You could give primary emphasis to military centers, and your viceroy would know to crank out military units first, before anything else.

Military Info

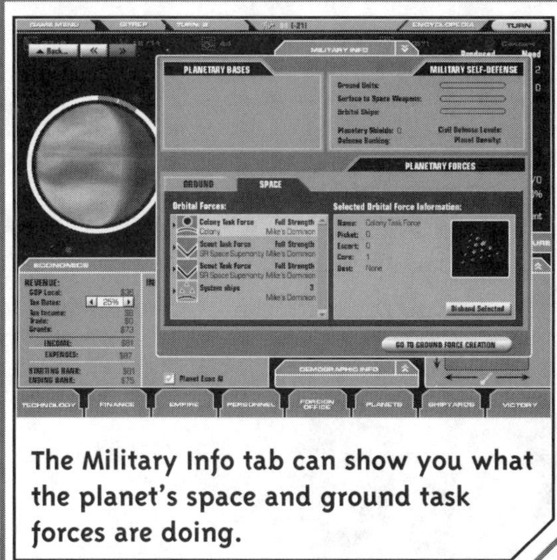

The Military Info tab can show you what the planet's space and ground task forces are doing.

For the full scoop on how well your military is performing on a given planet, click on the Military Info tab. A menu pops up with three main sections: planetary bases, military self-defense, and planetary forces. Planetary bases simply lists the bases on your planet—missile, beam, etc.—but the other two you'll refer to often.

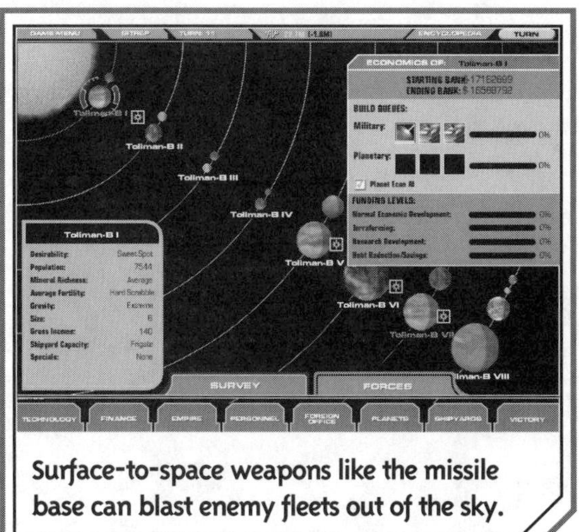

Surface-to-space weapons like the missile base can blast enemy fleets out of the sky.

Military self-defense shows the planet's maximum capacity for ground units, surface-to-space weapons, and orbital ships. It also notes whether you have planetary shields and rates your defense ranking and civil defense level. To balance your planet's military, stagger your builds between ground units, STS (surface-to-space) weapons, and orbital ships.

Military builds can get out of hand while running an empire—that's why you have viceroys—so you can always check this screen for the breakdown percentages. If the ground units are at 15 percent to orbital ships' 55 percent, train more troops. Keep a balance, but you need to start with orbital ships (to protect the system from enemy ships) and ground units (to secure your government seat), and then supplement them with STS weapons as extra firepower.

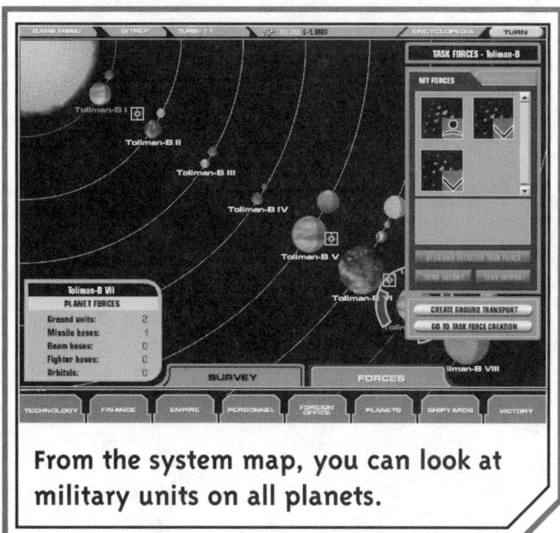

From the system map, you can look at military units on all planets.

The planetary forces section lists all ground and space forces, along with their missions and strength levels. It's probably more than you need to know, unless you're waging a war campaign from that planet. At the bottom of the screen, you can click on "Ground Force Creation" to organize any grunts you might have created.

All the Marbles

Those tiny blue marbles in space might not look like much in the distance, but they're the heart of your empire. Learn how to run planets efficiently and you'll have all the money and military you need to rule the galaxy. Treat them like so much rock and all the diplomatic cooing in the universe won't save your bacon. If you're playing *Master of Orion III*, after hundreds of turns exploring the galaxy, planets should feel just like your children.

Chapter 4: Technology

Energy is the most studied school.

Given the choice between 10,000 troops and a nuclear bomb, I'll take the bomb. Modern wars are won on technological superiority, whether it's gun over club, jet over biplane, or satellite surveillance over binoculars. Not to mention the boost technology gives everyday life. Where would we be without engines or computers?

In *Master of Orion III*, the Technology breaks down into six separate schools: economics, energy, biological sciences, mathematics, physical sciences, and social sciences. Each school influences a particular aspect of your empire. Some are more useful than others, though it all depends on how you want to evolve your civilization. You can't master all 380 different advances, so focus on two or three schools.

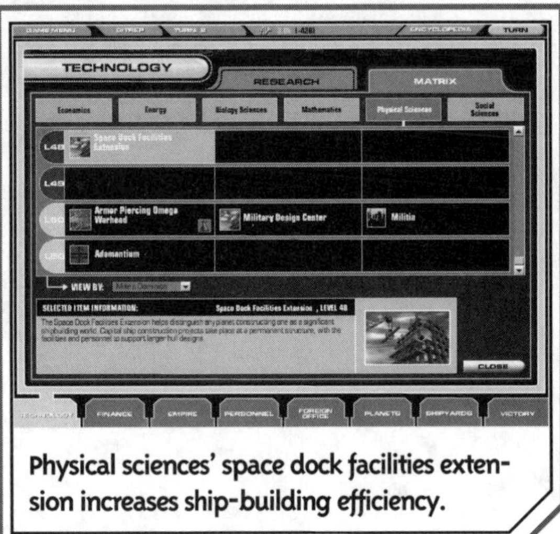

Physical sciences' space dock facilities extension increases ship-building efficiency.

Research

Click on the Technology menu and it opens to the research tab. On the top left, all six schools are represented with expenditure percentages next to them. You can't touch them the first turn—your Chief Scientist can't make up his mind where he wants to spend your money—but adjust them early in your planet's development.

To accelerate and get the jump on your fellow alien powers, concentrate in two areas, devoting at least 30 to 40 percent to each. Split whatever is left to one or two other schools. For example, let's say you want to concentrate on economics and biological sciences. Slide both up to 40 percent, then spend the remaining 20 percent on whichever other school you think best complements your direction. Once you have all your percentages figured out, lock them in place so the viceroy doesn't fiddle with them later.

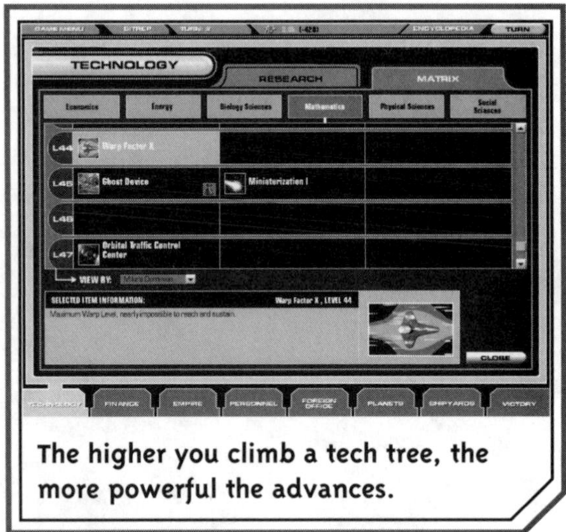

The higher you climb a tech tree, the more powerful the advances.

To the right of the schools, "upcoming possibilities" previews the next advance in that field. "Research items" (bottom left) shows how many turns you have left to change one of your discoveries into a practical application to use in your empire. At the bottom, "total Research points available" displays how many points you're using this turn. The "Research points expected next turn number" helps you decide whether your advances are proceeding quickly enough. If the points next turn are low, devote more finances to your research centers, and contemplate purchasing a new Research DEA in the empire.

The Matrix

You're not going into a 3-D virtual reality environment. In *Master of Orion III*, the matrix charts all six schools and your discoveries to date in those schools. If you click on a school, the bottom information box displays what level you've successfully studied and the percentage you've completed on the next level. Depending on the school, there are 40 or 50 levels to research, so be patient and check back often to update your choices.

It's not called the matrix for its virtual-reality karate moves.

Economics

Economics is more than just businesses making money. It also includes trade, budgets, law, process engineering, and even education. The economics school has nine advances dedicated to government and eight to Manufacturing. Three advances help Mining, two tax collection, and two miscellaneous breakthroughs—one for Research and one for space ports—round out the list. If you score a good or superior rating in Manufacturing, or want your government to be the strongest in the galaxy, then invest percentage points in the economics school.

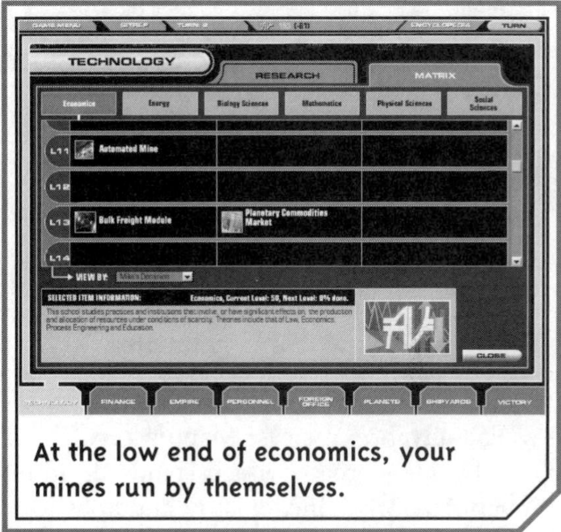

At the low end of economics, your mines run by themselves.

Starting with the securities board, there are five advances that increase your government DEA by one. The mid-range lending associations, higher-level reserve banks, government robot, and mints are the other four. Government DEAs increase the efficiency of taxation, and reduce planetary unrest. Each Government DEA advance on its own isn't powerful, but the cumulative effect can eliminate unrest and roll in the tax dollars.

By level 30, you'll collect all four of your heavy foot of government reducers. Anti-redundancy structuring, institutional checks and balances, legal engineering, and fiscal ubiquity help negate the penalties of setting your Oppressometer high, thus keeping out spies and keeping the local peace. By the time you reach fiscal ubiquity, you can reduce the heavy foot by 17 percent and, literally, get away with murder.

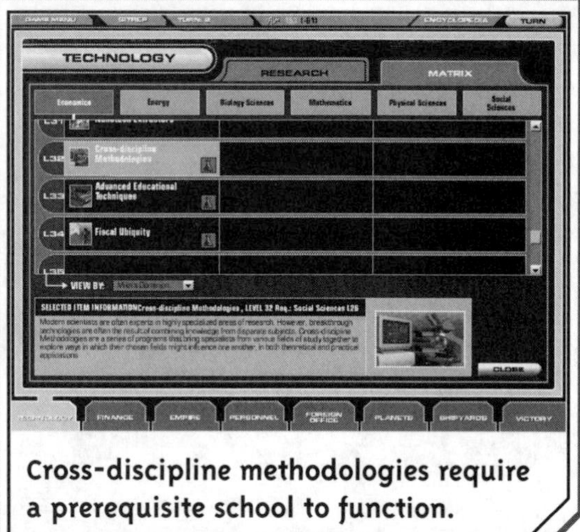

Cross-discipline methodologies require a prerequisite school to function.

Five advances increase Manufacturing DEAs by one—broader usage, standardization, miniaturization, refined quality, and holistic planning. Manufacturing-centric races should exploit these advances. However, don't neglect these five if you're suffering in that department; they might be the boost your economy needs to survive.

Harmonic construction techniques cheapen the building cost of structures like the mint.

Also in the realm of Manufacturing, harmonic construction techniques reduce building costs by one, which allows for cheaper and faster industry. The awesome imperial university and advanced educational techniques increase food, mineral, industry, *and* test tube production by 10 percent.

CAUTION

Advances like imperial university are incredible. Unfortunately, they rely on progress in two schools—in this case, mid-level economics and level 20 mathematics.

Mining can gain a shot in the arm with only three advances on the board. The three cumulative-bonus advances—automated mine, robo mining plant, and nanotech extractors—add one, two, and three bonuses, respectively. Reach the early 30s and your Mining efficiency can be up by six points.

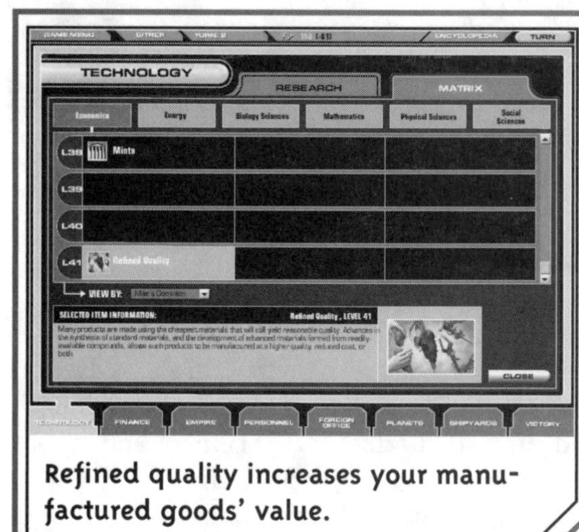

Refined quality increases your manufactured goods' value.

If your trade avenues are slow or you run a few planets that don't accept high taxes, squeeze every AU out of your tax revenue. That's where planetary commodities market and system stock exchange come in. The commodities market increases tax collection by 15 percent, while the system stock exchange raises tax collection by 10 percent, *but* across the entire system. It's particularly useful if you've colonized many planets in your home system.

Two miscellaneous advances shouldn't be counted out. The mid-teen bulk freight module increases space port efficiency by one. Even better, cross-discipline methodologies—which, unfortunately, relies on a level 26 social sciences to function—increases your Research DEAs by *three* points!

Economic Advances

Advance	DEA/Resource Affected	Adjustment
Advanced Educational Techniques	Food, Minerals, Industry, Test Tubes	+10%
Anti-Redundancy Structuring	Heavy Foot of Government	-3%
Automated Mine	Mining DEA	+1
Broader Usage	Manufacturing DEA	+1
Bulk Freight Module	Space Port	+1
Cross-discipline Methodologies	Research DEA	+3
Fiscal Ubiquity	Heavy Foot of Government	-5%
Government Robot	Government DEA	+1
Harmonic Construction Techniques	Building Cost	-1
Holistic Planning	Building Cost	-1
Imperial University	Food, Minerals, Industry, Test Tubes	+10%
Institutional Checks and Balances	Heavy Foot of Government	-4%
Legal Engineering	Heavy Foot of Government	-5%
Lending Associations	Government DEA	+1
Miniaturization	Manufacturing DEA	+1
Mints	Government DEA	+1
Nanotech Extractors	Mining DEA	+3
Planetary Commodities Market	Tax Collection	+15%
Refined Quality	Manufacturing DEA	+1
Reserve Banks	Government DEA	+1
Robo Mining Plant	Mining DEA	+2
Securities Board	Government DEA	+1
Standardization	Manufacturing DEA	+1
System Stock Exchange	Tax Collection	+10%

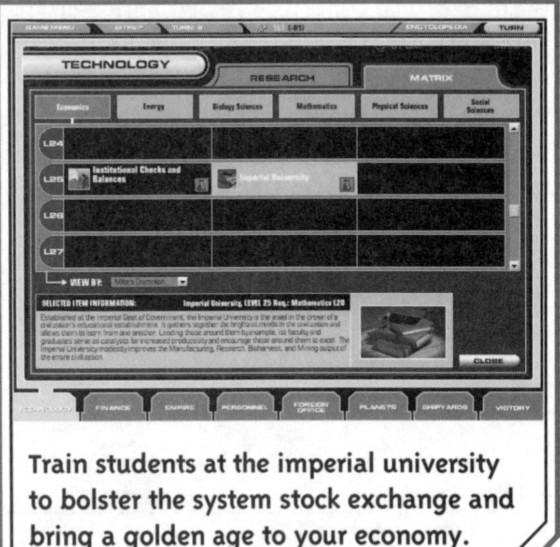

Train students at the imperial university to bolster the system stock exchange and bring a golden age to your economy.

Energy

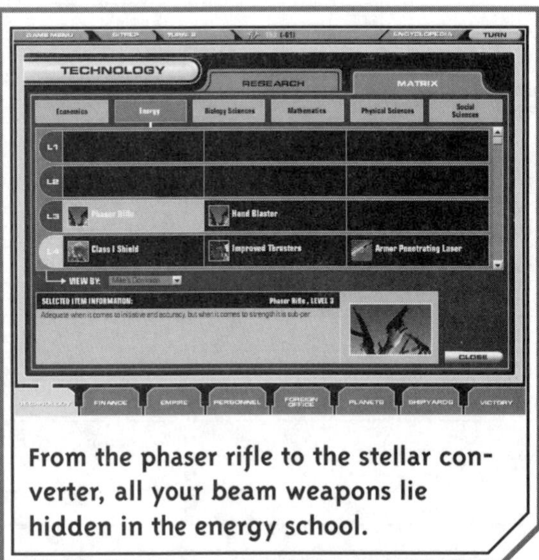

From the phaser rifle to the stellar converter, all your beam weapons lie hidden in the energy school.

Delve into relativistic physics or quantum mechanics and you touch upon the subatomic universe that is energy's domain. This school's studies include matter-energy conversion, transwarp physics, optronics, and transdimensional electronics. It touts the most advances of any school, and probably for that reason—sheer quantity—it should be one of your chosen pursuits. If that doesn't convince you, the energy school aids your military with all kinds of weapons and ship shields.

Weapons

Don't throw sticks at your opponent. Weapons increase the effectiveness of your military and deliver an edge when equal forces meet. It's another reason why the energy school commands your attention.

Weapons have four types: ground, ship, fighter, and missile. Ground weapons can only be used by your infantry to defend and lay siege to planets. Ships carry most of the weapons; a ship-designated weapon goes on any space vessel, except for fighter weapons, which apply specifically to that small subclassification. Missiles deliver a physical payload, affecting ship's defenses differently than the standard laser-based weapons.

Fighter weapons don't go on regular ships, only their miniature fighter versions.

As you progress up the scale, weapons deal more damage and have a better chance to hit. To give you an idea of weapon effectiveness, each weapon has a combat value based on its energy level.

Six special abilities apply to weapons. Accuracy increases range by 50 percent, while super range allows you to hit anything on the screen. Armor-piercing capability reduces armor effectiveness by 25 percent. Weapons equipped with autofire get three shots off to a regular weapon's one. Double damage does just that—it doubles a weapon's damage-dealing at close range, plus it increases damage up 10 percent at long range. Shield penetration capabilities reduce a ship's shield effectiveness by 50 percent.

Don't worry about special abilities on ground troops' weapons—they don't have any. For infantry weapons, the higher the energy level, the higher the combat value. Your first weapon is a phaser rifle (energy 2), followed shortly by a fusion gun (energy 6). Middle-of-the-school weapons include the multi-synch phaser rifle (energy 22) and chemical blaster (energy 24). At the top of the destruction heap, the plasma pod cranks out at energy level 38.

Ship's weapons take up the rest of the weapons on the chart. It's not a stretch to tie armor piercing into all the armor-penetrating weapons, such as the armor-penetrating phaser beam (energy level 26), or link autofire to the autofire-named weapons, such as the autofire disruptor cannon (energy level 36). The continuous series of weapons improve accuracy, like the continuous graviton beam (energy level 26) or the continuous plasma cannon (energy level 31). Enveloping weapons, such as the enveloping fusion cannon (energy level 11), offer shield penetration and should be used against ships with light armor and heavy shields. Improved weapons, such as the improved neutron blaster (energy level 29), deal double damage.

A damper field, the most effective shield known to the Orion system, depowers incoming laser blasts.

Those are all laser-based ship weapons. The hercular warhead missiles pack a different punch. Ones like the scatter pack warhead (energy level 33) are armor piercing. They all destroy armor, but have more trouble versus shields.

The smaller fighter vessels have a series of weapons designed just for them. The earliest one, the fighter fusion cannon, can be discovered as early as level six. The most powerful weapon, the fighter disruptor, is found at energy level 35.

The pinnacle of ship weapon technology rests in the energy level -40 mauler. Equip your ship with this beauty and you won't take no for an answer.

Energy Advances: Weapons

Advance	Type	Tech Level	Special
Armor-Penetrating Fighter Laser	Fighter	3	Armor Piercing
Armor-Penetrating Phaser Beam	Ship	26	Armor Piercing
Armor-Penetrating Laser Beam	Ship	3	Armor Piercing
Armor-Piercing Hercular Warhead	Missile	23	Armor Piercing
Armor-Piercing Scatter Pack Warhead	Missile	33	Armor Piercing
Autofire Disruptor Cannon	Ship	36	Autofire
Autofire Fighter Laser	Ship	7	Autofire
Autofire Ion Pulse Cannon	Ship	22	Autofire
Autofire Laser	Ship	5	Autofire
Autofire Phaser Beam	Ship	27	Autofire
Blaster Rifle	Ground	14	—
Chemical Blaster	Ground	24	—
Continuous Fighter Fusion Cannon	Fighter	14	Accuracy
Continuous Fighter Laser	Fighter	8	Accuracy
Continuous Fusion Cannon	Ship	11	Accuracy
Continuous Graviton Beam	Ship	26	Accuracy
Continuous Laser	Ship	7	Accuracy
Continuous Neutron Blaster	Ship	17	Accuracy
Continuous Phaser Beam	Ship	26	Accuracy
Continuous Plasma Cannon	Ship	31	Accuracy
Disruptor Cannon	Ship	34	—
Enveloping Fighter Fusion Cannon	Fighter	16	Shield Penetration
Enveloping Fusion Cannon	Ship	11	Shield Penetration
Fighter Disruptor	Fighter	35	—
Fighter Fusion Cannon	Fighter	8	—
Fighter Graviton Beam	Fighter	19	—
Fighter Ion Cannon	Fighter	22	—
Fighter Neutron Cannon	Fighter	15	—
Fighter Particle Cannon	Fighter	21	—
Fighter Phaser Beam	Fighter	25	—
Fighter Plasma Cannon	Fighter	29	—
Fusion Accelerator	Ground	16	—
Fusion Cannon	Ship	9	—
Fusion Core Launcher	Ground	36	—
Fusion Gun	Ground	6	—
Gatling Laser	Ground	21	—
Graviton Beam	Ship	19	—
Hand Blaster	Ground	4	—
Hercular Warhead	Missile	18	—

Advance	Type	Tech Level	Special
Improved Fusion Cannon	Ship	23	Double Damage
Improved Graviton Beam	Ship	23	Double Damage
Improved Laser	Ship	11	Double Damage
Improved Neutron Blaster	Ship	29	Double Damage
Improved Phaser Beam	Ship	30	Double Damage
Improved Plasma Cannon	Ship	37	Double Damage
Ion Pulse Cannon	Ship	20	—
Laser Assault Rifle	Ground	10	—
Mauler	Ship	40	—
Multi Blaster	Ground	34	—
Multi Fusion Rifle	Ground	27	—
Multi-Sync Phaser Rifle	Ground	22	—
Neutron Blaster	Ship	15	—
No Range Penalty Fighter Laser	Fighter	8	Super Range
No Range Penalty Laser	Ship	7	Super Range
Particle Beam	Ship	21	—
Phaser Assault Rifle	Ground	12	—
Phaser Rifle	Ground	2	—
Phaser Beam	Ship	24	—
Plasma Cannon	Ship	29	—
Plasma Enveloper	Ground	18	—
Plasma Gun	Ground	28	—
Plasma Pod	Ground	38	—
Plasma Projector	Ground	6	—
Pulse Laser	Ground	32	—
Scatter Pack Warhead	Missile	31	—
Tri-Sequence Phaser Rifle	Ground	32	—

Shields

Shields are the first line of defense. They stop laser firepower before it damages your ship. Stockpile bigger and better shield classes to withstand the enemy's guns and be able to return fire. As you climb the energy tree, the shields get better, all the way up to the dampening field.

One of your first energy advancements is class I shields. With a shield strength of 100, you'll take them, but you won't install many before moving on to the responsibly priced class IV shields, which are four times more effective. The exponential pattern stops there, however. Class V shields have a strength of 650 to the IV's 400, and class VII's climb up to 1,800. Though class X shields, the highest in the series, tops out at a 7,700 strength and weighs in at energy level 50, dampening field reveals around energy level 44 and exhibits a *32,000* shield strength!

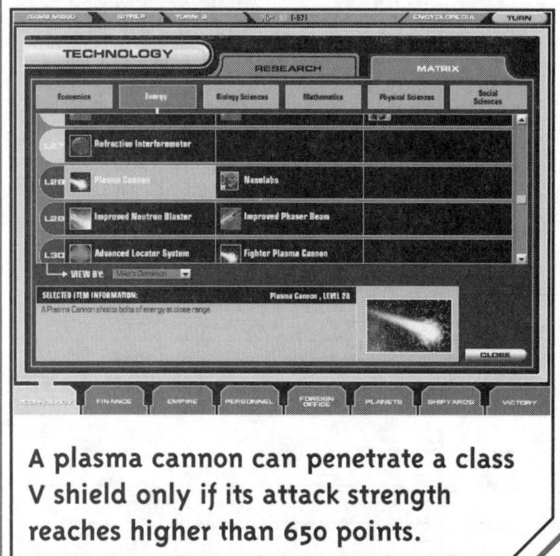

A plasma cannon can penetrate a class V shield only if its attack strength reaches higher than 650 points.

A matter conversion module enables you to build bigger warships, but your world won't need protecting once it installs a planetary shield generator.

You also can purchase shield generators as you work your way up the tree. The large variety doubles shield strength on ships, and the planetary version does the same for whole planets. Because the equipment on a missile shield generator is much smaller, it only increases shield strength by one-third.

Energy Advances: Shields

Advance	Shield Strength
Class I Shield	100
Class II Shield	150
Class III Shield	250
Class IV Shield	400
Class V Shield	650
Class VI Shield	1,150
Class VII Shield	1,800
Class VIII Shield	2,950
Class IX Shield	4,750
Class X Shield	7,700
Damper Field	32,000
Large Shield Generator	Ship's Shield Strength Doubled
Missile Shield Generator	Missile's Shield Strength Increased by One-Third
Planetary Shield Generator	5x Planet's Shield Strength

Detection and Evasion

At energy level 17, the x-ray transponder system doubles the range of your sensors.

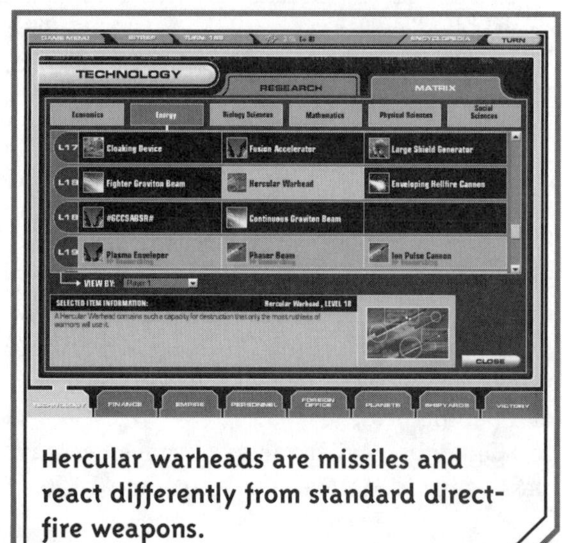

Hercular warheads are missiles and react differently from standard direct-fire weapons.

Two dozen levels later, the ultimate detector system brings scanner range up to four times efficiency. For those who want to know where the enemy is at all times, the energy school has your detection devices.

On the opposite end of the spectrum, the various cloaking devices hide your ship from the enemy. The way they function is to increase your ship's apparent range, so your enemy's scanners can't pick you up. The plain old cloaking device multiplies your range by 2.2, phased cloaking device multiplies it by 3.3, and the reactive cloaking device multiplies it by 4.95. The best cloaker, however, sits in mathematics. The ghost device increases your range by a multiplier of 7.425.

One of your first energy advances is improved thrusters.

The matter conversion module (energy 25) allows you to build one hull level larger on your planet. A size seven world would become a size eight world in terms of shipyard capacity. Nanolabs (energy 29) increase Research DEAs 1.5 points. The T.R.A.P.S. logistics system (energy 33) bumps up military DEAs by one point. Matter facilitators (energy 39) add one point to space port efficiency.

The last series of energy advances center around stardrives. The base speed of all your vessels is 1,500 NSUs (near space units). You can upgrade technology to better outmaneuver your opponent's ships. Improved thrusters give a 300 NSU boost; the king, though, is the transwarp drive, which zooms a ship up to 4,200 NSUs.

Do you go for sensors or all-out artillery? You won't have room for everything.

Energy Advances: System Engines

Advance	System Speed
Improved Thrusters	1,800
Hydrogen Fuel Cells	2,100
Impulse Engine	2,400
Iridium Fuel Cells	2,700
Dotomite Crystals	3,000
Uridium Fuel Cells	3,300
Reajax Fuel Cells	3,600
Trilithium Crystals	3,900
Transwarp Drive	4,200

Biological Sciences

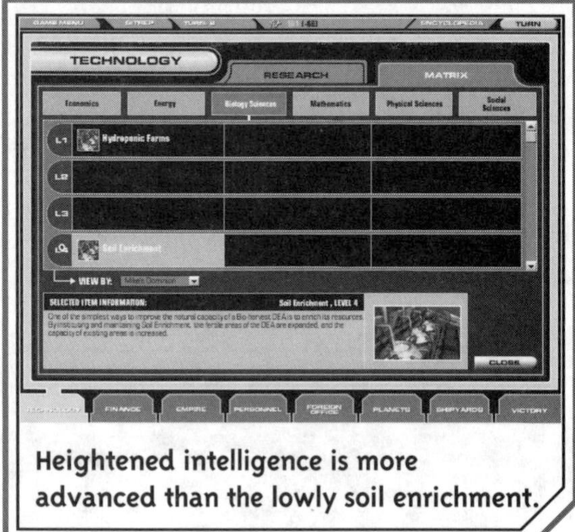
Heightened intelligence is more advanced than the lowly soil enrichment.

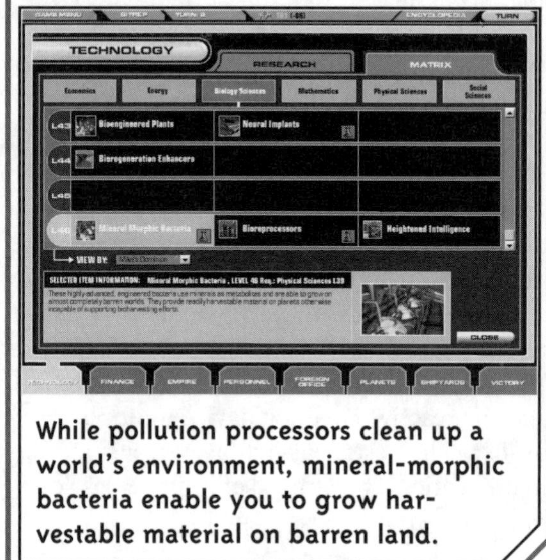
While pollution processors clean up a world's environment, mineral-morphic bacteria enable you to grow harvestable material on barren land.

Looking within, biological sciences investigates the structure and functioning of living organisms and life processes. From genetic engineering to bio-organic cultivation, it benefits farming, population growth, pollution control, and espionage.

When thinking biology, the first race trait that should come to mind is Bioharvesting. Biological sciences, like automated biocare (level 10 biology) and orbital biomonitoring (level 23 biology), grant a +1 bonus. One step up, byproduct reprocessing (level 20 biology) increases Bioharvesting by two and genetic engineering (level 30 biology) by three. Atmospheric containment (level 18 biology) might only grant one point to terraforming, but the powerful bio-engineered life (level 42 biology) terraforms whole planets into paradises.

Hand in hand with Bioharvesting, food DEAs supply your population with nourishment and can eventually be turned into economic profit. Controlled environment farming (level 15 biology) increases food DEA by 1, soil rejuvenators (level 25 biology) notch it up by 1.5, and the ecosystem controller (level 35 biology) raises food DEAs by 2.

When you take into account your food DEAs, terraforming, pollution, and planetary environment, you're talking about the ecological infrastructure. Four advances—bio-organic monitoring station, regional weather controller, moisture regulators, and bioregeneration enhancers—give a plus one to the ecological infrastructure.

Biology Advances: Ecosystem

Advance	Effect
Atmospheric Containment	Terraforming +1
Automated Biocare	Bioharvesting +1
Bio-Engineered Life	Terraforms planets into paradises
Bioharvesting Robot	Food DEA +1
Biomorphic Fungi	Bioharvesting +1, Terraforming +2
Bio-organic Monitoring Station	Ecological infrastructure level +1
Bioregeneration Enhancers	Ecological infrastructure level +1
Byproduct Reprocessing	Bioharvesting +2
Controlled Environment Farming	Food DEA +1
Ecosystem Controller	Food DEA +2
Genetic Engineering	Bioharvesting +3
Mineral-Morphic Bacteria	Bioharvesting +2, Terraforming +1
Moisture Regulators	Ecological infrastructure level +1
Orbital Biomonitoring	Bioharvesting +1
Organic Composites	Bioharvesting +1
Regional Weather Controller	Ecological infrastructure level +1
Soil Enrichment	Food DEA +.5
Soil Rejuvenators	Food DEA +1.5

Each turn, you have to spend money to keep pollution from ruining your planet. Why pay the extra cash? Decomposition centers (level 5 biology), pollution processors (level 16 biology), and atmospheric renewers (level 27 biology) all reduce pollution by one-third. Recycling microbes increases pollution cleanup by .25 points.

Inside your sleeping mind, dream inducers dramatically increase a civilization's research potential.

To staff all your DEAs and colonize far worlds, your population must grow at a steady rate. Cloning complex (level 13 biology) increases population growth by .025 points. For a population explosion, try smart drugs (level 25 biology) and antiagathics (level 38 biology), which grow population by 25 and 50 percent, respectively.

The numbers on biological sciences' espionage advances don't seem to make sense, but you can take advantage of this. Genetic mutagens can be discovered at around level 13, yet it gives a +1 bonus to a spy's Cloak, Dagger, and Luck values. Telepathic training (level 28 biology) and Psionics (level 41 biology) give one point to Cloak and Dagger, and the level 33 neural scanners only give a +1 to Dagger. The level 16 training resistance compensator allows spies to be trained one turn faster.

Biology Advances: Espionage

Advance	Cloak	Dagger	Luck	Special
Genetic Mutagens	+1	+1	+1	—
Neural Scanners	—	+1	—	—
Psionics	+1	+1	—	—
Psi-Signature Dampening Field	—	—	—	Less likely to be detected
Telepathic Training	+1	+1	—	—
Training Resistance Compensators	—	—	—	-1 Turns to spy training

Turn excess food into extra income by selling it. Several biology advances help in this area, such as level 26's organic factories (+.5 to Manufacturing DEAs), level 36's recycling facilities (+1 to Manufacturing DEAs), and level 46's bioreprocessors (+1.5 to Manufacturing DEAs).

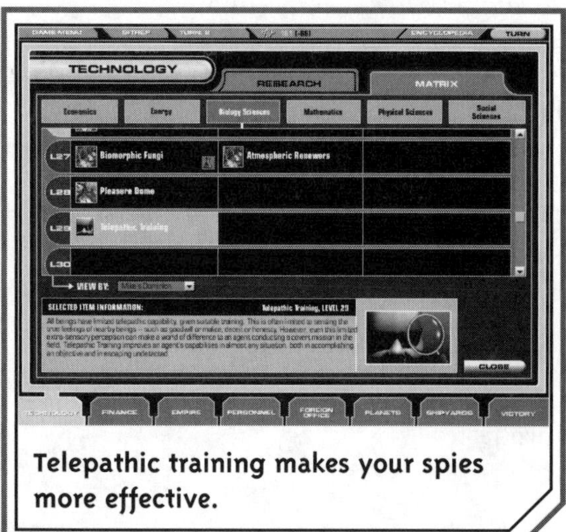

Telepathic training makes your spies more effective.

The stranger biology advances help your civilization without you being aware they're working. Dream inducers (level 34 biology) increase research efficiency a whopping *nine* points, while heightened intelligence (level 46 biology) inches it up a modest three points. Pleasure dome (level 27 biology) increases recreation DEAs by one point, hypersleep nexus (level 34 biology) expands space port capacity by one, and inter-organizational evolution (level 8 biology) reduces the heavy foot of government by three percent. One of the better biology advances, level 42's neural implants increases food, minerals, industry, and test tubes by 50 percent!

Mathematics

Computer science. Number theory. Artificial intelligence. Robotics. Mathematics covers a lot of ground. It helps to fill in a lot of holes in your empire. On the flipside, mathematics doesn't offer many powerful series other than miniaturizations, electronic countermeasures, and warp drives.

Zero right in on the universities. You need economics levels to unlock the advances, but the astro university (level 9 mathematics) and system university (level 16 mathematics) offer the greatest value. Astro increases food, minerals, industry, and test tubes by 40 percent; system modifies the same stats by 30 percent. Other miscellaneous advances to consider: catalyst design (+1 manufacturing conversion), geo-harmonic principle (+1 Mining), experiment replicators (+1 to positive overrun), and Z storage and basing facilities (+1 to military DEAs).

Fourteen miniaturization advances enable mathematics to shrink your equipment to unprecedented levels. Fit another weapon in your starship. Don't let a heavier engine drag you down. From the level 4 mass driver miniaturization I to the level 33 plasma cannon miniaturization II, each advance reduces the appropriate unit space by 30 percent.

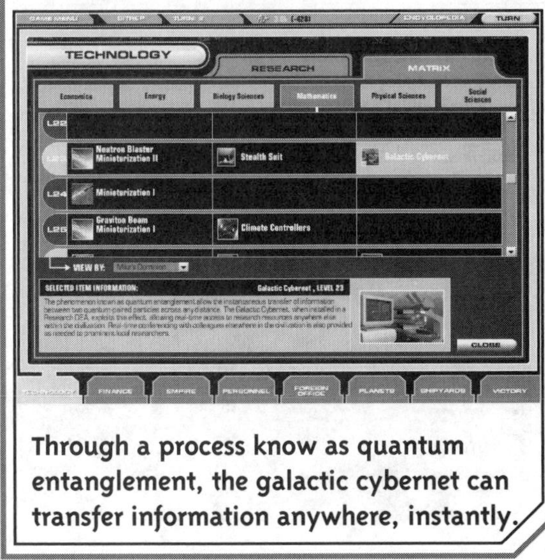

Through a process know as quantum entanglement, the galactic cybernet can transfer information anywhere, instantly.

Your sensors are honed in the mathematics school. Military DEAs benefit from the level 11 thetaplex scanning array, which increases sensor strength by 100 units, and the level 34 subspace motion analyzer, which extends sensor range by 400 units. Electronic countermeasures, such as ECM II (level 13 mathematics), hide your ships from enemy scanners, while electronic counter-countermeasures penetrate ECMs, like level 17's ECCM III.

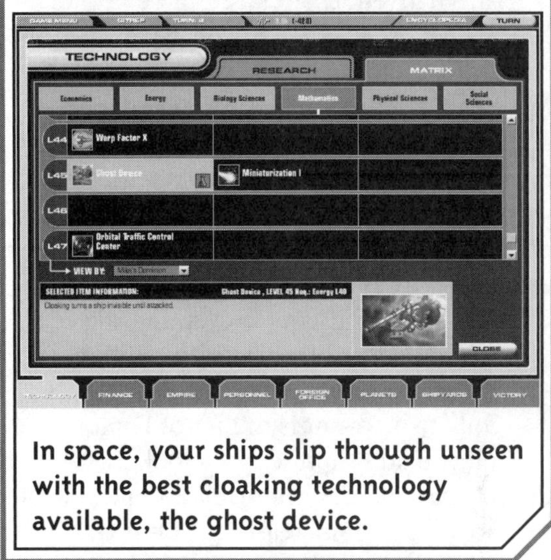

In space, your ships slip through unseen with the best cloaking technology available, the ghost device.

Mathematics Advances: Countermeasures

Advance	Effect
ECCM II	+25% to sensors
ECCM III	+40% to sensors
ECCM IV	+55% to sensors
ECCM V	+70% to sensors
ECM II	-35% to enemy's sensors
ECM III	-65% to enemy's sensors
ECM IV	-90% to enemy's sensors
ECM V	-120% to enemy's sensors

Some of your main race traits can be augmented with mathematics. Amplify research with five different advances: regional research network (+3), galactic cybernet (+6), planetary research network (+3), planetary supercomputer (+6), and research robot (+1 to Research DEA). With 18 pluses to your Research trait and a boost to Research DEAs, mathematics can be a great complement to science-minded races like the Psilons and the Trilarians.

Alternatively, espionage can be heightened. At level 18, backwater navigation makes it easier to get your spies into enemy territory (+5 to spy insertion). Border scanning array (level 35 mathematics) and fine-edge scanning (level 43 mathematics) work the opposite way—they decrease the chances of enemy spies infiltrating your empire (-5 each to spy insertion). The level 19 cyber security link gives a spy's Dagger skill +1, and level 24's stealth suit enhances a spy's Cloak value by one.

Only two advances influence Diplomacy, though you still should take a look. Level 35's dialect universal translator might take a while to discover, but it increases the odds of successful diplomatic negotiations by 20 percent. Level 39's ambassadorial androids increase the chance of success by 25 percent.

The ability of mathematics to eliminate paperwork contributes to a decrease in the heavy foot of government score. Interchangeable policy structures (-2 percent), advanced policy theory (-2 percent), netizenship (-5 percent), and adaptive administration techniques (-4 percent) can knock off 13 percent by the time you reach level 20.

Ironically, mathematics and not energy power your stardrives. If you want to get from system to system quickly, build your ships with drives from this school. Level 5's nuclear engine only hits a speed of 105; however, by the time you reach level 30's anti-matter drives (speed of 336) or level 39's hyper drives (speed of 532), you'll be in your neighbor's backyard before they fire up their first satellite.

Mathematics Advances: Stardrives

Advance	Maximum Warp
Nuclear Engine	105
Sub-Light Drives	133
Fusion Drives	168
Impulse Drives	211
Ion Drives	226
Anti-Matter Drives	336
Inter-Phased Drives	422
Hyper Drives	532
Warp Factor X	672

The thetaplex scanning array aids military DEAs.

Physical Sciences

From the rocks within the core of your homeworld to the plotting of star courses in distant galaxies, physical sciences branches out into many disciples. Astro-engineering, astrophysics, material science, mineral extraction, and planetology all add to the physical sciences' strengths in building, mining, and construction. Where the energy school emphasizes space-based military, physical sciences determines your ground forces.

Space Tech

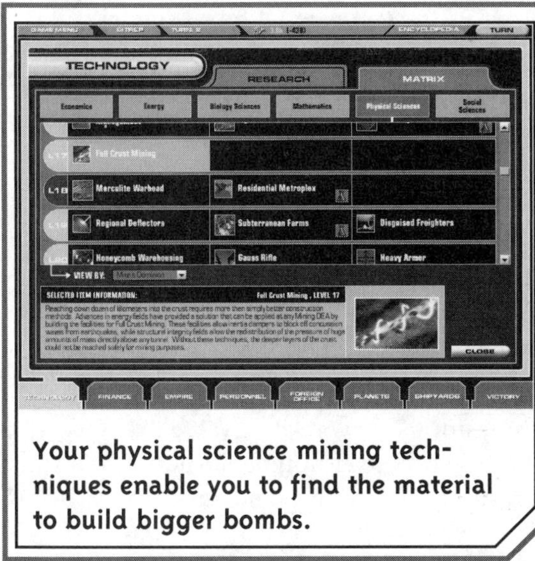

Your physical science mining techniques enable you to find the material to build bigger bombs.

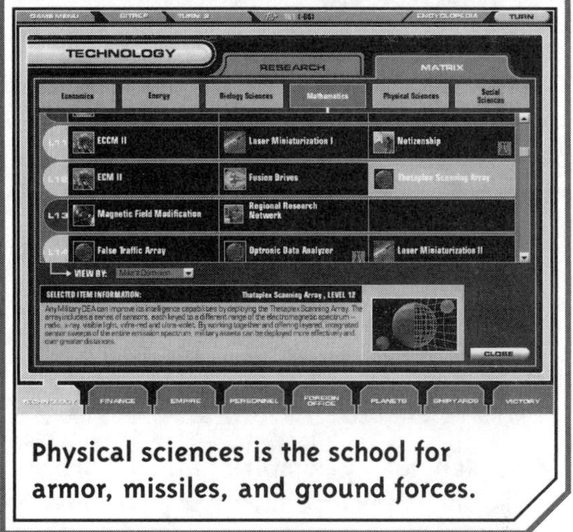

Physical sciences is the school for armor, missiles, and ground forces.

Energy has the lion's share of ship-based advances, but the physical sciences contribute heavily with more weapons and armor. The gauss series of weapons, such as level 25's fighter and regular gauss cannons, deal significant damage and can be upgraded with armor piercing (level 25's armor-penetrating gauss cannon) and autofire (level 26's autofire gauss cannon). Also look for level 9's point defense—cuts your fire delay in half and increases near and far damage by 50 percent—and level 30's fighter dual phaser pod, which doubles a fighter's rate of fire.

Weapon effectiveness can be increased with mounts. Level 12's heavy mount doubles damage with a 40 percent fire delay penalty. Level 28's improved spinal mount triples damage, but you fire more than three times slower. The most expensive mount, level 38's ultra spinal mount, fires five times slower but for five times the damage.

Fifteen missiles occupy the physical sciences chart. Your first, level 3's armor-piercing nuclear warhead, does minor damage, while level 49's armor-piercing omega warhead can wipe out a ship in a single blast. Each ship carries a limited number of missiles, but they pack a bigger wallop than direct-fire weapons. You also can beef up missile defense with level 4's missile armor (+50% armor and deflect) or improve damage with level 27's heavy missile chassis (x4 damage).

Ship's armor is the last line of defense before you take it to the crew quarters, so you want a tough ship. The higher the armor strength, the more damage the ship can withstand before critical systems start going down. If you have deflection, it can avoid the attack completely if the attack value doesn't exceed the deflection value. Your initial armor, level 4's duranium, has a 200 armor strength and 3 deflection. But it's weak compared to level 36's neutronium (armor strength 800, deflection 7) and level 50's adamantium (armor strength 1,600,

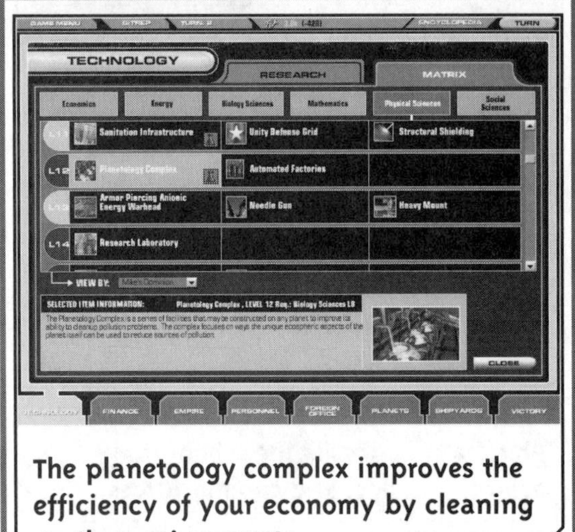

The planetology complex improves the efficiency of your economy by cleaning up the environment.

deflection 9). For super protection, try level 44's ultra heavy armor, which increases armor strength sixteen-fold and doubles the deflection value.

Fast as they are, needle guns have trouble penetrating armor.

Physical Advances: Armor

Advance	Armor Strength	Deflection Value
Duranium	200	3
Titanium	400	5
Heavy Armor	400	5
Neutronium	800	7
Adamantium	1,600	9
Medium Armor	x2	—
Very Heavy Armor	x8	+75%
Ultra Heavy Armor	x16	x2
Fighter Armor	+50%	+50%

It's meant to show relative value to each other. Those exact numbers will not be a stat you can check in the game.

Planetary Improvements

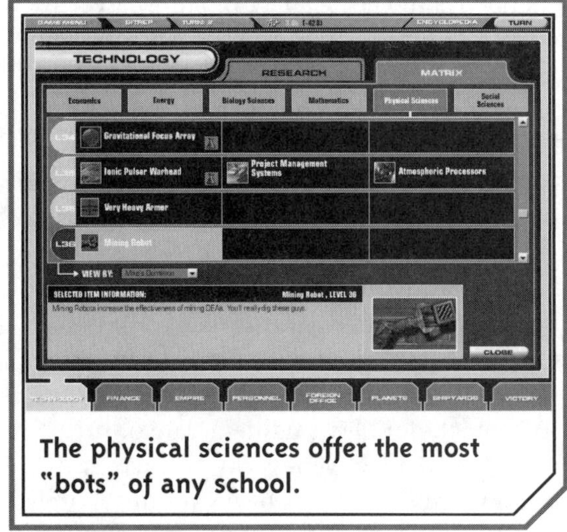

The physical sciences offer the most "bots" of any school.

The physical sciences help you create your ground troops. You can't win a military campaign with just infantry. Even a simple upgrade to level 6's marine gives you troops three times stronger than your basic infantry. The potent level 31 battleoids are fourteen times more effective than normal grunts, level

Physical Advances: Ground

Advance	Infantry Strength	Special
Marine	x3	—
Mobile	x6	—
Needle Gun	—	High Initiative, Poor Accuracy
Gauss Rifle	—	Higher Initiative
Armor	x10	—
Commandos	—	Armies +50% More Effective
Gauss Automatic Rifle	—	Highest Initiative
Battleoids	x14	—
Combat Robot	x8	Ignore Environment Restrictions

21's commandos can increase combat efficiency by 50 percent, and—if you can climb that high—level 50's militia converts the planet's population into weaker infantry units. Throw a level 24 gauss automatic rifle on any one of them and you have the highest initiative ground troops can gain.

In case of attack, physical sciences build up your defensive infrastructure. Structural shield (level 10 physical), regional deflectors (level 20 physical), reinforced construction (level 30 physical), and concussion redirection system (level 40 physical) all add 10,000 points to your buildings' defenses to toughen them against ground assaults and planetary bombardment.

You also can improve the infrastructure economically with developments such as sanitation (level 11 physical), transportation (level 23 physical), power (level 34 physical), and communications (level 43 physical). Combined, they add +1 to the infrastructure.

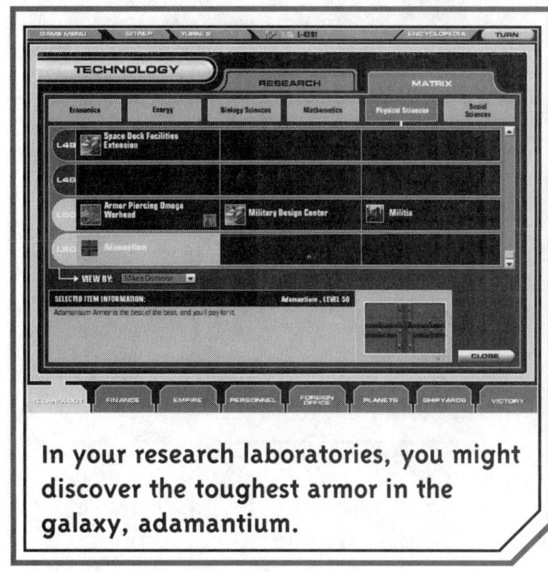

In your research laboratories, you might discover the toughest armor in the galaxy, adamantium.

With all those buildings being constructed, it's no wonder you have seven advances that contribute to ship hull size. From level 29's materials processor to level 50's military design center, you gain cumulative +1 increments to hull building and can create giant space vessels on smaller planets.

You also can increase your economy with physical sciences. Seven mining and eight manufacturing advances populate the tech tree. For mining, you start off with the modest level 7 deep extraction mining, which inches up your Mining DEA by .5. You continue to raise your stats with level 27's complete mantle mining (Mining DEA +1.5) and the bargain deep core mining at level 35 (Mining DEA +2). Manufacturing follows similar trends. Level 11's automated factories clicks up Manufacturing DEAs by .5, level 31's nanofactories by 1.5, and level 42's matter converters by +2.

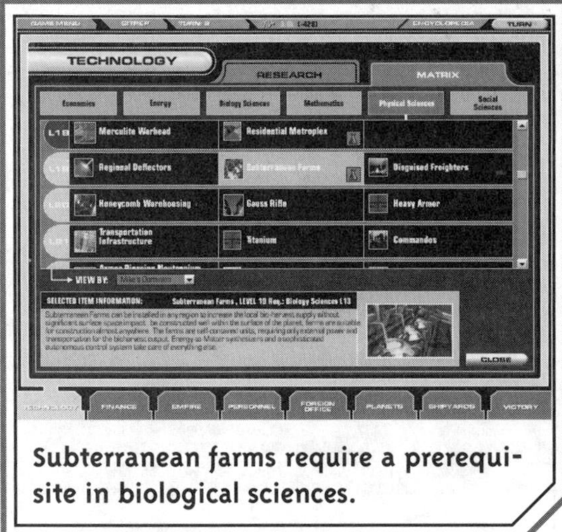

Subterranean farms require a prerequisite in biological sciences.

To further maximize profits, physical sciences helps you clean up pollution, increase population, and open interstellar trade. You can cut pollution with level 10's planetology complex (cleanup increased +.5), but you want level 38's core waste dumps, which reduce pollution across the board by 33 percent.

Whether it's the lack of pollution or all your other advances, physical sciences brings in the people. Level 16's residential metroplex increases maximum population by one, and level 35's biospheric urbanization module goes one better and increases population growth by .67 point.

The ever-important space port, with all the advances that modify it and increase trade, shows up around physical science level 8. Especially if you don't have flowing diplomatic trade agreements, pick up the space port achievement as soon as possible.

Physical Advances: Mining and Manufacturing

Advance	Effect
Automated Factories	Manufacturing DEA +.5
Complete Mantle Mining	Mining DEA +1.5
Deep Core Mining	Mining DEA +2
Deep Extraction Mining	Mining DEA +.5
Extractor Assemblies	Manufacturing +1
Full Crust Mining	Mining DEA +1
Manufacturing Robot	Manufacturing DEA +1
Matter Converters	Manufacturing DEA +2
Microlite Construction	Manufacturing DEA +.5
Mineral Analysis Network	Mining +2
Mining Robot	Mining DEA +1
Nanofactories	Manufacturing DEA +1.5
Orbital Lithoscanners	Mining +1
Robotic Factories	Manufacturing DEA +1
Scanning Resonance Collectors	Manufacturing +1

Phys Ed

With sunlight redirection and subterranean farms, physical sciences can actually help your food situation. Level 5's sunlight redirection increases terraforming by one, as does level 36's atmospheric processors, except the processors can expand the terraform ring all the way to paradise level. For Bioharvesting efficiency, look toward level 18's subterranean farms (+1) and level 40's helio regulator (+2).

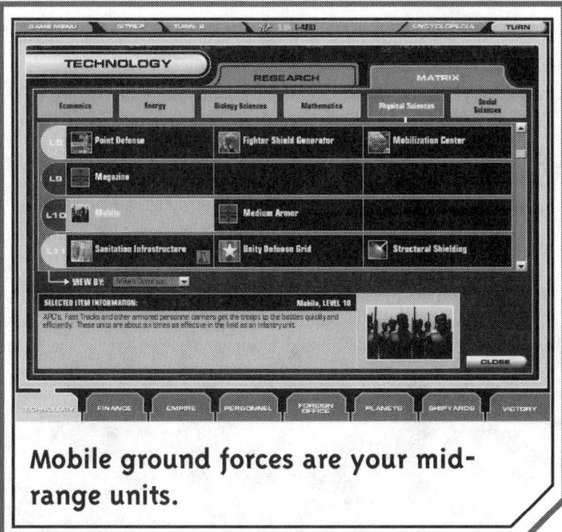

Mobile ground forces are your mid-range units.

Your trade can shoot up if you nab a space port, then follow it with enhancements. Level 20's honeycomb warehousing and level 30's asynchronous docking system increase Space Port DEAs by one point and two points, respectively. To help your entire economy, invest in level 16's mass synthesizer and level 35's gravitational focus array. They both drop the gravity penalty by one, which is especially useful on planets with extreme environments.

Military is not just ships and ground troops. Some of the miscellaneous physical sciences advances can enhance performance. Level 12's unity defense grid and level 23's tri-planar command center both increase military DEAs by one. For more weapons and devices, level 19's battlepod and level 50's megafluxer each increase ships' capacities by 20 percent. Maybe the ultimate military improvement—though it takes level 25 energy and level 33 mathematics, as well—is level 40's advanced damage controls. The controls reduce the maintenance cost of your *entire fleet* by 25 percent!

Social Sciences

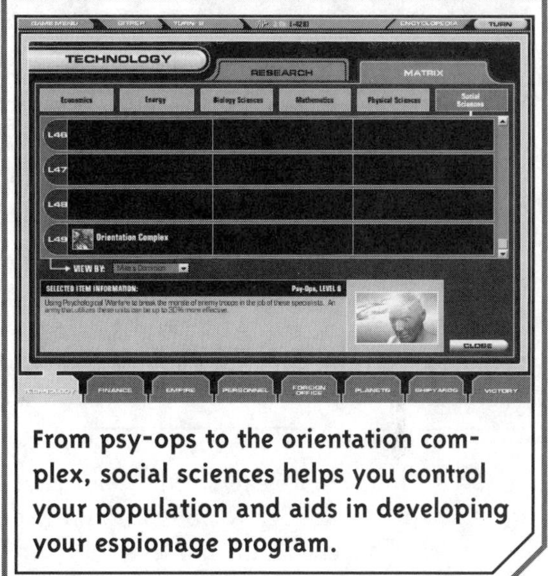

From psy-ops to the orientation complex, social sciences helps you control your population and aids in developing your espionage program.

Social sciences investigate the thoughts, behavior, and institutions of sentient life. Yes, it dwells on psychology, philosophy, political science, and social happiness, but that doesn't mean it's useless. With pursuits in criminology and espionage, you'll want to study here for the latest spy technology, diplomatic edges, and recreational activities.

If you're thinking aggressively, social sciences offer a lot through its espionage tools. Level 9's espionage training requirement and level 29's espionage youth movement both reduce the cost of spies by 25 percent. Spy defense, the number checked to see if an enemy agent can infiltrate your empire, can be increased in increments of +5 with level 20's automated criminal background checks, level 31's foreign spy recognition database, and level 42's institutional paranoia. Spy offense can be increased by five points with level 24's nonlinear thinking.

Entertain people with your hospitality campus.

On the individual agent level, two advances bump up spy Loyalty by five points—level 15's deep Loyalty indoctrination and level 29's base fear indoctrination. To increase Luck by five, invest in level 7's xeno-survivor academy, and to increase your agents' Cloak skills by one, discover level 33's xeno-evasion doctrine.

Social Advances: Espionage

Advance	Effect
Automated Criminal Background Checks	Spy Defense +5
Base Fear Indoctrination	Loyalty +5
Deep Loyalty Indoctrination	Loyalty +5
Espionage Training Requirement	Cost -25%
Espionage Youth Movement	Cost -25%
Foreign Spy Recognition Database	Spy Defense +5
Institutionalized Paranoia	Spy Defense +5
Nonlinear Thinking	Spy Offense +5
Xeno-Evasion Doctrine	Cloak +1
Xeno-Survivor Academy	Luck +5

Your first social sciences advance is level 4's psy-ops. Along with its brother disciplines, mathematics' hackers and physical science's commandos, psy-ops can improve an army's effectiveness by up to 30 percent. An important advance, level 11's command center eliminates the bonuses by an enemy's commandos,

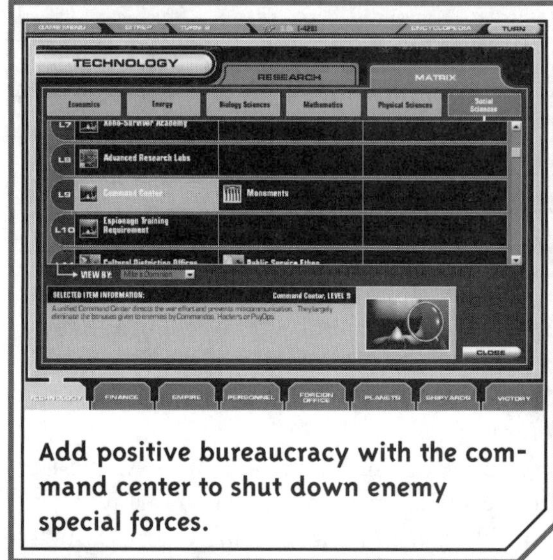

Add positive bureaucracy with the command center to shut down enemy special forces.

hackers, and psy-ops.

If you can't beat them militarily, talk your enemies out of a fight with Diplomacy. Level 13's cross-cultural reference library improves negotiations by 10 percent, while level 23's frame of reference simulator increases diplomatic relations by 15 percent.

As with the five other schools, social sciences helps with space ports, research, and government. Three advances improve space port efficiency: level 25's commuter transport docks, level 32's planetary customs office, and level 45's megaresort facilities. Two advances increase Research DEAs: level 8's advanced research labs (+.5) and level 19's research campuses (+1). Four advances aid government, adding +1 to civic capacity: level

8's monuments, level 17's media outlets, level 27's academies, and level 37's capitals.

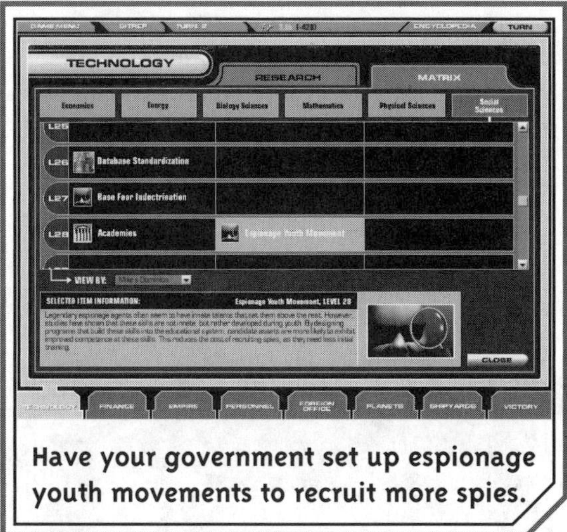

Have your government set up espionage youth movements to recruit more spies.

Social sciences' second strongest trend lies in recreation. With a focus on your population's happiness, you can virtually eliminate unrest and generate extra income. Level 9's cultural districting offices have a double effect, increasing Recreational DEAs by .5 and subtracting one from the unrest level. Level 42's arts and entertainment megalopolis does the same, except it increases recreation DEAs by 1.5 points. To increase recreation efficiency, pick up level 14's hospitality campus (+1), level 35's media output center (+2), and level 47's orientation complex (+3).

Social Advances: Recreation

Advance	Effect
Arts and Entertainment Megalopolis	Recreation DEA +1.5, -1 Unrest
Cultural Districting Offices	Recreation DEA +.5, -1 Unrest
Hospitality Campus	Recreation Efficiency +1
Media Output Center	Recreation Efficiency +2
Orientation Complex	Recreation Efficiency +3
Social Robot	Recreation DEA +1

Tech-nique

It's overwhelming. How are you supposed to absorb 380 different advances and decide which are the right ones for you? Even if you know what your race is good at, you might have a tough time deciding which tech tree best synchs with your game plan.

Support Your Skills

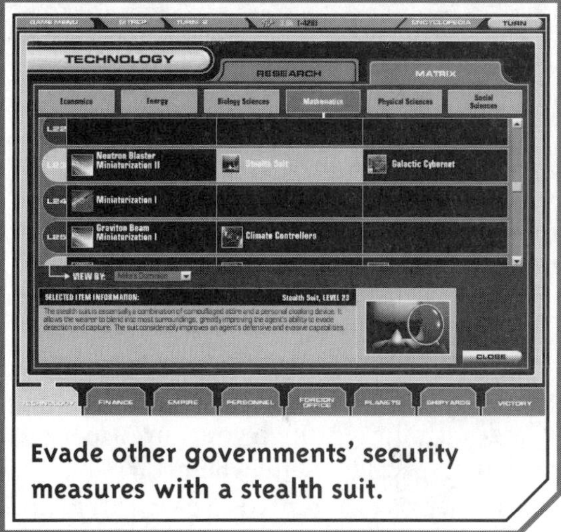

Evade other governments' security measures with a stealth suit.

There are two schools of thought regarding how to best use the technology schools. One is to look at your race's weaknesses and try to cover them up. The Eoladi, for example, are superior in Bioharvesting and poor in Mining, so you could designate physical sciences as your primary tech school to help balance your lack of minerals. However, unless you manage things properly, you probably will end up with average production. Instead, exploit a particular trait and ride that advantage as far as it will go. Eoladi's superior Bioharvesting plays into the strengths of the biological sciences, so devote most of your points to advances such as genetic engineering and soil rejuvenators.

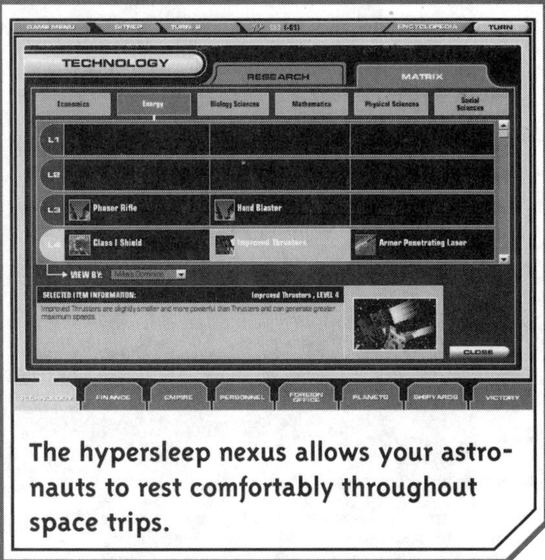
The hypersleep nexus allows your astronauts to rest comfortably throughout space trips.

If you're playing Human, go with economics. Your specialty is turning average production and decent trade agreements into a huge cash flow through your investment skill. It's especially useful when you're cut off from other races and need to earn extra AUs through your own ingenuity.

The Evon are the only race to pursue the social sciences early. They do almost everything at an average level, except espionage, which is at the dangerous level. Maximize your spy potential with advances such as base fear indoctrination and xeno-survivor academy.

The masters of science, the Psilon, should start out in mathematics. All the schools offer research bonuses, and mathematics leads the way. If you have extra points, you can't go wrong with biology's level 34 dream inducers and its +9 to research efficiency.

The Meklar are hurting as a race, so when in doubt, go with military. Energy offers the quickest potential because it builds ships that explore and conquer other systems. Energy's military advances support the Meklar's superior Accuracy, average Reflexes, and good Toughness traits.

A refractive interferometer scans for enemy weapon systems.

In contrast, the other cyborg race, the Cynoid, don't need help. To further exploit their superior Mining and Manufacturing traits, head into physical sciences.

The brute force races, the Sakkra and Grendarl, rely on military and, for the same reasons as the Meklar, should accelerate in the energy school. Their Saurian brethren, the Raas, should choose economics to better exploit their superior Manufacturing.

Like the Psilon, the Trilarian pursue mathematics to increase their superior Research skills. Their fellow Ichthytosian race, the Nommo, could go the same route—they also have a superior Research trait—but should probably opt for biological sciences to gain the early advantage with their superior Bioharvesting.

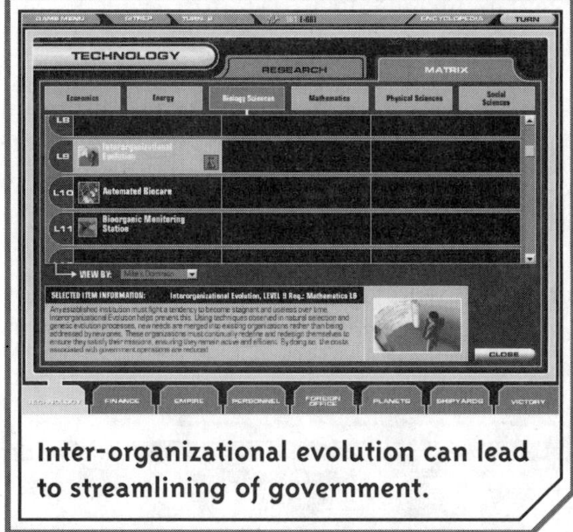

Inter-organizational evolution can lead to streamlining of government.

Like the Nommo, the Etherean Imsaeis and Eoladi head into biological sciences. They need to play off their superior Bioharvesting and Environmental traits because of their weak military.

Silicoids eat minerals, so physical sciences with all its Mining advances is the way to go. The Insecta races, Klackon and Tachidi, follow suit, hoping that physical sciences help their superior Mining inject some life into their economies.

The Ithkul, harvesters that prey on the other races, are strong enough to go several directions. They could master energy for military or economics for Manufacturing bonuses; instead, they'll choose biological sciences to grow their Bioharvesting trait into a huge moneymaker.

Schools by Race

Race	Starting School
Human	Economics
Evon	Social Sciences
Psilon	Mathematics
Meklar	Energy
Cynoid	Physical Sciences
Sakkra	Energy
Raas	Economics
Grendarl	Energy
Trilarian	Mathematics
Nommo	Biological Sciences
Imsaeis	Biological Sciences
Eoladi	Biological Sciences
Silicoid	Physical Sciences
Klackon	Physical Sciences
Tachidi	Physical Sciences
Ithkul	Biological Sciences

Joint Endeavors

Looks can be deceiving. Just because that nifty advance has been exposed doesn't mean you'll be seeing a practical application anytime soon. Many of the advances have prerequisites—you need to have a certain level in a second or third school to use that particular advance. Powerful advances might seem like bargain at their level, but only if they don't have a prerequisite or it's one in a school you already study. Economics' level 24 imperial university improves four stats—food, minerals, industry, and test tubes—but only if you know level 20 mathematics, too.

At first glance, physical sciences would seem the most difficult path to learn, with 20 prerequisite advances. That's misleading. Six of those prerequisites are its various warheads, which rely on a partner in energy. If you're pursuing warheads, chances are

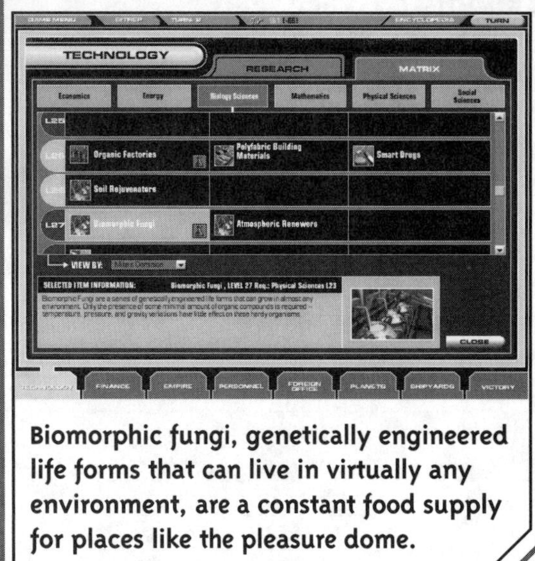

Biomorphic fungi, genetically engineered life forms that can live in virtually any environment, are a constant food supply for places like the pleasure dome.

you're into military and, consequently, the energy school. Most people want the ground troops and weapons included with physical sciences, and none of these require a prerequisite.

In fact, you don't have to worry about a single prerequisite until level 11, and that's sanitation infrastructure (population booster) and planetology complex (pollution control). The one you care about is advanced damage controls. It reduces your empire's fleet maintenance by 25 percent, but only if you learn mathematics level 33 and energy level 25, too.

The easiest to advance is the energy school. Out of 107 advances, just three have prerequisites. Level 11's planetary shield generator requires mathematics level 8. It's nice, with superior space power, you don't worry about shielding your planet. Level 32's phased cloaking device and level 33's reactive cloaking device require mid-level mathematics; skip them and just use the regular cloaking device (level 19), which doesn't require any help.

The social sciences don't rely on the other schools either. Only three out of 34 advances need prerequisites. Since they require assistance from three different schools—economics, mathematics, and physical sciences—disregard them. None of the three are worth worrying about, and ignoring them doesn't jeopardize the school's strength in espionage and recreation.

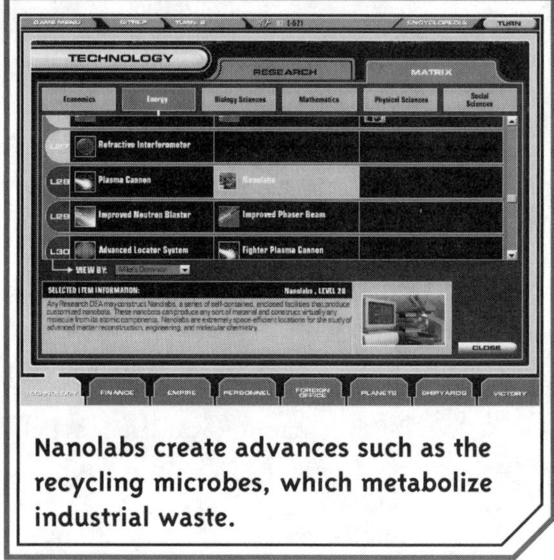

Nanolabs create advances such as the recycling microbes, which metabolize industrial waste.

Approximately 20 percent (12 out of 64) of mathematics' advances require a partner. Half of those are early advances that need low-level assistance, and thus are easy to acquire. Once you get up to advances like level 28's advanced polymerization and require level 22 biological sciences assistance, things get tough. You'll have to give up many of these advances unless you played with plans to team up with another school.

Nearly a quarter of biological sciences' advances (9 out of 43) can't be learned alone.

On the upside, only one advance, level 7's inter-organizational evolution, has a prerequisite prior to level 21. On the downside, many of your better advances, such as level 33's dream inducers and level 41's neural implants, fall short without help from social sciences and mathematics.

The toughest school to progress in without help is economics. Nine out of its 24 advancements need help from three different schools—biology, mathematics, and social sciences. To master the school, spend points in the other non-military schools. If you plan to win with technologically advanced infantry and fighters, kiss economics goodbye.

The Final Analysis

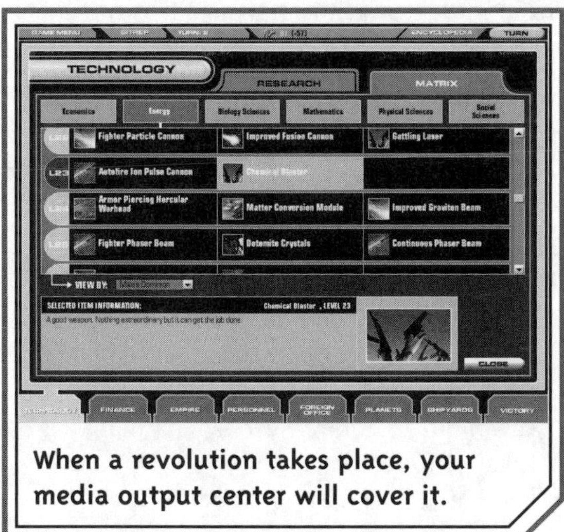

When a revolution takes place, your media output center will cover it.

By this point you should have an idea of how to tackle the tech tree. The game is deliberately designed so that you can't master all six schools. You need to plan how you want your empire to evolve and pick accordingly.

Choose three schools, spend 30 to 40 percent in your primary and secondary schools, and the remainder in the third school. Sometimes you can dip into a fourth school, but only if you need a low-level prerequisite to activate one of your necessary advances. Spending a percentage point or two across the board won't develop into much by game's end.

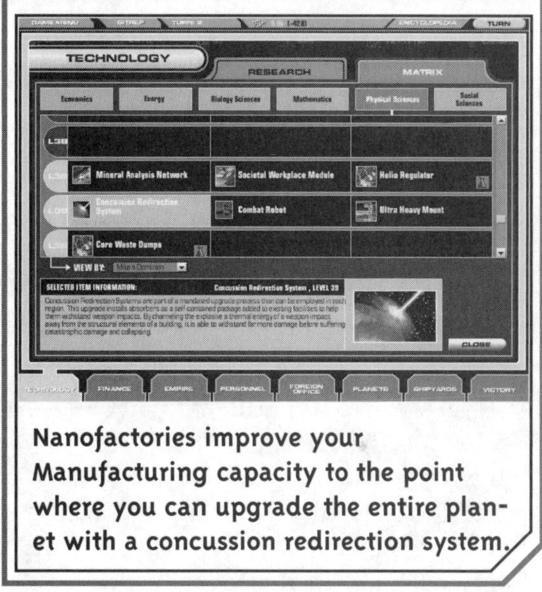

Nanofactories improve your Manufacturing capacity to the point where you can upgrade the entire planet with a concussion redirection system.

TIP

Energy and physical sciences are the two most important tech schools.

In most games, you start with energy and physical sciences as one and two. Their military values are immense—you probably can't win without at least one of them, they have the most advances, and they're easy to progress in. With your remaining 20 or 30

percent, dip into whatever you feel your race needs most. Social sciences provide additional espionage power. Mathematics helps your military with sensors and countermeasures for your ships. Economics gives a boost to your Manufacturing and overall revenue. Use a three-pronged approach to advance at a reasonable rate and catch the slower races with their pants down.

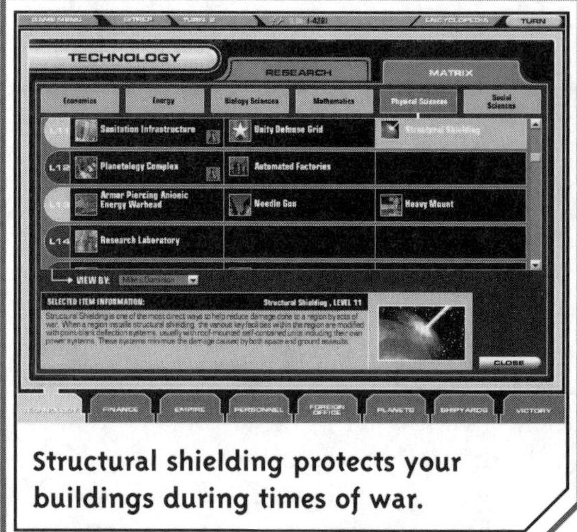

Structural shielding protects your buildings during times of war.

ECONOMICS SCHOOL (24 ADVANCES)

All the economics advances are given below. A random factor at the start of the game might alter the level of each advance plus or minus two levels.

- Level 7: Securities Board
- Level 8: Anti-Redundancy Structuring (requires level 7 biological sciences)
- Level 9: Broader Usage, Holistic Planning
- Level 11: Planetary Commodities Market
- Level 12: Automated Mine
- Level 14: Bulk Freight Module
- Level 18: Lending Associations
- Level 19: Standardization (requires level 16 social sciences)
- Level 22: System Stock Exchange, Robo Mining Plant
- Level 25: Institutional Checks and Balances (requires level 22 social sciences)
- Level 26: Imperial University (requires level 20 mathematics)
- Level 28: Legal Engineering (requires level 25 mathematics)
- Level 29: Reserve Banks
- Level 31: Cross-discipline Methodologies (requires level 26 social sciences), Miniaturization
- Level 32: Nanotech Extractors
- Level 33: Fiscal Ubiquity (requires level 28 social sciences), Advanced Educational Techniques (requires level 29 mathematics)
- Level 36: Government Robot
- Level 38: Mints, Harmonic Construction Techniques
- Level 40: Refined Quality

ENERGY SCHOOL (112 ADVANCES)

All the energy advances are listed below. A random factor at the start of the game might alter the level of each advance plus or minus two levels.

- Level 1: Phaser Rifle
- Level 2: Armor-Penetrating Laser
- Level 3: Class I Shield, Armor-Penetrating Fighter Laser
- Level 4: Hand Blaster
- Level 5: Plasma Projector
- Level 6: Improved Thrusters, Autofire Laser, Continuous Laser, Missile Shield Generator, Fusion Gun
- Level 7: No Range Penalty Laser, Continuous Fighter Laser, No Range Penalty Fighter Laser
- Level 8: Hydrogen Fuel Cells, Autofire Fighter Laser
- Level 9: Fighter Fusion Cannon, Laser Assault Rifle, Fusion Cannon
- Level 10: Planetary Shield Generator (requires level 8 mathematics), Class II Shield, Improved Laser
- Level 11: Enveloping Fusion Cannon
- Level 12: Phaser Assault Rifle, Continuous Fusion Cannon
- Level 13: Blaster Rifle
- Level 14: High-Caliber Detection System, Class III Shield, Impulse Engine
- Level 15: Continuous Fighter Fusion Cannon
- Level 16: Fighter Neutron Cannon, Neutron Blaster, Continuous Neutron Blaster, Enveloping Fighter Fusion Cannon, Large Shield Generator
- Level 17: Cloaking Device, X-Ray Transponder System, Fusion Accelerator, Plasma Enveloper
- Level 18: Hercular Warhead
- Level 19: Fighter Graviton Beam, Graviton Beam
- Level 20: Fighter Particle Cannon, Class IV Shield, Iridium Fuel Cells, Particle Beam, Gatling Laser
- Level 21: Ion Pulse Cannon
- Level 22: Armor-Piercing Hercular Warhead, Fighter Ion Cannon
- Level 23: Multi-Sync Phaser Rifle, Improved Graviton Beam, Improved Fusion Cannon, Autofire Ion Pulse Cannon
- Level 24: Fighter Phaser Beam, Dotomite Crystals
- Level 25: Matter Conversion Module, Continuous Graviton Beam, Phaser Beam, Chemical Blaster, Lightning Field Generator
- Level 26: Class V Shield, Autofire Phaser Beam, Armor-Penetrating Phaser Beam, Continuous Phaser Beam
- Level 27: Multi Fusion Rifle, Refractive Interferometer
- Level 28: Plasma Gun
- Level 29: Class VI Shield, Uridium Fuel Cell, Improved Neutron Blaster, Improved Phaser Beam, Nanolabs
- Level 30: Phased Cloaking Device (requires level 20 mathematics), Advanced Locator System, Fighter Plasma Cannon, Plasma Cannon, Continuous Plasma Cannon, Planetary Core Heat Pumps, Dark Energy Beam
- Level 31: Scatter Pack Warhead, Energy Reclamation, Pulse Laser
- Level 32: Tri-Sequence Phaser Rifle, T.R.A.P.S. Logistics System
- Level 33: Reactive Cloaking Device (requires level 30 mathematics), Armor-Piercing Scatter Pack Warhead

- Level 34: Reajax Fuel Cells, Disruptor Cannon, Multi Blaster
- Level 35: Disintegrater Beam, Megabolt Cannon
- Level 36: Fighter Disruptor, Class VII Shield, Hardened Shields, Torpedo Missile Chassis
- Level 37: Fusion Core Launcher, Matter Facilitators, Autofire Disruptor Cannon
- Level 38: Improved Plasma Cannon
- Level 39: Plasma Pod, Mauler
- Level 40: Ultimate Detector System, Trilithium Crystals, MicroGrav Pallets, Tachyon Beam
- Level 41: Class VIII Shield
- Level 44: Transwarp Drive
- Level 45: Damper Field
- Level 46: Class IX Shield
- Level 49: Class X Shield, Stellar Converter

BIOLOGICAL SCIENCES SCHOOL (43 ADVANCES)

All the biological science advances are given below. A random factor at the start of the game might alter the level of each advance plus or minus two levels.

- Level 1: Hydroponic Farm
- Level 5: Soil Enrichment
- Level 6: Decomposition Centers
- Level 9: Automated Biocare, Inter-Organizational Evolution (requires level 6 mathematics)
- Level 11: Bio-Organic Monitoring Station
- Level 13: Cloning Complex
- Level 14: Genetic Mutagens
- Level 15: Training Resistance Compensators
- Level 16: Controlled Environment Farming, Pollution Processors
- Level 18: Atmospheric Containment
- Level 19: Psi-Signature Dampening Field
- Level 21: Byproduct Reprocessing, Regional Weather Controller
- Level 22: Recycling Microbes (requires level 15 physical sciences)
- Level 24: Polyfabric Building Materials, Orbital Biomonitoring, Soil Rejuvenators
- Level 26: Smart Drugs, Pleasure Dome, Atmospheric Renewers
- Level 27: Organic Factories (requires level 20 physical sciences)
- Level 28: Telepathic Training
- Level 29: Biomorphic Fungi (requires level 23 physical)
- Level 31: Moisture Regulators, Genetic Engineering
- Level 33: Hypersleep Nexus
- Level 34: Neural Scanners
- Level 35: Recycling Facilities (requires level 30 physical sciences), Dream Inducers (requires level 29 physical sciences), Ecosystem Controller
- Level 37: Organic Composites
- Level 38: Bioharvesting Robot
- Level 39: Antiagathics
- Level 41: Psionics
- Level 42: Bio-Engineered Life
- Level 43: Neural Implants (requires level 37 mathematics)
- Level 44: Mineral-Morphic Bacteria (requires level 39 physical sciences), Bioregeneration Enhancers
- Level 45: Bioengineered Plants
- Level 46: Bioreprocessors (requires level 40 physical sciences)
- Level 47: Heightened Intelligence

MATHEMATICS SCHOOL (64 ADVANCES)

Listed below are all the mathematics advances. A random factor at the start of the game might alter the level of each advance plus or minus two levels.

- Level 3: Interchangeable Policy Structures (requires level 2 economics)
- Level 4: Mass Driver Miniaturization I
- Level 5: Nuclear Engine, Advanced Policy Theory (requires level 2 physical sciences)
- Level 9: Sub-Light Drives, Astro University (requires level 5 economics), Catalyst Design, Mass Driver Miniaturization II
- Level 10: Netizenship (requires level 10 social sciences)
- Level 11: ECCM II, Magnetic Field Modification, Laser Miniaturization I, Thetaplex Scanning Array
- Level 13: ECM II
- Level 14: Fusion Drives, False Traffic Array, Fusion Cannon Miniaturization I, Laser Miniaturization II
- Level 15: Optronic Data Analyzer (requires level 10 physical sciences), Hackers, Regional Research Network
- Level 16: System University (requires level 13 economics)
- Level 17: ECCM III, Backwater Navigation
- Level 19: ECM III, ECM IV, Cyber Security Link, Fusion Cannon Miniaturization II
- Level 20: Impulse Drives, Neutron Blaster Miniaturization I
- Level 21: Adaptive Administration Techniques (requires level 14 social sciences)
- Level 23: Neutron Blaster Miniaturization II, Climate Controllers
- Level 24: Stealth Suit, Graviton Beam Miniaturization I
- Level 25: Ion Drives, Galactic Cybernet
- Level 26: Planetary Research Network
- Level 27: Phaser Beam Miniaturization I
- Level 28: ECCM IV, ECM IV, Displacement Device
- Level 29: Graviton Beam Miniaturization I, Advanced Polymerization (requires level 22 biological sciences)
- Level 30: Anti-Matter Drives, Geo-Harmonic Principle
- Level 31: Phaser Beam Miniaturization II
- Level 33: Plasma Cannon Miniaturization I, Plasma Cannon Miniaturization II
- Level 34: Subspace Motion Analyzer
- Level 35: Inter-Phased Drives, Border Scanning Array, Dialect Universal Translators (requires level 22 biological sciences)
- Level 38: ECCM V, Experiment Replicators, Economic Robot
- Level 39: Hyper Drives, Ambassadorial Androids (requires level 25 social sciences), Research Robot
- Level 41: Molecular Resequencing (requires level 35 energy)
- Level 42: Planetary Supercomputer
- Level 43: Z Storage And Basing Facilities, Fine-Edge Scanning
- Level 44: Ghost Device (requires level 40 energy), Warp Factor X
- Level 47: Orbital Traffic Control Center

PHYSICAL SCIENCES SCHOOL (108 ADVANCES)

All the physical sciences advances are shown below. A random factor at the start of the game might alter the level of each advance plus or minus two levels.

- Level 2: Armor-Penetrating Mass Driver
- Level 3: Armor-Piercing Nuclear Warhead
- Level 4: Missile Armor, Duranium
- Level 5: Fighter Armor, Sunlight Redirection
- Level 6: Anionic Energy Warhead, Marine
- Level 7: Deep Extraction Mining, Mobilization Center
- Level 8: Fighter Shield Generator, Space Port
- Level 9: Mobile, Magazine, Point Defense
- Level 10: Structural Shielding, Planetology Complex (requires level 8 biological sciences)
- Level 11: Sanitation Infrastructure (requires level 8 biological sciences), Medium Armor, Automated Factories
- Level 12: Unity Defense Grid, Heavy Mount
- Level 13: Armor-Piercing Anionic Energy Warhead, Needle Gun
- Level 15: Research Laboratory
- Level 16: Neutronium Warhead, Extractor Assemblies, Residential Metroplex (requires level 14 social sciences), Mass Synthesizer (requires level 13 energy)
- Level 17: Biosphere Housing Management, Full Crust Mining
- Level 18: Subterranean Farms (requires level 13 biological sciences)
- Level 19: Battlepod, Gauss Rifle, Light Missile Chassis
- Level 20: Merculite Warhead, Honeycomb Warehousing, Regional Deflectors, Armor, Robotic Factories, Disguised Freighters
- Level 21: Titanium, Commandos, Heavy Armor
- Level 22: Armor-Piercing Neutronium Warhead
- Level 23: Transportation Infrastructure, Tri-Planar Command Center
- Level 24: Fighter Gauss Cannon, Scanning Resonance Collectors, Gauss Automatic Rifle, Orbital Lithoscanners
- Level 25: Gauss Cannon, Armor-Penetrating Gauss Cannon
- Level 26: Armor-Piercing Merculite Warhead, Autofire Gauss Cannon
- Level 27: High Energy X-Ray Laser Warhead, Heavy Missile Chassis, Complete Mantle Mining
- Level 28: Improved Spinal Mount
- Level 29: Materials Processor, Very Heavy Mount
- Level 30: Fighter Dual Phaser Pod, Armor-Piercing High Energy X-Ray Laser Warhead, Asynchronous Docking System, Automated Assembly Module, Reinforced Construction, Disruptor Cannon
- Level 31: Battleoids, Nanofactories
- Level 33: Pollution Control Center (requires level 27 biological sciences)
- Level 34: Power Infrastructure (requires level 24 energy)
- Level 35: Deep Core Mining, Biospheric Urbanization Module, Microlite Construction, Very Heavy Armor, Gravitational Focus Array (requires level 28 energy)
- Level 36: Ionic Pulsar Warhead (requires level 30 energy), Atmospheric Processors, Neutronium
- Level 37: Project Management Systems, Mining Robot
- Level 38: Combat Robot, Ultra Spinal Mount, Core Waste Dumps (requires level 32 biological sciences)
- Level 39: Societal Workplace Module, Concussion Redirection System, Manufacturing Robot
- Level 40: Helio Regulator (requires level 32

mathematics), Advanced Damage Controls (requires level 25 energy), Ultra Heavy Mount
- Level 41: Armor-piercing Ionic Pulsar Warhead (requires level 35 energy), Energy Pulsar Warhead (requires level 40 energy), Mineral Analysis Network
- Level 42: Matter Converters
- Level 43: Orbital Access Module, Communications Infrastructure (requires level 33 mathematics)
- Level 44: Omega Warhead (requires level 44 energy), Nanodisassemblers (requires level 36 mathematics), Ultra Heavy Armor
- Level 45: Dark Matter Projector
- Level 46: Armor-Piercing Energy Pulsar Warhead (requires level 45 energy)
- Level 48: Space Dock Facilities Extension
- Level 49: Armor-Piercing Omega Warhead (requires level 49 energy)
- Level 50: Military Design Center, Militia, Adamantium, Gyro Destabilizer, Megafluxer (requires level 33 energy and level 33 mathematics)

SOCIAL SCIENCES SCHOOL (34 ADVANCES)

Given below are all the social sciences advances. A random factor at the start of the game might alter the level of each advance plus or minus two levels.

- Level 4: Psy-Ops
- Level 7: Xeno-Survivor Academy
- Level 8: Advanced Research Labs, Monuments
- Level 9: Cultural Districting Offices, Espionage Training Requirement
- Level 11: Command Center
- Level 12: Public Service Ethos, Science Guilds
- Level 13: Cross-Cultural Reference Library
- Level 14: Hospitality Campus
- Level 15: Deep Loyalty Indoctrination
- Level 17: Media Outlets
- Level 19: Research Campuses
- Level 20: Automated Criminal Background Checks
- Level 23: Frame of Reference Simulator
- Level 24: Nonlinear Thinking
- Level 25: Commuter Transport Docks
- Level 27: Academies, Database Standardization
- Level 29: Base Fear Indoctrination, Espionage Youth Movement
- Level 31: Foreign Spy Recognition Database
- Level 32: Planetary Customs Office
- Level 33: Xeno-Evasion Doctrine
- Level 34: Mass Vertical Urbanization
- Level 35: Media Output Center
- Level 37: Capitals
- Level 38: Social Robot
- Level 39: Entertainment Robot
- Level 42: Arts and Entertainment Megalopolis
- Level 45: Megaresort Facilities
- Level 47: Orientation Complex

chapter 5

Finance

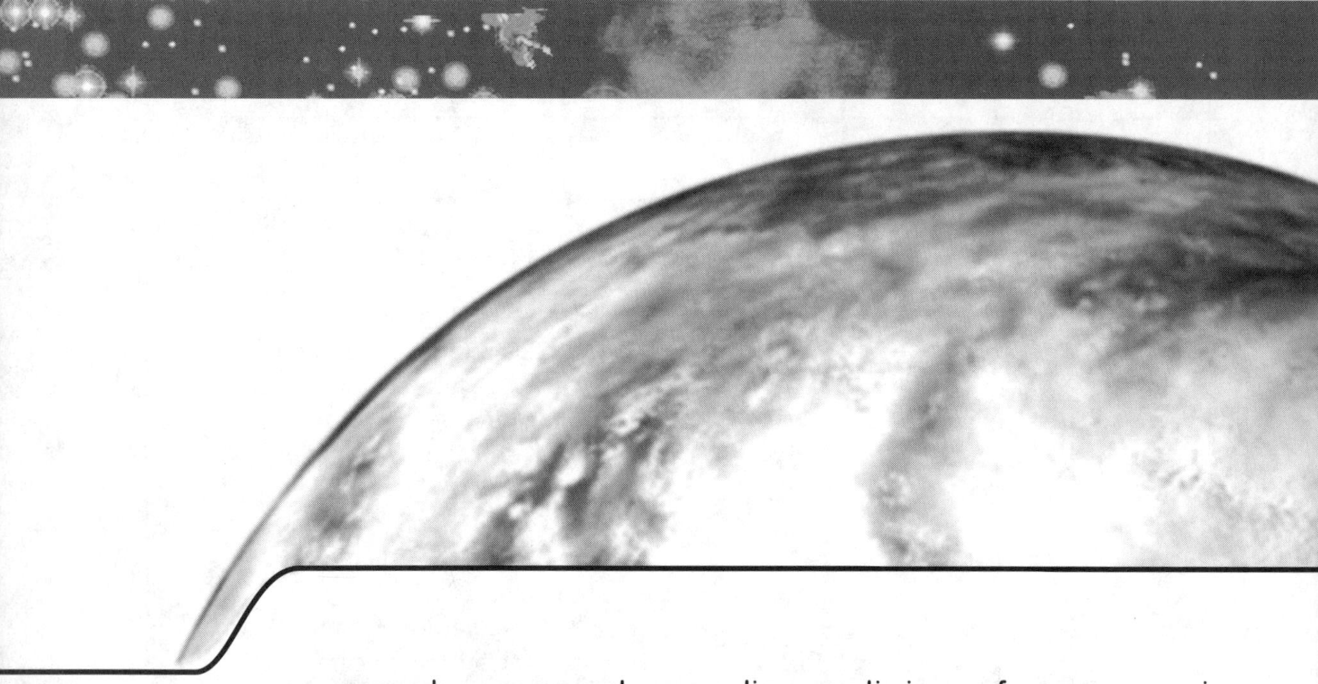

The general spending policies of your empire are set at the Finance menu. These principles will apply to all your planets, not just one. You can still levy higher taxes on a more opulent world to squeeze out some more cash; however, when you want to increase taxes throughout the realm or alter your military-political economy, look no further.

No fleets get built without proper financing.

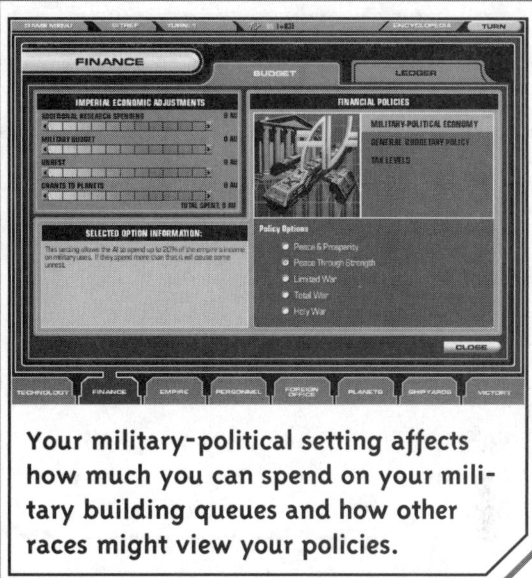

Your military-political setting affects how much you can spend on your military building queues and how other races might view your policies.

The Budget

The first screen you'll see is the budget. Let's skip that right now, since it's the nitty gritty stuff, and click on the Ledger tab. The ledger tells your planetary viceroys exactly how to spend their money, whether it's political policies, budgetary policies, tax level, or what to do with the excess treasury.

Military-Political Economy

You start off the game in a state of "peace and prosperity." Your viceroy will spend up to 10 percent of his budget on military uses, and the people won't complain if he stays within this range. Spend 12 percent and you'll have a mob of angry protestors torching the imperial palace. Until you're ready to go to war with someone, click it up one notch to "peace through strength." This gives you greater flexibility for spending on military—up to 20 percent—and doesn't alarm the general populace.

Your other settings spend even more on military. "Limited war" allows 15 to 30 percent for military spending—but you must spend in that range! Decide not to crank out ships one turn and spend less than 15 percent and your population will begin to lose faith in your political statements (leading to eventual unrest). "Total war" raises the level even higher to 25 to 50 percent military spending. If you have nothing but money and neighbors to burn, call a "holy war" and raise military spending to 33 to 67 percent.

General Budgetary Policy

For the most part, leave this policy right in the middle where it starts—on "balanced." Balanced spending means your viceroy will try to spend only the money he makes that turn. Switching the policy to "spending" allows the viceroys to burn through money and buy whatever their planet needs. This can

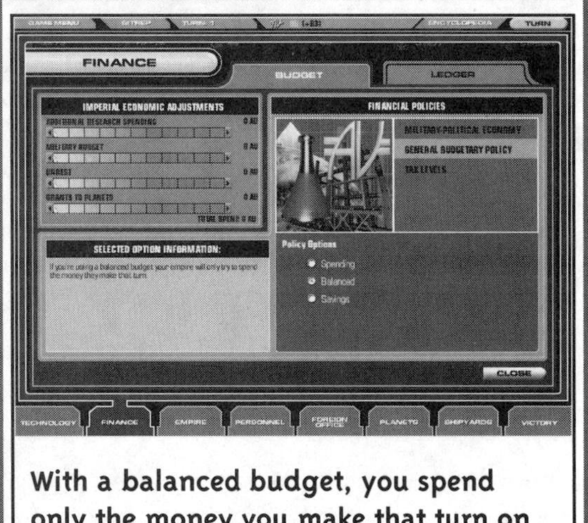

With a balanced budget, you spend only the money you make that turn on improvements like research labs.

give a huge boost to an economy . . . at the expense of the surplus in your treasury. "Savings" is just the opposite. Your viceroys will cut back on spending and some needs will wait as you stockpile some reserve cash.

If you elect to choose "savings" for your budgetary policy, you'll save money but might put some research projects on hold.

Tax Levels

Governments like to set them as high as possible, and no one likes to pay them. At the tax levels option, you set system and empire taxes. Charge too much and the people will revolt. Charge too little and you won't be able to support what the people want. Depending on your race, economic factors, and social perks, you can get away with setting taxes so you can gobble up planets like candy or cut back until you're washing your own dishes.

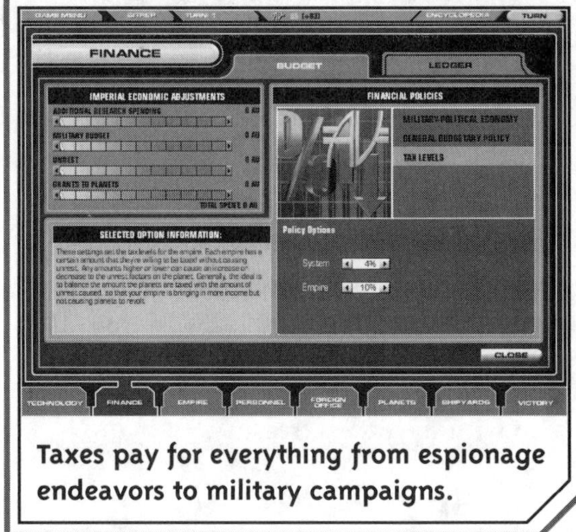

Taxes pay for everything from espionage endeavors to military campaigns.

Aim high. It's always easier to scale back the taxes than it is to make up a big budget deficit. Shoot for the 17–20 percent range at first. Remember that you can adjust the individual planet's tax rate on the Planets menu. Over time, your viceroy will adjust the tax rate to a comfortable level.

Imperial Economic Adjustments

Once you have AUs to spare, you'll be back to the Imperial Economic Adjustment sliders often. The imperial sliders help you spend your surplus cash with ease. You can throw extra funds to research, military, help quell unrest, and dump grants on planets, which allow the viceroy to spend it where he thinks it will do the most good. As with all spending, try to keep the sliders in the green, where you spend on a one-for-one basis.

The Imperial Economic Sliders enable you to spend your treasury on key areas, such as unrest or research.

An important advance almost in range? Adjust your research slider to the one-third position and you'll have a practical application in no time. Want to crank out ships faster? Pour money into the military budget. Experiencing unrest after a disaster event? A few clicks on the unrest slider should quiet everyone down. Whatever extra cash you have left over should go to the Grants to Planets slider; that way, you can let the viceroys take over and not worry about every little adjustment on each planet.

The Ledger

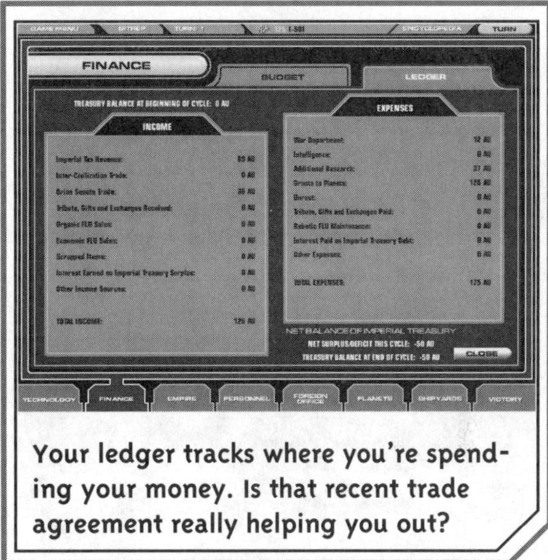

Your ledger tracks where you're spending your money. Is that recent trade agreement really helping you out?

All your income and all your expenses are listed on the Ledger screen. It's simple math. If your income exceeds your expenses, your economy's doing just fine. You don't even have to exceed expenses by that much—any positive number indicates that your economic strategies are fruitful.

Income

If you don't know where you're making money, you won't know what's working right. Early on, and possibly for your whole game, imperial tax revenue will generate your biggest cash flows. The more planets you control and the higher the tax rate, the larger this number will climb. In cases of high unrest, though, be prepared to lose some of this cash when you slash taxes.

Inter-civilization trade and Orion Senate trade draw in revenue from the trade agreements you strike in the Foreign Office screen. You take a hit from trade agreements the first few turns—costs involved in setting up and expanding trade infrastructure eat away any early profits—but they can prove lucrative over the long haul. Track your progress on these two lines and continue striking bargains if you feel it favors your empire.

You can earn income from trade within the Orion Senate.

If it's Christmas time in the galaxy and an alien neighbor decides to give you a gift, it'll show up on the fourth line. Below that, revenue shows up on the next two lines for the sale of items produced by economic and organic FLUs. When you scrap an item that has already been built, you can recoup up to 50 percent of the item's original cost on the "scrapped items" line.

Expenses

Are you wasting money on useless ships? Your expenses menu will tell you.

You don't like to look at this side of the Finance screen; it's where all your money goes down the drain. The top line, the war department, will probably rack up the biggest costs. Each turn, whenever you build an infantry unit, exploration ship or attack fighter, the expense enters the war department line. Watch the war department number to ensure you stay within your military-political choice on the budget screen.

Intelligence isn't a measure of your brain power. No, it's the amount of money you spend on maintaining spies. A few spies will amount to pennies; churn them out every turn, however, and the intelligence fee will become an annoying expense.

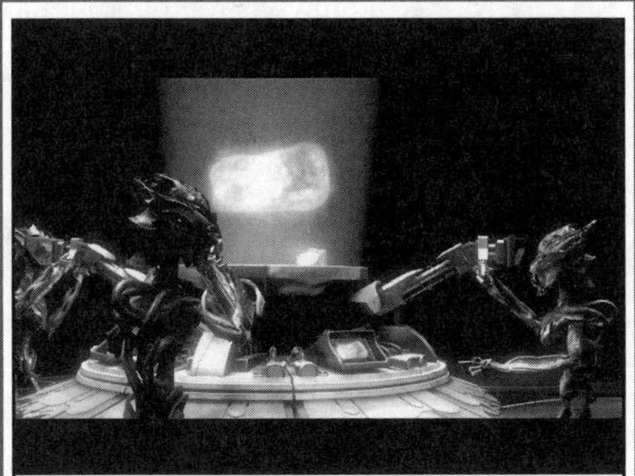

Your Imperial Economic sliders add Research points to a planet that might not develop them naturally.

Donate gifts to foreign powers for political influence. Make sure you monitor how much is going out on the expense screen.

Additional research shows how much money you sink into research's imperial slider. As the name implies, this is extra money spent only through the slider. If you want to pump up your science endeavors, watch this line carefully and spend to a productive and comfortable level.

As we mentioned before, grants to planets serve as bandages to patch up whatever the planet most needs. When a world suffers because of lack of food, and Bioharvesting is nonexistent on the planet's surface, dump AUs into grants and you can alleviate the harm done. If you don't have a particular goal in mind at the moment, it's best to put your hard-earned cash into grants and let the viceroys run the show.

When the people are unhappy and your revolt number climbs into the teens, it's time to spend a few AUs on the unrest line. Click your imperial slider two or three times and you should calm all civil unrest.

Should you enter into a trade agreement with another power, don't be alarmed if you see AUs in the "tribute, gifts, and exchanges paid" column. To spark trade, you need to set forth some bribe money. To woo a potential ally to your side, exchange valuable items and the AU amount will show up here.

The more robotic forced labor units you have, the more maintenance you have to pay, which shows up on the line below tributes. "Interest Paid on Imperial Treasury Debt" only occurs in timed games. If you take longer than your opponents, your interest on debt climbs.

Balancing Act

Your green AU number along the top-strip menu bar displays the total AUs in your bank account. If this number turns red, you're in a depression and need to turn things around quickly or planets will start drying up. A quick glance at the net surplus number at the bottom of the Finance menu will tell you how your spending is going for the turn. In times of financial panic, adjust your spending so the number becomes positive.

Without planets, your empire's treasury would be nothing more than rocks and potatoes.

Once your economy gets rolling, you may not return to the Finance screen often. Even so, it's a good idea to check in and tweak your imperial sliders. Throughout the later turns, you'll really only care about the war department, additional research, and grants to planets. Spend the maximum your empire can afford and you'll accelerate at a pace other powers will find very difficult to catch.

chapter 6

Empire Options

From colonization to labor conditions, the Empire menu sets broad polices for all your planets at the same time. Instead of clicking on each planet individually, the Empire options allow you to govern from afar. Whether it's deciding on how much

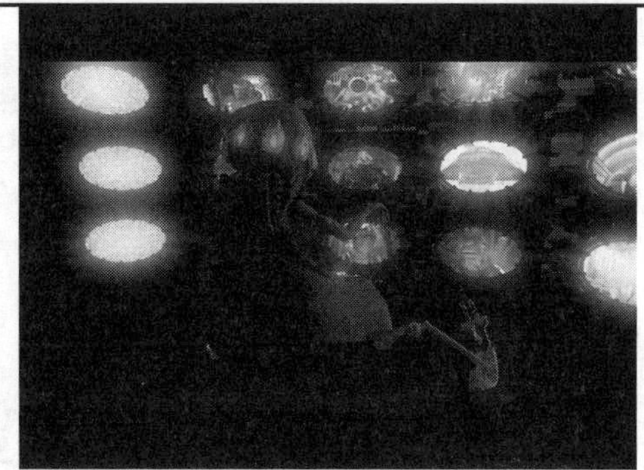

You have so much information at your fingertips, the Empire screen organizes many facets of your government for you so you can concentrate on flying ships around the universe.

military force you use to control your citizens or what sort of government will run the show, you'll spend your first turn or two here making choices that will have ramifications for the rest of the game.

Colonization

Make sure you switch the colonization AI on so you don't miss a colony ship launch opportunity.

Under the Colonization tab, you select your expansion policy. In reality, all you're doing is turning the computer AI on or off for colonization. If you select on, the AI will send the next colony ship to one of the best planets within reach. Remember, you chose the planets you want colonized under the Planets menu. The AI will only send ships to those colonies. If no planet has been selected for colonization, it will wait for one to be selected.

You don't have to flag planets while the AI is turned on. Once the AI is turned on, player flagging of colonies is no longer necessary. Player flagging of colonies works best when the colonization AI is off—think of it as a short cut for a one-shot colonization AI request.

Set your military spending in the building queue to produce two or three colony ships out of the gate.

If you select off for colonization, the computer AI will be deactivated and it will be up to you to send your colony ships manually. Why do all the work? Well, it's usually not a good idea. Keep colonization on if you can help it, especially early in the game (say, the first 50 turns). The only time it might be safe to switch it off is if you have many different possible colony spots and you want to make sure the next available colony ship heads to a specific world. Other than that, let the computer control your colonies.

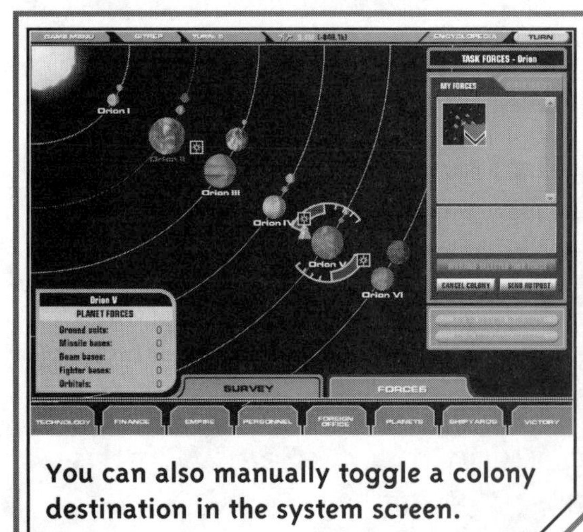

You can also manually toggle a colony destination in the system screen.

Oppressometer

How much will you oppress your people? Set it high and you won't have to worry about enemy spies, but unrest raises its ugly head. Set it low and foreign powers will have spies in every building, but your people will be happy.

Notice the two black guidelines above the Oppressometer slider. These arrows show you the minimum and maximum thresholds for oppression—the range your population will let you get away with. Depending on your race, these minimums and maximums will swing all over the place.

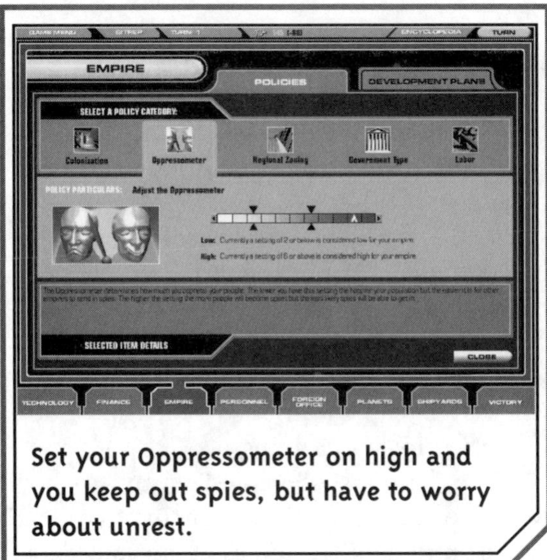

Set your Oppressometer on high and you keep out spies, but have to worry about unrest.

If you want to play it safe, click your Oppressometer right in the middle of the race guidelines. This gives you a little control without sacrificing money to quell unrest. Early in the game this is fine, since you probably won't have enemy spies infiltrating your borders. Once the first spy shows up, click to just below your maximum, or your maximum if you have lots of funds in the treasury. When you're at war, it's very important spies don't cut down your production, steal technology, or assassinate your leaders. Spend the extra AUs on the Imperial Unrest slider to balance out the high Oppressometer.

Regional Zoning

The regional zoning policies dictate how your worlds will develop. You start out on "natural." A natural planet will build according to its current needs; once those needs are fulfilled, it'll concentrate on the planet's strength, such as mineral or food production. When you need to watch your budget, this is the best option because it keeps the planets surviving first, then worries about exploiting conditions for extra cash.

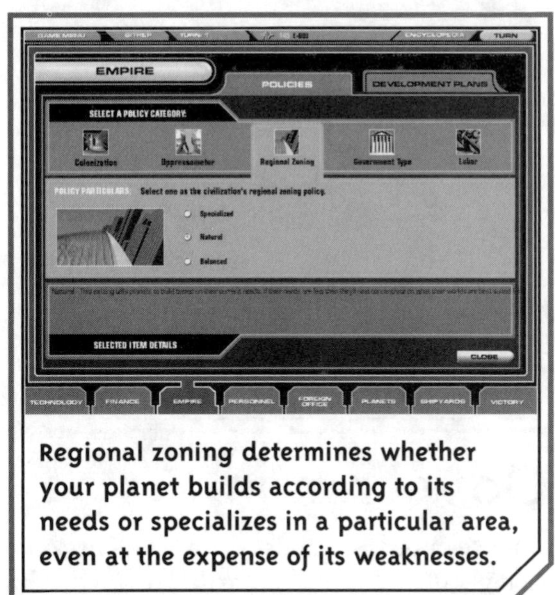

Regional zoning determines whether your planet builds according to its needs or specializes in a particular area, even at the expense of its weaknesses.

"Specialized" increases production in the world's strengths, even at the expense of its weaknesses. A world that's good at research will spin out those test tubes; however, it might lose revenue in its industry regions. To maximize profit later in the game, you'll want to switch to specialized. Your worlds will concentrate on what they're best at, and you can supplement each planet's weaknesses with healthy grants from the Finance menu.

Never switch to "balanced." A balanced planet does a little bit of everything, but isn't really proficient at anything. Though this might make for a self-sufficient and happy independent colony, it doesn't help your empire. You want each world chipping in where it can do the most good.

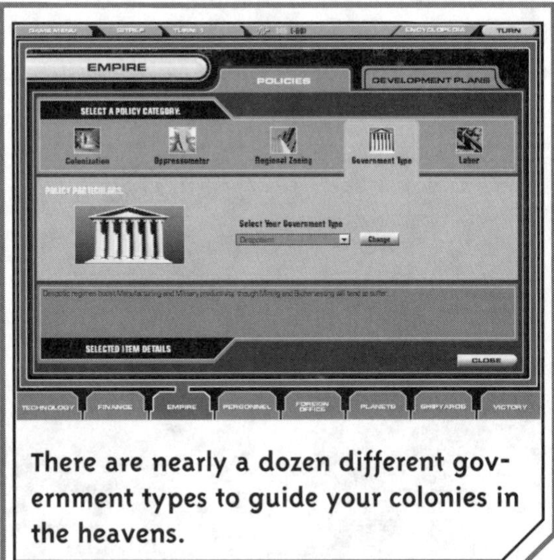

There are nearly a dozen different government types to guide your colonies in the heavens.

Government Type

There can be thousands of governments on a single planet—look at Earth. Fortunately, *Master of Orion III* has simplified things so there's only one main government per planet. Not all types are available to you at the start of the game.

Your race will determine whether you begin with an Absolutist, Representative, or Collectivist government type. Your choice is already picked for you, right? Not exactly. You can always switch government types, if you can handle the unrest such a move will cause in your people.

Some races begin with only the basics, such as the Raas. At the other end of the spectrum, the Klackons begin with a Collectivist government—the best there is, and better than any Absolutist model. Changes in government type will cause unrest. Don't make too many changes to the setting because the ramifications are severe. You can only change to another type in the same level.

Absolutist Series

The Absolutist governments consist of despotism, monarchy, oligarchy, and constitutional monarchy. In other words, you don't argue with the man!

A military dictator has absolute authority in a despotism. Power is generally kept in the hands of a few, thus government is highly centralized. When running such a society, your military and Manufacturing efficiency will see a boost. On the downside, your Bioharvesting and Mining take a hit.

The right of succession determines who will be king or queen in a monarchy. Leaders either outrank other nobles or are considered a "living gods" by their loyal subjects. Manufacturing and military tend to flourish in a monarchy, while food production—the peasants need to eat—and research need more attention than usual.

A military oligarchy is known as a "junta." When the social elite run a government it's called an "aristocracy." If the scientific elite govern, it may be labeled a "technocracy." No matter the terminology, oligarchies determine the course of a whole world based on the words of a few. Expect a slight increase in Research at the expense of Manufacturing.

When you're in a transition state between monarchy and a representative government, you're in a constitutional monarchy. The "monarch" shares power with an elected parliament. Usually this means your economy is average across the board, though you might experience a slight dip in Manufacturing.

Collectivist Series

Everyone does their part. In hive and unification societies—the two government types in the Collectivist series—subordinates obey every order from their superiors.

Hive governments have little to fear from unrest. Because subjects do their duty, little bureaucratic infrastructure is needed to keep the peace. Races like the Klackon thrive in hive governments, but don't count on recreation to entertain them. It's generally shunned. Bioharvesting, Mining, and military are very efficient, and Manufacturing can be quite improved.

Very difficult to achieve, unification governments work under the premise that there is universal agreement among citizens about how the civilization should run. Unification leaders don't hold any more power than their neighbors; they just speak for the people. This may be the best overall government, since it increases efficiency in Bioharvesting, Mining, Manufacturing, and military without any penalties.

Representative Series

We've been in a representative government since we were born. Democracy, parliamentary, republic, and corporate are among the most popular of the "freedom"-based governments on our planet.

In a democracy, popular voting determines executive and legislative decisions. Once a nation gets too big, it's difficult for the average citizen to carry out all their democratic responsibilities and it might develop into a republic. Bioharvesting, Mining, and Manufacturing tend to thrive in a democracy, while military suffers.

Prime ministers guide parliamentary governments. They lead the majority party, while the minority coalitions try to rally the popular vote to their cause. Parliamentary governments help out Bioharvesting and Mining, and they lend a big increase to Manufacturing.

A republic elects a leader, or chief executive, to run the government. That leader might not have as much personal power, since he must secure legislative support on important decisions. In a republic, Bioharvesting and Mining do well, and Manufacturing thrives.

Big business runs a corporate government, and their number one goal is profit. Taxes drive the economy, and any sort of privilege comes with a price tag. Mining and Manufacturing are extremely efficient under a corporate regime. Not so with Research, Bioharvesting, and recreation.

Government Influence

Government	Bioharvesting	Mining	Manufacturing	Research	Military	Recreation	Space Port	Oppression Cost
Despotism	-20%	0	+20%	-5%	+30%	-5%	0	-7%
Monarchy	-20%	0	+30%	-10%	+10%	0	+5%	-6%
Oligarchy	-10%	-10%	0	+20%	0	0	+5%	+1%
Constitutional Monarchy	0	0	0	0	0	+20%	0	0
Corporate	+20%	+20%	+10%	+5%	-20%	-20%	+20%	-4%
Democracy	+15%	+10%	+10%	+5%	-10%	+20%	0	+12%
Parliamentary	0	+20%	+30%	+5%	0	0	0	+9%
Republicanism	0	+20%	+20%	+5%	+20%	0	-5%	+11%
Hive	+30%	+40%	+20%	+5%	+40%	-15%	-15%	-12%
Unification	+20%	+30%	+10%	+20%	+30%	0	-5%	-10%

Labor

Organic and robotic forced labor units are allowed or disallowed under this tab. If it's allowed, whenever you capture an enemy world, you automatically create a labor force—sort of like prison colonies. You can also gain robotic forced labor units (FLUs) from the Technology schools.

The higher you move the Labor slider on this screen, the faster the forced labor units work. It also decreases their lifespan. When you want to accelerate production across the empire, FLUs can do the job.

Set the forced labor bar low and you make your people happy. Set it on high and you get a cheap work force.

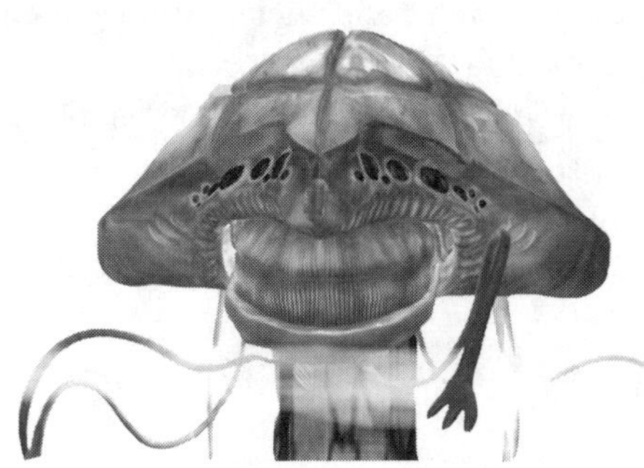

It all sounds good, right? Well, if you don't care about the moral implications and aren't worried about the social backlash, then sure. FLUs help your workforce, but increase unrest. If you choose to allow FLUs, you'll need to balance the money saved with some of that pumped back into shutting down unrest.

Development Plans

Admit it, you hate when your viceroys ignore your orders. Don't be too harsh on them—with running a planet, they have a lot on their plates. To save yourself time from tweaking economies on each individual world, the *MOO* designers invented the "Development Plans" menu. You will come to love this thing.

At the Development Plans screen, you can set the types of emphasis you want your planets to have.

There are three options along the right side of the screen: planet classification, development policy, and emphasis. Planet classification determines to which sort of planet the new plan applies, from all planets to starving worlds. The development policy tells the world in what category they should concentrate, from planetary defense to increasing morale to Mining. Emphasis can be primary, secondary, or tertiary, so you can stack policies on different worlds and the viceroy will carry them out in order—to the best of his ability.

If you set your emphasis to terraforming under the development policy, the selected worlds will spend money on perfecting their environments.

If you want to customize brand-new worlds to match your homeworld climate, select "newly acquired" under planet classification, "terraforming" under development policy, and "primary" under emphasis. Now all new planets will make terraforming their primary objective. If you fear attack from your neighbors, set planet classification to "frontier," development plan to "military," and emphasis on "primary." It's that easy.

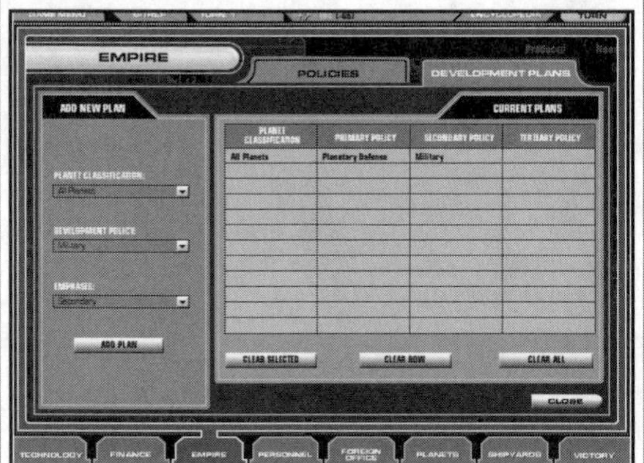

If you set your primary policy on planetary defense and your secondary emphasis on military, your planet will concentrate first on building missile bases and infantry and then fleets.

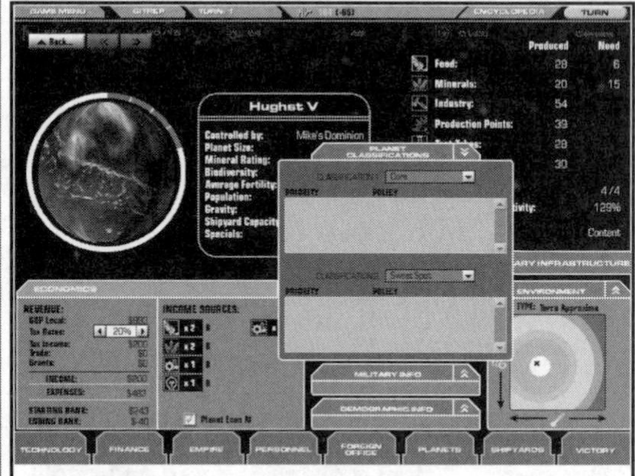

The Planet Classification tab can help you tag planets to better apply your development plan.

For a more complicated example, let's look at the sweet spot worlds. These worlds are already prime real estate, so you don't have to worry about terraforming. Since they're so valuable to the race, set the primary development policy on "planetary defense." Click on "manufacture" for your secondary policy—you might as well take advantage of the great conditions and make a ton of money. With your tertiary policy, you could go a number of ways. We'll choose "infrastructure" to tweak the economy to perfection.

NOTE

There are five user-defined planet classifications. Under the Planet Classifications tab in the Planets menu, you can define your world. Type "rogue" for colonies that have trouble with unrest, and then under the Empire menu you can use that classification to give orders to a specific group of planets.

chapter 7

PERSONNEL

Viceroys control your planets, leaders control your empire. A leader can improve your diplomatic channels, increase production, create better quality military troops, and keep the people happy. Sometimes, leaders

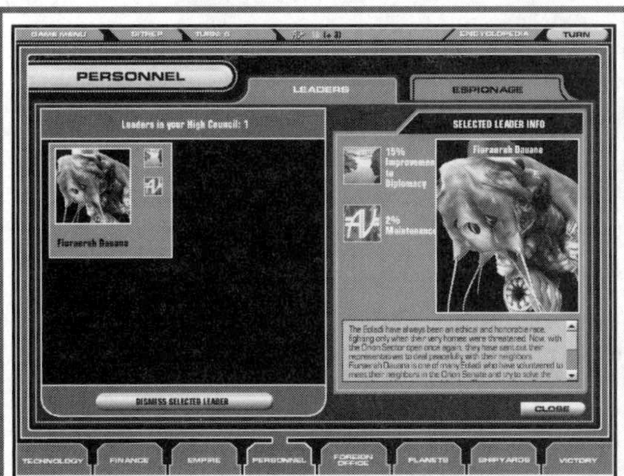

Would you rather have an improvement to Diplomacy or ground forces? Your leaders can have a profound effect on your whole civilization.

come with a cost attached, whether it be higher taxes or increased maintenance costs. Coupled with espionage, the two make up your Personnel files.

Leaders

Leaders come in all shapes and sizes. You can recruit an Eoladi who improves diplomatic relations by 15 percent, a Trilarian who aids Research by five percent, or an Evon leader who trains spies to have 15 percent better cloaking skills.

TM-217-ZEAP gives you a 10 percent increase to factory output.

Your high council can only hold four leaders. Early in the game, this won't be a problem. As the turns progress, you may need to dismiss a leader to make room for a better one to come along. Holding four denies you the chance to recruit any new leaders.

TIP

If your high council is full, you won't get a chance at recruiting any new leaders.

Watch for negative effects. If your empire is vulnerable to unrest and a leader comes along with an unrest penalty, think twice before accepting his aid. Always weigh the pluses and the minuses and make an informed decision.

Most leaders provide one or two bonuses, and come with at least one drawback, such as increased unrest.

You'll take help wherever you can get it. Accept the first three leaders that come your way (again, provided one doesn't have a huge disadvantage), then start being selective. Ask yourself what your empire needs. Are you looking to expand your empire through military conquest? You want one or two leaders who increase infantry effectiveness or lower fleet costs. Even a leader who affects production helps; a recreation-based leader does not. Do you need more income? Try a leader who collects more taxes or one who adds a diplomatic bonus to trade negotiations.

The Psilon Atresisi boosts Research output by 20 percent.

Espionage

When you can't reach your foes militarily and need to stop them, you turn to your espionage division. Sneak an agent into enemy territory and he can blow up buildings, cut supply lines, or assassinate a high-level scientist. Just watch out for those double agents . . . .

Leaders can go solo, but if you can team up their bonuses, the cumulative effect can be monstrously powerful.

On the Espionage screen, you can recruit six different types of spies: military, political, economic, social, diplomatic, and scientific. Below the recruitment selection, your current spies in training are displayed. It shows the time remaining until the spy is ready for field work. You can train only one agent at a time. Unless you're in a financial bind, you want to roll out four agents at all times.

On the right, one tab lists your spies, where you can check on their stats and current mission status, and another tab shows how many spies you have infiltrated in each foreign empire. Should you ever want to recall an agent—if you made peace with your one-time enemy—you'll have that option as well.

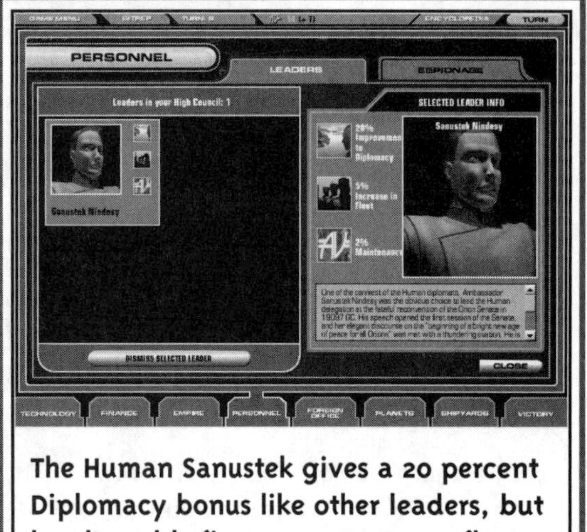
The Human Sanustek gives a 20 percent Diplomacy bonus like other leaders, but he also adds five percent to your fleet building.

Skills

Each of your spies, whether he's military or economic, has four basic stats. A spy's Cloak rating represents how invisible he is to the enemy government. The higher the Cloak rating, the more likely he is to overcome certain obstacles in his mission.

The offensive Dagger rating determines how successful an agent is at completing his tasks—destroying buildings, killing leaders, or swiping technology. Luck represents a spy's "lifespan." If your spy is good, you can expect him to last that many turns before he gets caught . . . if that many. Finally, Loyalty affects how likely it is that the spy will crack under interrogation and spill the beans on you. A spy with high Loyalty will sometimes commit suicide rather than talk.

Don't worry so much about a spy's Luck value—there are plenty more where he came from—but you can benefit from increasing all your other skills. High Cloak and Loyalty ratings will prevent retaliation from your enemies. They won't even know your agents, or when your agents are caught, they won't crack and incriminate you. For maximum impact, raise your spies' Dagger skills so you can hit the enemy hard and often.

Remember that your biology science and social sciences have the most espionage-friendly advances. If you're a race like the Evon or the Raas and plan to undermine your enemy's plans with spies, try to reach some of the espionage advances quickly to gain an edge.

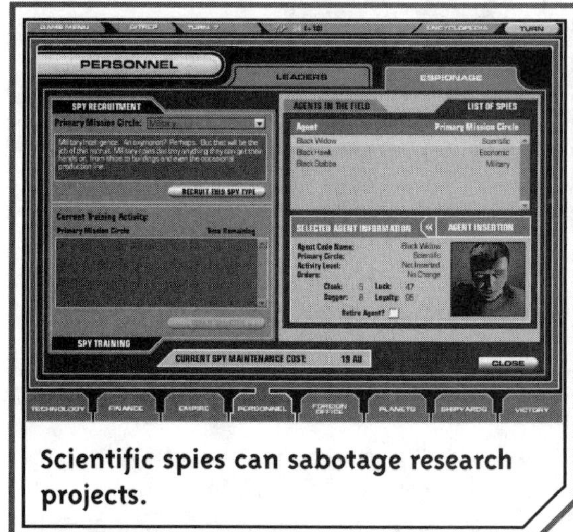
Scientific spies can sabotage research projects.

Mission

Your spy can only specialize in one task. You want a wide variety of spies; however, you should concentrate in military, political, and science, since they're the most powerful. Ignore economic and social unless you know the enemy has strong targets in those fields to eliminate.

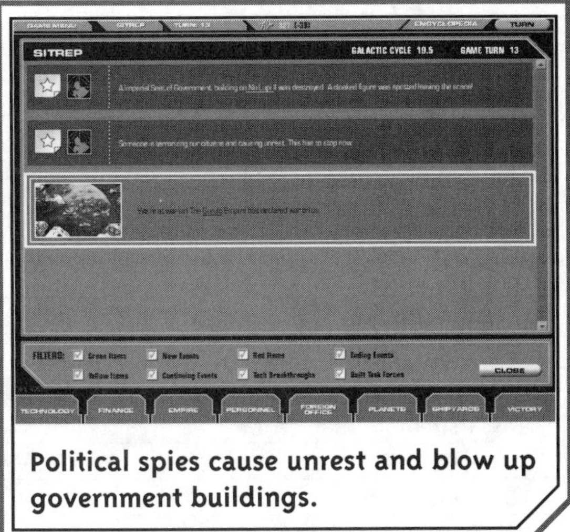

Political spies cause unrest and blow up government buildings.

With six different military tasks, your military agents can do the most damage. Most importantly, four missions slow the production of troops and ships. In an evenly matched conflict, every turn counts and your spies could make the difference in getting that one extra ship into a hotly contested system. Certain missions also cut down an enemy's Manufacturing by five percent and destroy military DEAs.

A common tactic is to generate tons of military spies then launch them at your enemy a few turns before you engage with a massive fleet. Unless you've misjudged your foe, the chaos to their military structure should set them back enough to give you an easy victory.

Political spies only have two agendas: Assassinate a leader or blow up a government building. Either one can be a critical strike against the enemy. With political spies, you have much more control over their missions. You don't have six different tasks, and so don't have to hope they complete the one you desperately need. Assassinating a leader hurts your enemy empire in all the areas the leader was supporting, and destroying a government DEA creates unrest and political chaos.

You can insert spies into any foreign power with which you have contact.

Much the same as military, science spies have five different tasks. Most involve slowing down your opponent's tech advances. Over the course of a long game, this can be a big advantage if you can move your own tech along. Destroying a Research DEA can set back an enemy a dozen turns, while stealing an advance from them can instantly strengthen an area that was once weak. Science espionage is more of a long-term, patient strategy. It's not a tactic you want to explore a few turns before you go to war; you won't see any benefit in that timeframe. Given time, a technologically advanced civilization will make mincemeat out of low-tech empires, and your science spies know just how to "dumb down" your enemy.

Espionage Missions

Mission Circle	Objective	Result
Economic	Economic Building	Weaken Economic Infrastructure 1 Turn
Economic	Civil Trade	Reduce Space Port Efficiency 1%–8%
Military	Training Depots	Slow Down Military Production 1 Turn
Military	Repair Facilities	Slow Down Military Production 1 or 2 Turns
Military	Support Lines	Slow Down Military Production 3 Turns
Military	Mobilization Center	Destroy Mobilization Center
Military	Military Building	Destroy Military DEA
Military	Production Sabotage	Reduce Manufacturing 5%
Political	Government Building	Destroy Government DEA
Political	Leader	Assassinate Leader
Science	Project Facility	Slow Down Research 1 Turn
Science	University Professor	Slow Down Research 1 Turn
Science	Major Government Research	Slow Down Research 4 Turns
Science	Science Building	Destroy Research DEA
Science	Technology	Steal Technology Advance
Social	Citizens	Unrest +5
Social	Recreating Building	Destroy Recreation DEA

Foreign Office

Traditional "empire conquest" games rely on who has the bigger cannon. Not *Master of Orion III*. Of course, you have the option of enslaving the galaxy through machines of mass destruction. You can also sip some tea, eat some

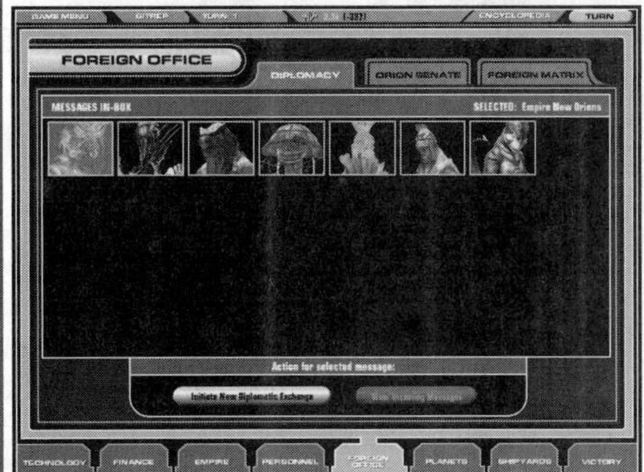

When you're a race that relies on trade, a single alien delegate weakens your chances while many delegates give you possible allies and economic partners.

alien pastries, and discuss matters diplomatically. It's possible to play through an entire game without pulling a violent move, unless you count booting someone off the Orion Senate.

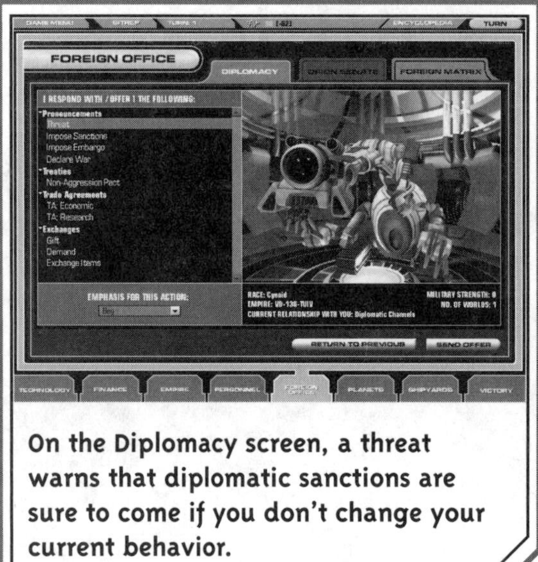

On the Diplomacy screen, a threat warns that diplomatic sanctions are sure to come if you don't change your current behavior.

Keep the Phones Open

One thing you don't do in this game is ignore the other players—breathing players or otherwise. You should always keep the lines of communication open. Someone who might be your enemy now may turn into an ally later against a larger threat. Plus, if you keep an enemy from unloading all his guns on you—maybe another enemy annoys him even more—you give yourself more time to recover.

The benefits of political alliances will help you win the game. Economic trade helps both sides with their debts. Research agreements generate extra Research points for both sides, resulting in advanced technologies for both parties. Depending on the military agreement—non-aggression pact, defensive alliance, or full alliance—you guarantee yourself peace of mind or extra warships in an intergalactic war. You can always offer a gift to your ally; it helps out that race's economy and scores you big diplomatic points for future negotiations.

Believe me, you'll pay the price if you keep hitting the turn button and ignore the Foreign Offices. In terms of game play, a "no answer" is worse than a stall tactic. If you reply immediately, your opponent will at least regard you seriously. A "stall" response outputs a negative reaction twice as bad as a regular reply, while a "no answer" is two and half times worse. Flat-out refusal generates a negative modifier three times that of a normal reply.

Declaring war puts both parties at the tops in the hatred scale.

Should talks break down, you have several recourses. You can demand something from the other alien power. Essentially, it's a bribe; if they don't pay up, they pay for it on the political or military front. A threat warns them and drops your diplomatic relation scores. The impose sanctions, impose embargo, and declare war options are identical to the decrees you can perform in the Orion Senate.

A non-aggression pact is the first step toward a military alliance.

Aliens vs. Aliens

Economic talks open up the trade routes between two powers.

Just like everyday life, space aliens have preconceptions about strangers, too. If you aren't of the same race—same race match-ups are treated as neutral—you fit into a "casus belli" category, and based on that category, your population either likes the other race, dislikes them, or sometimes has no feelings either way.

Casus Belli

State	Bonus/Penalty
Demand Exterminate	-200
Desire Exterminate	-191
Demand Surrender	-181
Desire Surrender	-169
Demand War	-154
Desire Conflict	-135
Accept Conflict	-111
Unfavorable	-81
Apathetic	-44
Favorable	+45
Accept End Conflict	+82
Desire End Conflict	+112
Demand Peace	+136
Desire Treaty	+155
Demand Treaty	+170
Desire Alliance	+182
Demand Alliance	+192

All this factors into *MOO's* diplomacy relations scale. Basically, it's a point system that tells what sort of reaction a race will have toward you in face-to-face conversations. The higher the number, the better the relations are. Anything over 100 means the two races treat each other with friendship and respect; hit -200 and you're going to war.

Diplomatic Tensions

State	Bonus/Penalty
Feud	-200
Loathing	-181
Hateful	-157
Jaundiced	-133
Troubled	-109
Tense	-85
Wary	-61
Uneasy	-37
Neutral	-13
Calm	+14
Relaxed	+38
Peaceful	+62
Cordial	+86
Amiable	+110
Friendly	+134
Harmonious	+158
Solidarity	+182

For example, Humanoids distrust Cybernetiks. They start off with an immediate -60 penalty to diplomacy relations. They aren't too fond of the Silicoid either; geodic races get a -38 penalty. However, they like the Ichthytosian (+50) and the Saurian (+30).

The Cybernetik races don't understand Humanoid (-60) and Etherean (-65), but do communicate with the Ichthytosian (+38). The Cybernetik are the most disliked "corporeal" race. We'll talk about the Harvester parasites in a second.

Saurian and Ichthytosian are natural enemies and rack up a whopping -140 rating against each other. They're an insult away from pulling the trigger. The Saurians like the Geodic and Humanoid races (both +30). The Ichthytosian get along with Humanoid (+50) and Etherean (+40).

The Ethereans play nice with the Ichthytosians and the Geodics (both +40) and not so nice with the Cybernetiks (-65). Out of all the starting races, the Ethereans start off with the best base relations.

The Geodics don't root for the Insectoids to come around (-64 diplomacy rating) and aren't happy about the Humanoids either (-38). The Ethereans (+40) and the Saurians (+30) get positive vibes.

The Insectoids are partially friendly with the Saurians (+24) and on an even keel with almost everyone else. The feeling is mutual with the Geodics—they don't like them either (-64 diplomacy rating).

Exchange trades one of your pieces of technologies for one of theirs.

The Harvesters hate everyone, even their own species. All races start out with a -150 penalty when meeting an Ithkul, so be very cautious.

Base Relations

Race Types	Humanoid	Cybernetik	Saurian	Ichthytosian	Etherean	Geodic	Insectoid	Harvester
Humanoid	0	-60	+30	+50	0	-38	+14	-150
Cybernetik	-60	0	-14	+38	-65	+38	0	-150
Saurian	+30	-14	0	-140	+14	+30	+24	-150
Ichthytosian	+50	+38	-140	0	+40	0	0	-150
Etherean	0	-65	+14	+40	0	+40	0	-150
Geodic	-38	+38	+30	0	+40	0	-64	-150
Insectoid	+14	0	+24	0	0	-64	0	-150
Harvester	-150	-150	-150	-150	-150	-150	-150	-150

Orion Senate

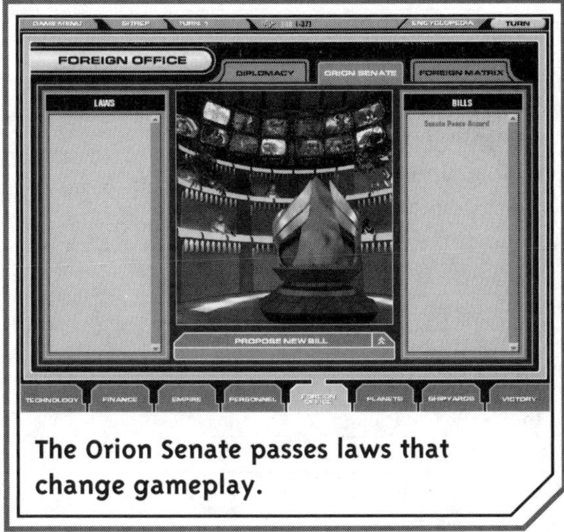

The Orion Senate passes laws that change gameplay.

The galactic congress, or Orion Senate, includes delegates from most of the game's races. You start off with a random chance to be on the Senate, unless you pay extra for it, and are at a big disadvantage if you aren't a member. Not only are you cut off from possible trade routes, but the Senate votes on proposals that can turn into laws that change the game. Most laws have a time limit, but some are permanent.

When you call up the Orion Senate, watch what the other powers vote on. Obviously, if a race sends a condemnation for your race, you can't trust that race. Conversely, propose commendations for your allies to bolster your voting power in the Senate. That way, if a particularly nasty proposal comes up against you, your allies can help you defeat it.

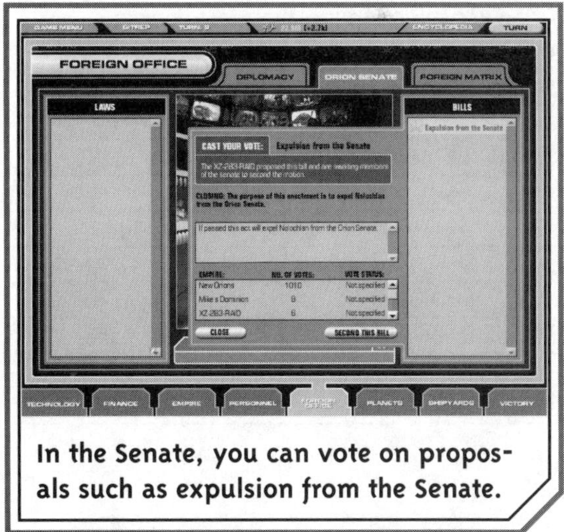

In the Senate, you can vote on proposals such as expulsion from the Senate.

If you choose to win through the second victory condition, being elected Senate President, try to earn as many votes as possible. The New Orions start out with 1,010 votes. As much as they may seem, you can surpass them. Think of the Senate as a popularity contest—make lucrative trade offers and throw gifts around to the other members, and your voting power will climb with your diplomatic points. Once you garner enough votes, you can force a call for a new leader. A "New President" proposal will show up and, hopefully, you and your allies can vote your way into history.

Senate Laws	Duration (in turns)	Result
Anti-cloning Initiative	25-1250	-20% Population Growth for All Members
Anti-Spying Initiative	6-24	+2 Spy Defense, +20% Spy Cost
Ban on Biological Weapons	3-60	+50% Unrest if Biological Weapons Used Previous Turn
Ban on Chemical Weapons	3-60	+50% Unrest if Chemical Weapons Used Previous Turn
Ban on Nuclear Weapons	3-60	+50% Unrest if Nuclear Weapons Used Previous Turn
Forced Labor Reparations	1	-500 Antaran Units
Galactic Relief Fund	2-12	-5% Tax Collection, -10 Unrest, +1 Diplomacy Point
Homeland Defense Bill	4-48	-20% Fleet Maintenance, +20% Oppression Cost
Humane Labor Law	5-30	-10% Oppression Cost
Interciv Holiday Declaration	25-1250	-1% Manufacturing, -5% Unrest
Jump Lane Tracking Law	4-40	+50% View on Galactic Map
Natural Preservation Initiative	25-1250	+20% Terraforming Cost
Orion Database Standardization	25-1250	-5% Heavy Foot, -2% Manufacturing, +5% Space Port
Orion Recycling Initiative	2-30	-15% Pollution
Orion Summit Meeting	1	+10 Diplomacy Points
Senate Audit	5-30	+.3 Heavy Foot of Government
Senate Farming Subsidies	4-40	+1 Bioharvesting, -2% Tax Collection
Senate Mining Subsidies	4-40	+1 Mining, -2% Tax Collection
Senate Peace Talks	3-27	-1 to Warfare Modifier
Senate Research Project	4-10	+30% Members Mineral Rarities
Senate Research Subsidies	4-40	+1 Research, -2% Tax Collection
Space Port Taxation	25-1250	+10% Space Port Efficiency
Standardized Working Hours	25-1250	+2 Manufacturing, -3 Unrest
Travel and Tourism Initiative	5-45	+2 Recreation, +10% Fleet Maintenance
Weapon Inspections Referendum	5-25	+2 Spy Insertion, +15% Oppression Cost

MILITARY

You can't get away from violence. Yes, it's possible to negotiate up to Orion Senate President, where you can call the shots. And yes, you can explore and trade with neighbors in the hopes of a galactic utopia. You might even win using one

Other races prepare for war, and so should you.

of these tactics, but somewhere along the line you'll get attacked and will need to defend yourself. It's a good idea to know the ins and outs of ground and space forces.

This chapter helps you build your units and wisely spend your military budget. If you want strategy tips on creating task forces and combat, refer to Chapter 13. Now, let's build some fleets and armies.

Building Spaceships

Upgrade your ship with the latest technology as soon as possible.

Fleets control space, planets, and the game. Without fleets, your five billion marines aren't moving off the planets where they're located. Fleets can initiate a planetary bombardment that eliminates enemy population, infrastructure, and military, or can transport ground forces for a land war. Pay attention to the type of mission for which you're designing the ship. You don't necessarily want to take a reconnaissance light cruiser into battle or a carrier on a recon mission.

Hulluva Ship

The bigger the ship, the more it can hold. Consequently, you can carry more weapons, shields, sensors, and big-screen TVs. The larger ships also have more hit points—a higher inherent hull strength—than smaller ships. It all comes down to your current tech level and cost; you need to have a lot of advances in physical sciences to build the larger ship hulls, and the money to pay for it when the design is submitted. There are 14 different base ships, and the more expensive ones are priced that way for a reason.

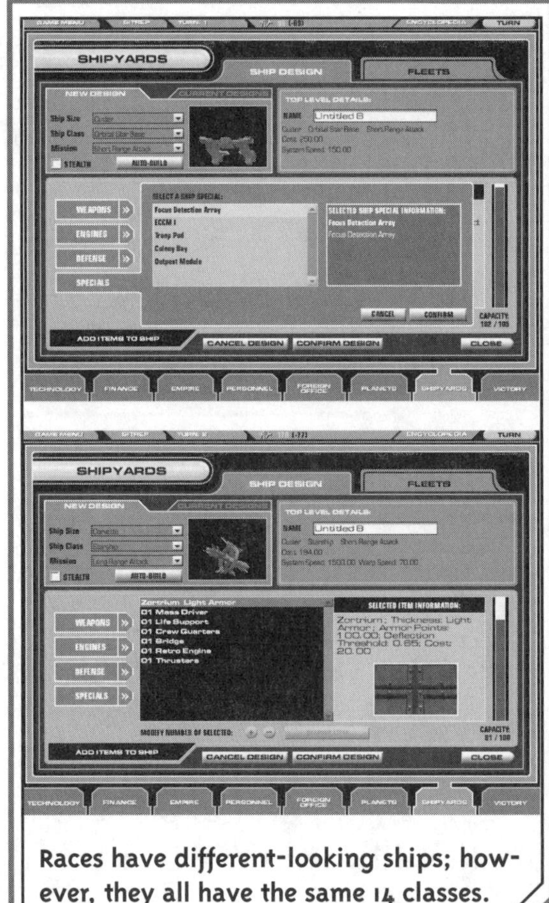

Races have different-looking ships; however, they all have the same 14 classes.

Base Ships

Name	Capacity	Base Hull Modifier	Marines Held	Cost (in AUs)
Lancer	50	+9%	2	100
Cutter	70	+12%	4	142
Corvette	100	+15%	6	204
Frigate	140	+19%	8	298
Destroyer	200	+24%	10	438
Light Cruiser	285	+31%	12	650
Cruiser	405	+39%	14	974
Battle Cruiser	575	+49%	16	1,458
Battleship	815	+62%	18	2,264
Dreadnought	1,155	+79%	20	3,502
Super Dreadnought	1,635	+100%	22	5,472
Titan	2,310	+125%	24	8,648
Behemoth	3,265	+158%	26	13,706
Leviathan	4,615	+200%	28	22,224

Weapons

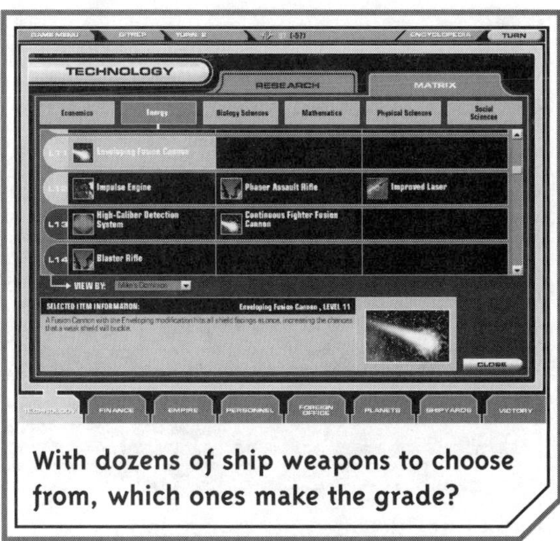

With dozens of ship weapons to choose from, which ones make the grade?

When it comes to space combat, weapons are your most important ship feature. If you can blast an enemy ship 100 times before it coasts into its range, who cares what armor it has? With so many choices, though, do you go with a mass driver over a graviton beam, or a particle beam over a mauler?

As you climb the tech tree, the weapons get better. The level 50 stellar converter blows away the competition! But there are some preferences to analyze.

Plasma weapons have the best accuracy and average damage.

Plasma weapons have the best accuracy. At maximum range, even the lowest plasma weapon, the level 5 fusion beam, operates at 80 percent effectiveness. Mass weapons are the opposite; they barely muster a 50 percent at maximum range. Beam weapons fall in the middle, but they have the best average range, with the level 20 ion pulse cannon shooting farther than level 25 weapons.

A ship's primary concern is blasting the enemy's hull. Plasma weapons do this best—the level 40 mauler hits for 679 damage—while the best of the weaker particle weapons deals 231 points.

That said, particle weapons are the cheapest and plasma weapons are the most expensive to build. When you have the cash in pocket, go with plasma.

Particle weapons can be bought cheap, for those on a budget.

Scan the weapons by level to find both oddities and bargains. The level 5 fusion beam is superior to the level 5 mass driver. From level 5 through level 10, you don't have much choice. The quark cannon and neutron blaster are decent weapons for the cost. The level 15 graviton beam is a bargain—it deals equal or greater damage than two of the three level 20 weapons.

Weapons get a little heftier when you pass level 20. The plasma cannon deals 213 damage per hit, five times more than the other similarly advanced weapons. The level 20 ion pulse cannon and the level 25 gauss cannon come equipped with great ranges, but the pulse cannon is inefficient against armor.

The disruptor cannon beats the particle beam at level 30. The cannon has an equal range and deals twice as much damage. The level 45 mauler usually spits out mega damage, but against ships with shields the damage is reduced by half. At level 50, the stellar converter weighs in with an awesome range, 100 percent accuracy and 1,000 damage. The only thing it doesn't have going for it is the cost.

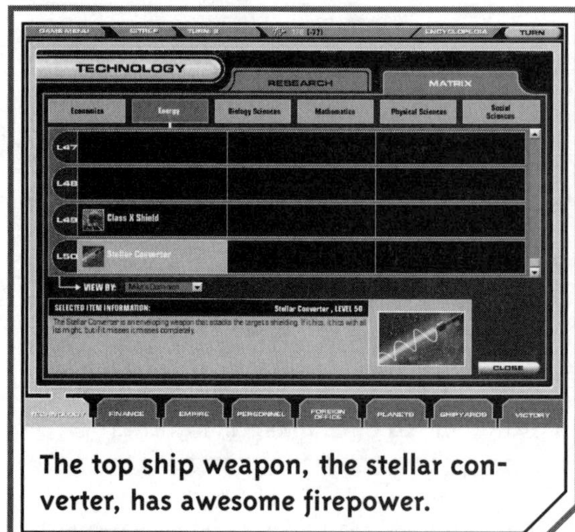

The top ship weapon, the stellar converter, has awesome firepower.

Ship Weapons

Weapon	Tech Level	Type	Accuracy	Max Range	Fire Delay	Damage	Shield Penetration	Armor Piercing	Cost (in AUs)
Laser	1	Beam	70%	3,750	2.5	7	100%	100%	5
Fusion Beam	5	Plasma	80%	5,590	2.5	31	100%	100%	21
Mass Driver	5	Mass	50%	3,000	2.5	14	100%	100%	9
Quark Cannon	5	Particle	70%	7,267	2.5	15	100%	100%	10
Neutron Blaster	10	Particle	70%	12,587	2.5	33	100%	100%	22
Hard Beam	10	Beam	70%	11,859	2.5	15	100%	100%	10
Rail Gun	10	Mass	50%	9,487	2.5	30	100%	100%	20
Graviton Beam	15	Particle	70%	14,534	2.5	49	100%	100%	33
Hellfire Cannon	15	Plasma	70%	9,682	2.5	67	100%	100%	45
Phasors	20	Beam	70%	18,750	2.5	48	100%	100%	32
Plasma Cannon	20	Plasma	70%	13,693	2.5	213	100%	100%	142
Ion Pulse Cannon	20	Beam	70%	16,771	5	33	100%	80%	22
Particle Beam	20	Particle	90%	14,534	2	49	10%	90%	33
Gauss Cannon	25	Mass	50%	15,000	2.5	97	100%	100%	64
Lightning Field Generator	25	Plasma	90%	12,500	2.5	36	70%	70%	24
Disruptor Cannon	30	Mass	50%	17,748	2.5	209	100%	100%	139
Dark Energy Beam	30	Particle	70%	17,801	2.5	107	100%	100%	71
Disintegrater Beam	35	Beam	70%	22,185	2.5	105	100%	100%	70
Megabolt Cannon	35	Plasma	70%	14,790	2.5	314	100%	100%	209
Tachyon Beam	40	Particle	70%	20,555	2.5	231	100%	100%	154
Mauler	45	Plasma	100%	15,811	4	679	50%	100%	453
Dark Matter Projector	45	Mass	50%	20,125	2.5	453	100%	100%	302
Stellar Converter	50	Beam	100%	26,517	8	1,000	100%	100%	666

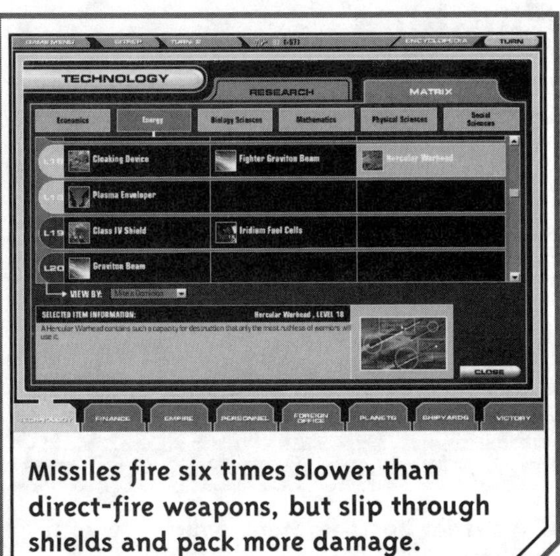

Missiles fire six times slower than direct-fire weapons, but slip through shields and pack more damage.

Missiles

Missiles don't care about shields, and they don't fizzle out like energy-based weapons. These physical, torpedo-like bombs deal significant damage to the enemy.

Missiles fire six times slower than the average weapon. Even so, they pack some firepower. A second-tier missile barely does more damage than it costs, unlike a tenth-generation warhead, which detonates for over 1,000 points of damage. Given extra space, load up on missiles to supplement the mainstay firing power of your energy weapons.

Missile Damage

Warhead	Damage	Cost (in AUs)
Nuclear Warhead I	112	28
Anionic Energy Warhead II	165	31
Neutronium Warhead	243	34
Hercular Warhead	357	38
Merculite Warhead	525	42
High Energy X-Ray Laser Warhead	773	46
Scatter Pack Warhead	1,137	51
Ionic Pulsar Warhead	1,673	56
Energy Pulsar Warhead	2,462	62
Omega Warhead	3,623	68

Armor

The low-end duranium can't stand up to the better armors.

If your ship's shields fail, you had better pack thick armor. Damage done through shields will be absorbed by armor, or you won't be coming home from the war. Deflectivity is a threshold value and if the damage is below that threshold, then no damage can get through. The only sure thing is a high armor value to cut down on the casualties.

Titanium offers moderate protection at a 400 armor strength. However, compared to the high-end neutronium (800) or adamantium (1,600), it's tinfoil. Medium armor can double the base value of your armor, while very heavy armor improves it by eight times.

Your latest armor tech is automatically applied to your ground forces.

For the complete breakdown on the armor tech advances, check out the physical sciences section in Chapter 4.

Fighters

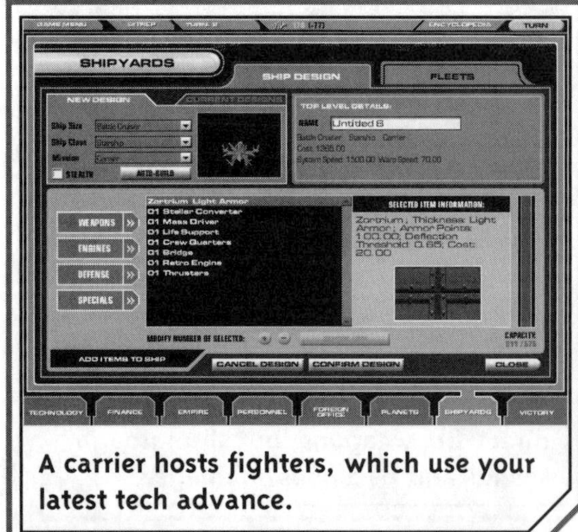

A carrier hosts fighters, which use your latest tech advance.

Fighters are tiny versions of their mother ships and follow similar patterns, but with reduced numbers. For example, the level 1 fighter fusion beam has a tiny range compared to its bigger counterpart, and deals five damage to its 31. Both plasma cannons fall in the level 20 range, except the fighter plasma cannon costs one-tenth the price of the regular plasma cannon and only deals 23 damage to 213. Apply the same logic as you do with normal ship-building and it'll make sense.

Fighter Weapons

Weapon	Tech Level	Type	Accuracy	Max Range	Fire Delay	Damage	Shield Penetration	Cost (in AUs)
Fighter Laser	1	Beam	70%	280	2.5	5	100%	5
Fighter Fusion Beam	1	Plasma	80%	80	2.5	20	100%	5
Fighter Mass Driver	5	Mass	50%	230	2.5	9	100%	5
Fighter Neutron Blaster	10	Particle	70%	450	2.5	22	100%	8
Fighter Graviton Beam	15	Particle	70%	550	2.5	32	100%	12
Fighter Ion Pulse Cannon	20	Beam	70%	870	2.5	22	50%	15
Fighter Phasers	20	Beam	70%	860	2.5	32	100%	10
Fighter Plasma Cannon	20	Plasma	70%	285	2.5	141	100%	15
Fighter Gauss Cannon	25	Mass	50%	500	2.5	64	100%	10
Fighter Disruptor Cannon	30	Mass	50%	550	2.5	138	100%	25
Fighter Particle Beam	30	Particle	70%	820	2.5	32	10%	35

The Shipyards

Customize ships to exact specifications at the Shipyards.

It's possible to customize your own ships. Maybe you want the latest cloaking technology or prefer one weapon over another? The Shipyards allows you to make changes to any ship in your arsenal.

In the Ship Design screen, you'll see several menus for altering your ship. First, pick a ship size. They range from cutter to leviathan, though you can't build the bigger ships until you've equipped a planet with enough ship-building advances (like energy level 25's matter conversion module) to field such a design.

Next, choose a ship class. You can be an orbital star base, system ship, or starship. Orbital star bases are stationary platforms that defend a world—good for shooting down the enemy, but with limited mobility. System ships can pursue enemies within a system, but without stardrives they can't jump to other systems. Starships can motor anywhere in the galaxy. If you choose the stealth checkbox at the bottom of the menu, your ships will be equipped with the latest cloaking technology—if they can fit it.

New warships get designated for certain missions in the Shipyards. Choose carefully—the mission will determine the equipment that goes on the ship.

Carefully choose a mission for your ship. Your ship will be outfitted with different parts depending on the type of mission—short-range attack, point defense, colony, etc. Don't go into battle with an outpost ship. Because most of the ship is devoted to navigation and living quarters, it lacks the space for extra weapons and armor. Point defense ships can protect your fleet from enemy missiles, but they don't have the heavy weaponry to go it alone.

When you design your ship, space is the main concern. It's hard to fit everything into each ship, so most ships have to be specialized. One will carry your heavy-duty weapons, while another will run the faster engine for maneuverability. It's critical to work your way up to the larger ships—their capacity is much greater, and they can carry the weapons, armor, and special instruments you'd like to cram in.

At the bottom of the Ship Design screen, you can add individual items to a ship. Select the appropriate category—weapons, engines, defense, or specials—and plug and play. We've already discussed strategy tips for weapons and defense (armor) in this chapter, so follow those principles to design your perfect vessels. For more information on engines and specials, check out Chapter 4 to read up on all the game's technologies.

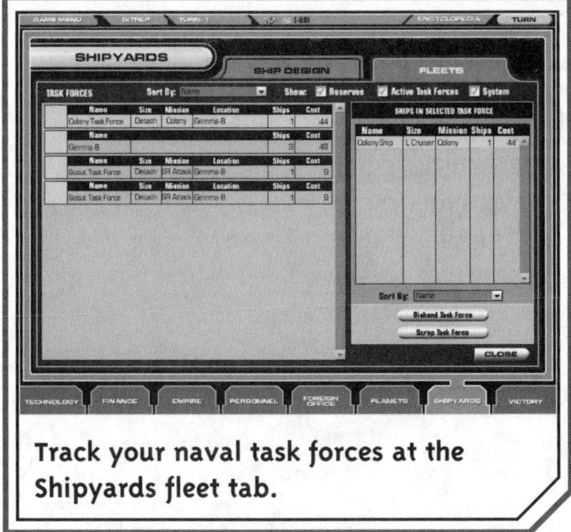

Track your naval task forces at the Shipyards fleet tab.

Finally, the fleets tab helps you to keep track of your naval task forces. It lists your current task forces and the individual ships in each force. Rather than scroll around the galactic map, you can identify the size, mission type, and location of your fleets here. Check back here often if you're having trouble visualizing your navy's epic scope.

Building Ground Forces

Each world can design its own ground forces to defend the planet or get carted off to fight on enemy territory.

The Imperial armed forces—the men and women who defend and conquer planets—are the underappreciated workers in this game. Your fleets get all the praise, until a particularly difficult planet won't roll over. That's when you send in the marines to combat the locals one-on-one.

Each ground force consists of a base unit (modified by your starting race's traits), armor for added defense (if they have any), and a weapon (optional, but preferred). Add dozens of abilities together and you have the "competency" of that unit. Let's examine some of the more notable ones.

Base Stats

Initiative figures out who shoots first. The higher the number, the more likely you'll put a hole through the other guy's armor first.

Number of attacks represents how many attacks you get each turn. Even if you have a low damage total, multiple attacks can hammer an opponent if they all hit.

Accuracy is how likely you are to hit. Doing massive damage or shooting 25 times doesn't mean squat if you aren't successful.

Evade represents your chances of dodging an attack. High evaders can bounce around the battlefield and live longer than they should.

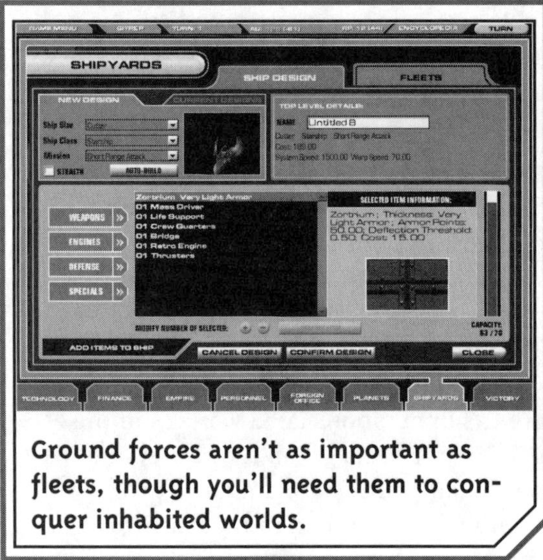

Ground forces aren't as important as fleets, though you'll need them to conquer inhabited worlds.

Attack strength helps determine whether a shot hits, misses, or is deflected. Any hit does one point of damage. A battle can be over quickly if this area is mismatched.

Armor increases a unit's defense. You may not shoot first or evade, but you can soak up the damage.

Hits stand for the amount of damage you can take. If the attack gets through armor, it's applied to hits.

Morale represents a unit's courage and willingness to stay in battle, even when the odds are stacked against it.

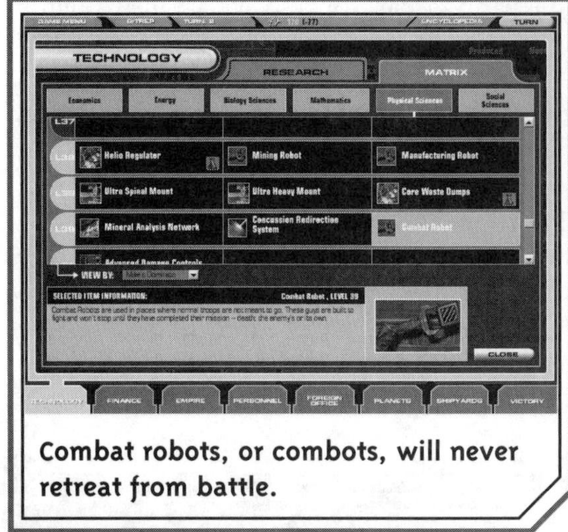

Combat robots, or combots, will never retreat from battle.

Humans or Sakkra?

Species are adapted for different environments. You wouldn't expect the gaseous Eoladi to wear natural armor, and yet they may surprise you in combat. The Sakkra are no-brainers for warriors, but are the Meklar?

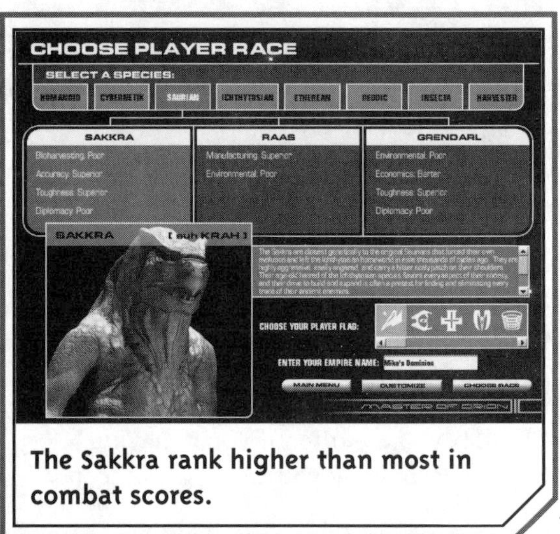

The Sakkra rank higher than most in combat scores.

In a comparison of the races, they all seem to be good at one particular item, except the Etherean and the Ichthytosians who are better at two. Etherians, like the Eoladi and Imsaeis, get a surprise +1 points to their number of attacks. Not really durable, they get the combat bonus for their many tentacles. The Ichthytosian are the quickest of the bunch and gain +30 to evade. Both the Ichthytosian and Etherian also improve 10 points on initiative.

The Humanoids' forte is in shooting first. The bipeds get the jump on everyone with a +20 to initiative. The machine-like Cybernetik, with all their technological enhancements and more than a few telescopic sights, gain +20 to accuracy. The hateful Harvesters, the Ithkul, will not stop until you're dead, and thus receive a +2 to morale.

On the combat side of things, the Saurians gain +10 attack strength and are likely to deal the most damage. On the other hand, the Geodics can take a hit or four. A +20 to armor and +2 hits ensures they can counteract with the best of them.

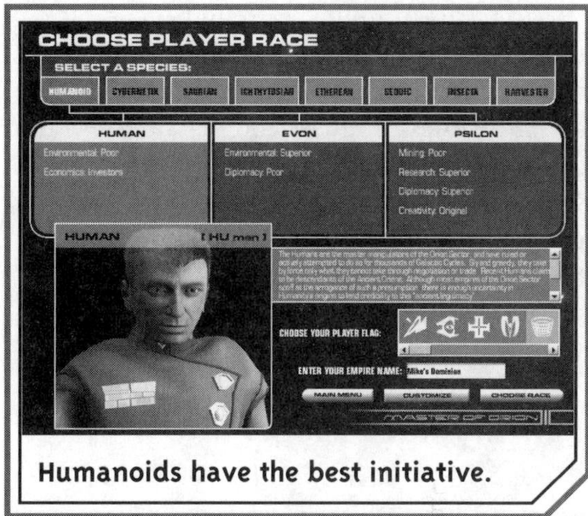

Humanoids have the best initiative.

Race Modifiers

Race Class	Initiative	Number of Attacks	Accuracy	Evade	Attack Strength	Armor	Hits	Morale
Humanoid	+20	0	0	0	0	0	0	0
Cybernetik	0	0	+20	0	0	0	0	0
Saurian	0	0	0	0	+10	0	0	0
Ichthytosian	+10	0	0	+30	0	0	0	0
Etherian	+10	+1	0	0	0	0	0	0
Geodic	0	0	0	0	0	+20	+2	0
Insectoid	0	0	0	0	0	0	0	0
Harvester	0	0	0	0	0	0	0	+2

In terms of military strength, each race starts with a base of three and adjusts the number according to their Accuracy, Reflexes, and Toughness bonuses and penalties. All the ground force bonuses affect this base combat score. You'll get a rough idea of how well that particular race's regular army can fight; however, there are many variables in combat, such as how fast they can build military and what effect their spies will have.

Military Race Scores

Race	Base Military Strength	Place
Ithkul	8	1st
Sakkra	7	2nd
Grendarl	7	3rd
Cynoid	6	4th
Meklar	6	5th
Evon	5	6th
Raas	4	7th
Tachidi	3	8th
Silicoid	3	9th
Klackon	3	10th
Trilarian	2	11th
Human	2	12th
Eoladi	1	13th
Psilon	1	14th
Nommo	0	15th
Imsaeis	0	16th

Basic Units

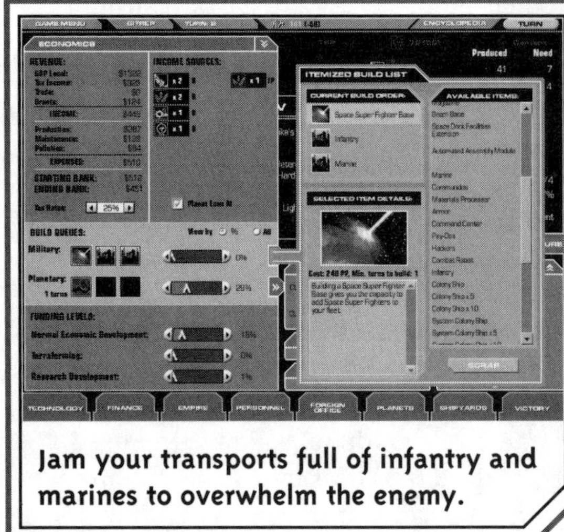

Jam your transports full of infantry and marines to overwhelm the enemy.

The type of ground force you have dictates your army's strength. Are you fast? Tough? Relentless? The type of unit will determine these factors more than the race.

Infantry and marines are quick. Infantry gives a +20 bonus and space marines +15. Other than infantry being the nimble ones and evading better (+30 to marine's +15) the space marines pack an extra attack, +10 accuracy, +5 attack strength, +5 armor, and an extra hit. As the cheapest ground forces on the list, you'll end up stockpiling these units. Pack them into transport ships, then use their numbers to overwhelm enemy resistance on targeted planets. The marines, in particular, offer a good value for the price.

Armored forces have a better accuracy than armor value.

Mobile units aren't as mobile as you'd think. They offer +10 initiative and no points to evade. They're tougher with four hits, supply two extra attacks, and +10 to attack strength. If you can't afford the big boys, the mobile units are solid mid-range units for defending your worlds.

Oddly enough, the armor units' accuracy (+30) is better than their armor (+15). Still, you can't argue with a unit that can take a hit and keep on ticking along. Four additional attack per round, +15 attack strength, and six extra hits makes this is the best unit, next to the elite sluggers.

If you want to kick butt, sink your money into battleoids. Battleoids are amazing. Other than zeroes in initiative, evade, and morale, they hit with six additional attacks, +40 accuracy, and +20 attack strength, and defend with +20 armor and eight additional hits.

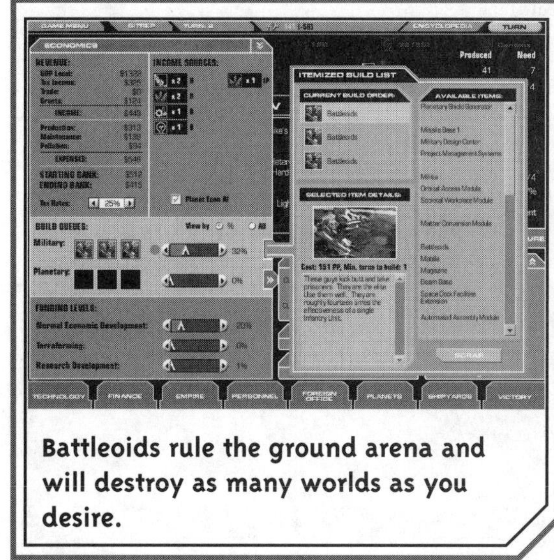

Battleoids rule the ground arena and will destroy as many worlds as you desire.

Ground Forces

Unit Name	Tech Level	Initiative	Number of Attacks	Accuracy	Evade	Attack Strength	Armor	Hits	Morale	Special Abilities	Cost (in AUs)
Infantry	1	+20	0	0	+30	0	0	2	0	—	20
Space Marine	6	+15	+1	+10	+15	+5	+5	3	0	—	50
Mobile	9	+10	+2	+20	0	+10	+5	4	0	—	80
Armor	20	+5	+4	+30	0	+15	+15	6	0	—	111
Battleoids	31	0	+6	+40	0	+20	+20	8	0	—	151
Combots	38	0	+1	0	0	+10	+10	+1	+99	Experience never gained or lost by combots	100
Militia	50	+5	0	0	0	0	0	2	0	—	10

Combat Support

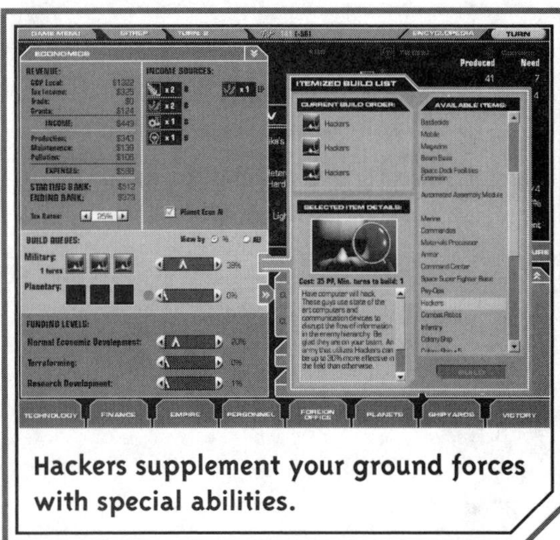

Hackers supplement your ground forces with special abilities.

A Pyrrhic victory is when you win a battle at a staggering cost to your own troops. You don't want that to happen in *MOO*, or you'll never recover for the next battle. That's where your ground support comes in. In an evenly matched contest, support can be the "X factor" you need to defeat the bad guys. They might not "fight" for you, but they will win for you.

Social sciences' psy-ops give a 10-point bonus to initiative to all your units and a +1 points to your enemy's rout checks. Even that little bit can be an edge for attacking first or sending enemies packing when they fail their morale check.

Mathematics' hackers are similar, offering +10 to initiative and +10 to accuracy. The best of the bunch, physical sciences' commandos, strengthen all your units' attack scores by +10. When in doubt, pound your opponent into submission.

What happens when all these bonuses soup up your opponent's forces? Invest in social sciences' command centers. They negate enemy commandos, hackers, and psy-ops bonuses, and allow the two forces to battle it out with annoying interference from support units.

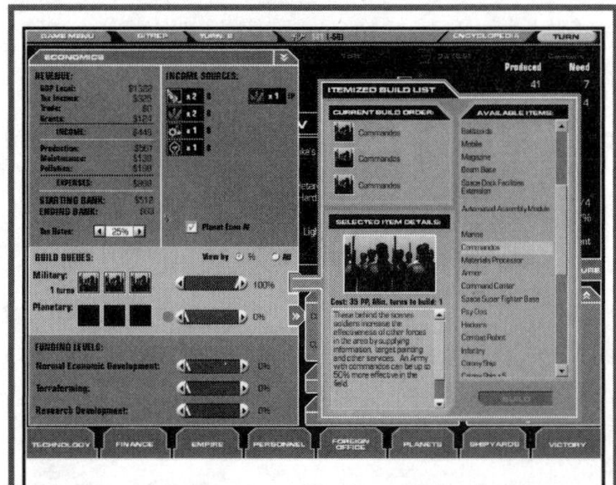

Command centers eliminate the bonuses from ground support units, so invest in them early.

Ground Support

Unit Name	Tech Level	Initiative	Accuracy	Attack Strength	Armor	Hits	Morale	Special Abilities	Cost (in AUs)
Psy-Ops	4	+10	0	0	0	2	+2	+10 Initiative, +1 rout on Enemy Morale Check	35
Magazine	0	0	0	0	+30	5	+10	Allows Isolated Troops to Fight at Full Effectiveness	35
Commandos	21	0	0	+10	0	2	+8	+10 Attack Strength	35
Hackers	15	+10	+10	0	0	2	+8	+10 Initiative, +10 Accuracy	35
Command Center		11	+10	+10	+10	+30	3	+10 Negates Enemy Commandos, Psy-Ops and Hackers	70

Armor Up

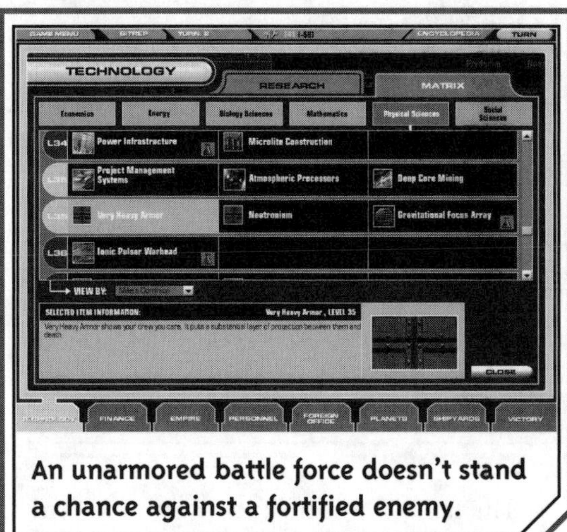

An unarmored battle force doesn't stand a chance against a fortified enemy.

Earth policemen wear bulletproof jackets for extra protection in the line of duty. Your space marines wear zortium to stop the laser blasts from singeing their chest hair. Suiting up makes a huge difference against armor-less opponents. Even a small force of armored units can decimate a technologically disadvantaged group three or four times their size.

Ground Armor

Armor Type	Armor
None	0
Titanium	+10
Duranium	+20
Tritanium	+30
Zortium	+40
Neutronium	+50
Adamantium	+60
Xintium	+70

Ground Weapons

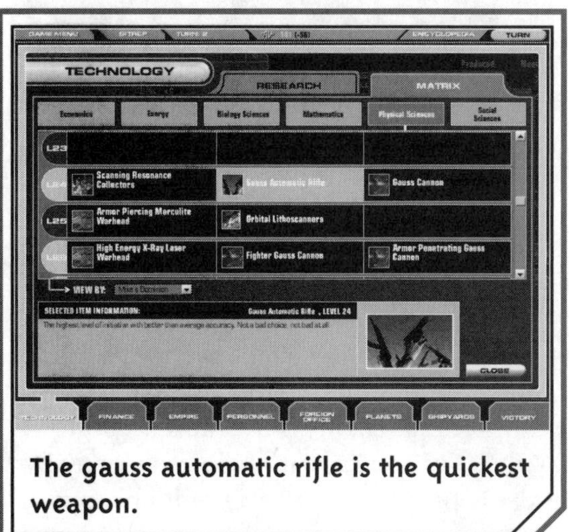

The gauss automatic rifle is the quickest weapon.

Improved speed, range, and damage come from owning a gun. Unravel the secrets of the energy and physical sciences tech trees and your troops will be second to none. Unless a freak occurrence mucks with your plans, your armed troops will always beat the enemy's unarmed goons.

The quickest of the weapons, the gauss automatic rifle, adds +16 to your units' initiative. The pulse laser holds its own at +14; and the gauss rifle increases unit weapon speeds by +13. Both the gatling laser and the tri-sequence phaser rifle provide a respectable +12.

The plasma projector, enveloper, gun, and pod all deliver four extra attacks per turn. The tri-sequence phaser rifle, multi blaster, and multi fusion rifle can throw three extra attacks around each round.

The tri-sequence phaser rifle ranks at the top of the accuracy field.

Some pistols can shoot fast, while others can launch multiple volleys, but the tri-sequence phaser rifle is the most accurate. With a +40 accuracy, it's followed closely by the +39 pulse laser and +39 multi blaster.

Don't count out the fusion core launcher, either, with its +36 accuracy.

The plasma weapons are best with damage capabilities. The plasma pod adds +13 to attack strength, just nipping the plasma gun and its +12. The fusion core launcher challenges the plasma enveloper, as they both contribute +11 to attack strength, and the multi fusion rifle and plasma projector hit for +10 apiece.

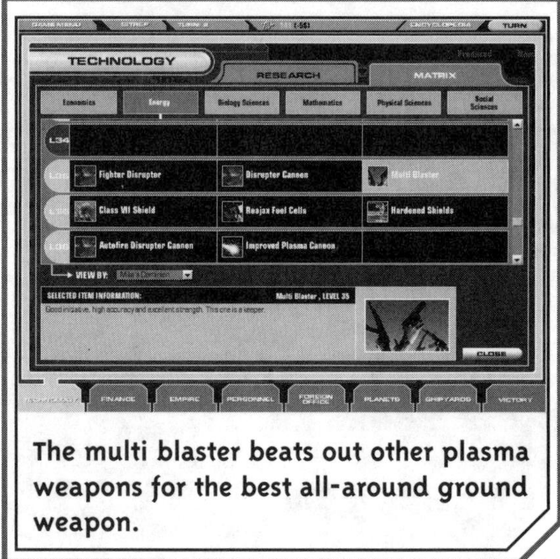

The multi blaster beats out other plasma weapons for the best all-around ground weapon.

The bang-for-your-buck weapon award goes to energy level 34's multi blaster. It floats near the top in every category. Your marines shouldn't pass up a +10 initiative, +3 number of attacks, +39 accuracy, and +9 attack strength weapon. If they do, ship them off on the next one-way colony ship.

Ground Weapons

Weapon	Tech Level	Initiative	Number of Attacks	Accuracy	Attack Strength
Assault Blaster	25	+7	+2	+31	36
Assault Rifle	9	+10	0	0	3
Blaster Rifle	13	+5	+2	+23	27
Fusion Accelerator	16	+3	+1	+12	33
Fusion Core Launcher	36	+8	+2	+36	54
Fusion Gun	6	+2	+0	0	27
Gatling Laser	20	+12	+2	+31	24
Gauss Automatic Rifle	24	+16	0	+24	30
Gauss Rifle	19	+13	0	+16	18
Hand Blaster	4	+4	+1	+15	21
Laser Assault Rifle	9	+9	+2	+23	15
Laser Rifle	12	+8	+1	+15	9
Multi Blaster	34	+10	+3	+39	48
Multi Fusion Rifle	27	+5	+3	+24	42
Multi-Synch Phaser Rifle	23	+9	+2	+30	30
Needle Gun	13	+11	0	+8	9
Phaser Assault Rifle	12	+7	+2	+20	21
Phaser Rifle	2	+6	+1	+10	15
Plasma Gun	28	+3	+4	+20	48
Plasma Enveloper	18	+1	+4	+10	39
Plasma Pod	38	+6	+4	+30	60
Plasma Projector	6	0	+4	+0	33
Pulse Laser	31	+14	+2	+39	36
Tri-Sequence Phaser Rifle	32	+12	+3	+40	42

Defense Spending

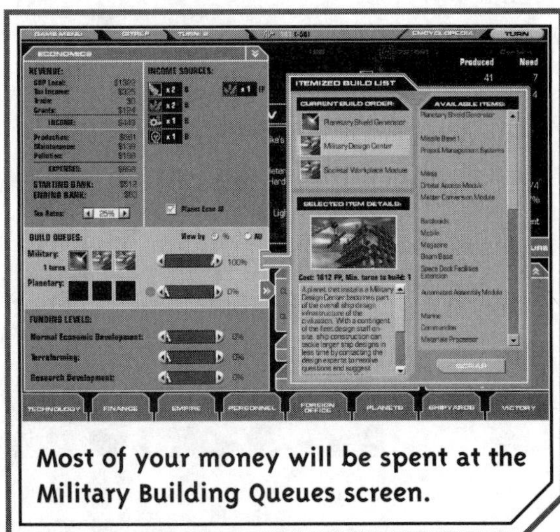

Most of your money will be spent at the Military Building Queues screen.

Unless you pursue a diplomatic win, you'll spend most of your money on military. That doesn't mean you want to buy everything in sight or purchase an overpriced frigate when a cutter will do.

Keep your military spending in the green when you're not at war. Your viceroys should handle this for you, but sometimes they get overzealous—or miserly—and you need to step in at the planetary level. Make sure your military build queues slider, under the planet's economic tab, stays green so you spend one AU for one military build point. This will produce the greatest amount of ships for the lowest cost.

When your war campaign gets under way, push that military spending bar into the yellow. That's two AUs for one military build point. Most of the time, you need to spend the extra money to get those ships and ground forces earlier. Don't let your spending violate the limits you've set in the military-political economy selection under Finance. In an emergency, you might have to push the military spending into the red, though it's not recommended for long-term financial survival.

To prevent other races from storming your castle, build up your military at key intersection systems you can defend.

Where do you want your military spending to occur? Ideally, you should set up planets in choke-point systems. You might have an efficient economy on a backwater world, but it'll cost you a lot more in time to ship those units to another system when they're complete. It's better to build up a military infrastructure on a planet in or near an important tactical system (a choke point) so you can quickly respond to needs and emergencies.

The only time you should violate this principle is for your home system. You don't have a choice where that starts, and it might be in a system with lots of open space lanes, or the homeworld might not be properly suited for large military production.

Work with what you've got. You must defend your homeworld—it starts off as your most profitable and important planet. Build up bases and fleets to defend this system before you go out on any big conquests. While you're out with all your forces, an enemy could sneak in the back door and ruin you. Start small and concentrated, then work your way out.

Don't stretch your home forces too thin; keep them in your home system and nowhere else. This keeps your defenses high and prevents individual fleets from being picked off, thus reducing your overall strength. Unless your homeworld is a choke point near your enemy's border—never a good thing—you should design a new military production center near your forward advance. From there, you can crank out an offensive threat that will quickly worry your enemy.

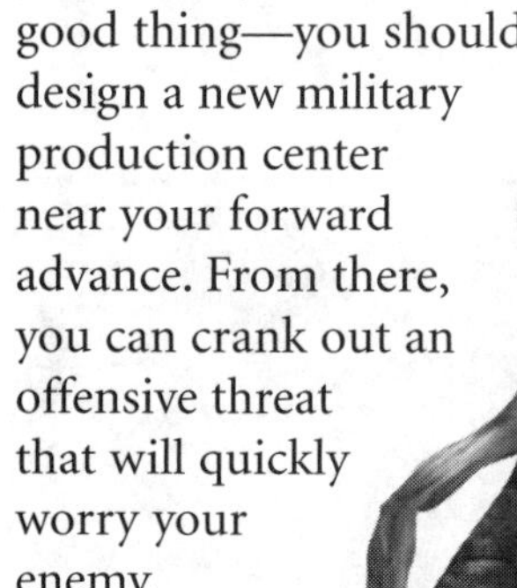

chapter 10

Victory Conditions

Space is huge, and you may not know how fast the other races are progressing. Stay in the dark. If you don't see a single alien race on your galactic map, you can still click on the Victory menu to see what's up with everyone in the

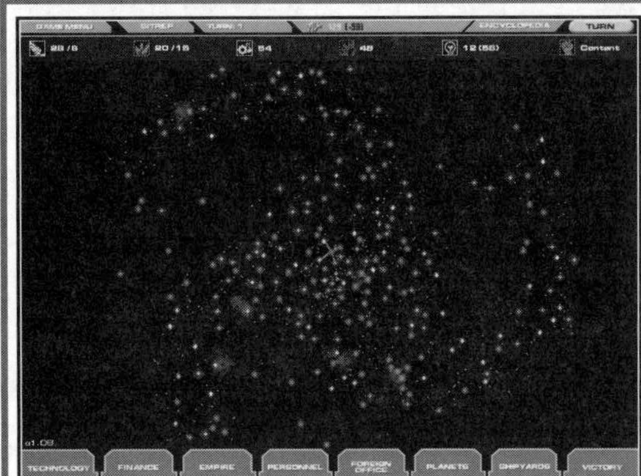

How many races are out there, and how fast are they gaining victory points? The Victory Conditions screen gives facts on the races you know about.

Orion Senate (if you're a member). Not only does it show what place you're currently in, it also provides a wealth of comparisons with your competitors.

Even if you don't see anyone out in space, you can toggle to the Victory Conditions screen for possible info on the hidden races.

Empire Overview

The Empire Overview screen displays how you, or any other race you currently have diplomatic ties to, compare to the other races. At the top, the powergraph rank instantly declares your place in the race for first. The powergraph is the sum total of four key stats: population, research, wealth, and military might. Population points are divvied out based on the percentage of your species across the galaxy. Note that population centers in unrest, revolt, or contested systems do not count. Research points come from advancement in the schools of physical sciences, energy, and mathematics, not economics or social sciences. Wealth points equal the amount in the Imperial Treasury divided by 100. Military might values all military units, including hull sizes, level of ground units, and planetary shields and bases. All that adds up to your total victory points, the number that appears on the Victory Conditions screen.

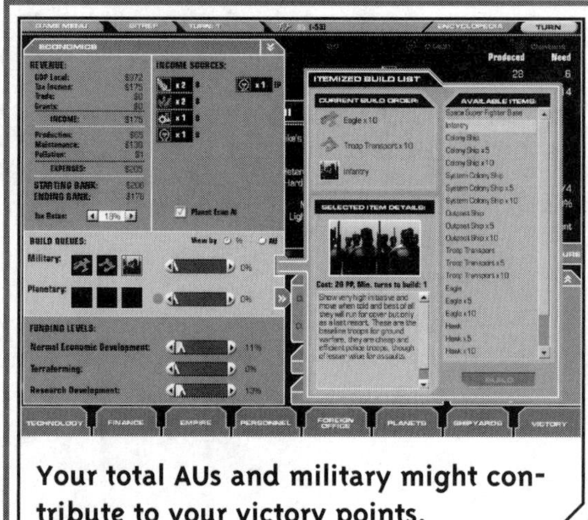

Your total AUs and military might contribute to your victory points.

TIP

Your exact victory point total can be found under the Victory Conditions screen. Once you play the game a few times, you'll be able to judge how well your civilization is progressing based on this number.

The next six lines are: species, Orion Senate status, interest rate, government type, military-political economy, and forced labor policy.

The next four lines are helpful. The "heavy foot of government" score is a combination of the Oppressometer and how much government bureaucracy affects the empire. The strongest allies list shows the powers with which we have better military and political ties. Conversely, the races that dislike us or are have declared war on us are listed on the worst enemies line. Rules of engagement show the empire's current policy toward us in times of war. This is a public statement and will affect diplomatic relations if violated. The three choices are quiet front (don't attack the other player), defensive front (attack only if confronted), and total war (always attack).

If you violate the rules of engagement, you'll annoy a lot of diplomats.

CAUTION

Don't violate your rules of engagement policy or your diplomatic relationship scores will suffer.

At the top right, the current balance of naval forces shows a fleet comparison between your forces and the selected race. It doesn't indicate the size of the ships or their technological level.

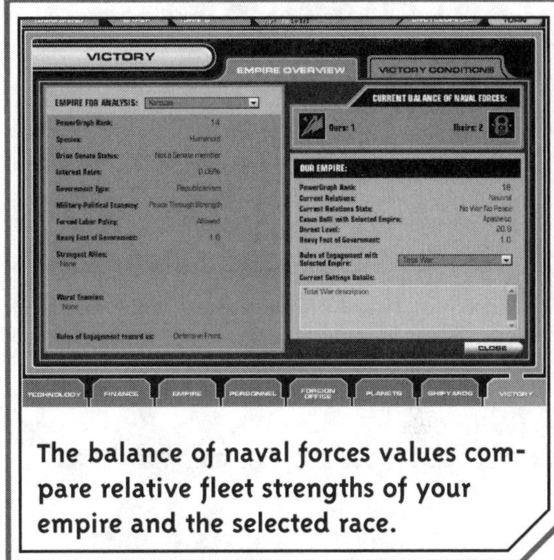

The balance of naval forces values compare relative fleet strengths of your empire and the selected race.

TIP

At a glance, you can gauge the enemy's fleet strength with the "current balance of naval forces" tab.

Under the "our empire" section, current relations measures the level of trust and understanding between you and the selected empire. There are 17 relation states, from solidarity (the best) to neutral (the middle) to feuding (the worst). This can be a key tool if you rely on your Diplomacy skill for trade and alliances. If you're unsure exactly where you stand with a race, click over here and you'll know whether or not you need to sweeten the deal.

There are 17 diplomatic relation states, ranging from solidarity to neutral to feuding.

Diplomatic Tensions

From worst to best, these diplomatic states clue you in on how another race feels toward you:

- Feuding
- Loathing
- Hateful
- Jaundiced
- Troubled
- Tense
- Wary
- Uneasy
- Neutral
- Calm
- Relaxed
- Peaceful
- Cordial
- Amiable
- Friendly
- Harmonious
- Solidarity

Next, the current relations state shows your formally established diplomatic relationship with the selected race. The five relationships are as follows: no contact, enforced peace (the parties were previously at war, but no longer), treaty (formal treaty between the two parties), no war/no peace (neutral with no formal ties), and war. Note that you cannot declare war if there is an enforced peace in place, and you can only trade if you have acquired treaty status with the other race.

TIP

Make sure your "current relations state" indicates "treaty" or you can't trade with that alien power.

"Casus belli" lets you know what your people think of the selected race. If your race was previously enslaved by the Grendarl, your people won't react favorably to them. Your military and diplomatic actions will be modified by this rating—it's difficult to declare war on a race your people like. If you go against the "casus belli" rating, you'll cause unrest throughout your empire.

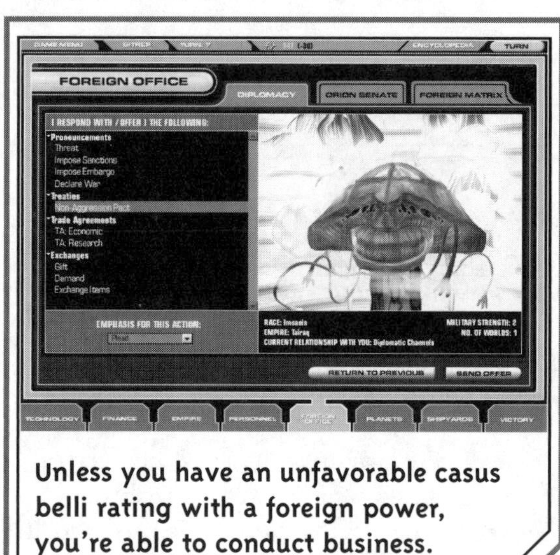

Unless you have an unfavorable casus belli rating with a foreign power, you're able to conduct business.

The unrest level is displayed below the "casus belli" rating. Negative numbers are good—your people are happy—while a high positive number means you need to pay immediate attention to the problem or you'll have a revolt or two on your hands.

Monitor your unrest level here—and on the Planets screen—to prevent a revolting experience.

Victory Conditions

The three ways to win the game are displayed, along with your total victory points under the Victory Conditions screen. "Sole Survivor" calculates how many other civilizations are left in the galaxy. To complete this victory condition, you must eliminate all others. "Senate President" shows you the percentage of the total votes you have in the Orion Senate. To win here, you must gain the majority of votes in the Senate, and considering that the New Orions start out with 1,010 votes to your 10, you have your work cut out for you.

"Antaran Xs" indicates how many Antaran artifacts you own. There are five of these super-powerful relics in the game, and you need to collect all five to win if you checked the box for Antaran X Victory at the start of the game. The Antaran Xs can be researched, stolen from other players, found on unexplored worlds, seized from one of the deadly five guardian spaceships, or accumulated through Antaran expeditions.

How others treat you, and whom you recruit to help out your empire, all affect your victory point total.

TIP

All games have the "Sole Survivor" victory condition. Remember that you can also win by holding the majority vote in the Orion Senate or discovering the five Antaran X artifacts.

Military Victory Points

Unit	Victory Point Value	Victory Points (Full Ally)	Victory Points (Defensive Ally)
Hull Sizes	1	0.4	0.2
Infantry	1	0	0
Space Marines	1.1	0	0
Mobile	1.5	0	0
Armor	2	0	0
Battleoid	3.5	0	0
Support	0.2	0	0
Planet Shield	4	0	0
Planet Base	1	0	0

Antaran Expeditions

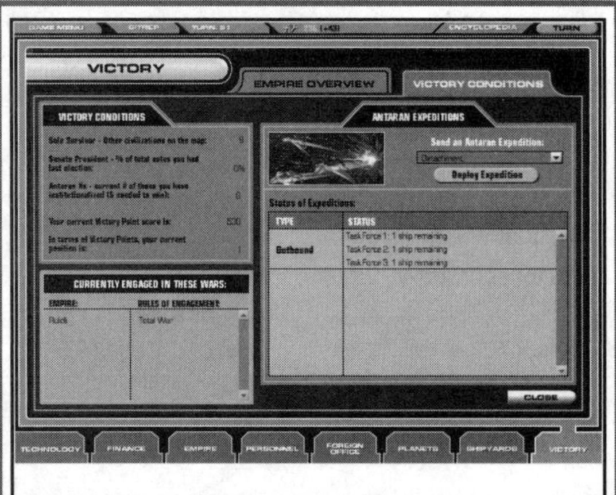

Track how well you're doing on the three game-ending conditions or send out Antaran expeditions from the Victory Conditions screen.

Prepare to spend a lot of money and waste a lot of ships. To search out the five Antaran Xs and complete that victory condition, you need luck and perseverance. Use the Antaran Expeditions menu to send out groups of ships to search for the ancient relics. Send heavily armed warships to ensure that your fleets return. Be patient—it takes a long time to hear anything and, even then, you have to be fortunate to capture one. The more recon ships you send, the better the chances of scoring a prize.

Sending anything less than a full armada is suicide; you're wasting resources. If you choose to embark on this expensive pursuit, send two armadas or more. Even then, you have a 10 percent chance of success.

There are five ruined homeworld planets in the galaxy belonging to the anciet races of the Orion Sector. One of these may have one of the five Xs on it. The planet will be protected by an Orion Guardian, a powerful ship left behind by the Antarans. You can't get past the Guardian until later in the game so avoid the system until you have built up the strength to defeat the Guardian.

chapter 11

Managing Your Homeworld

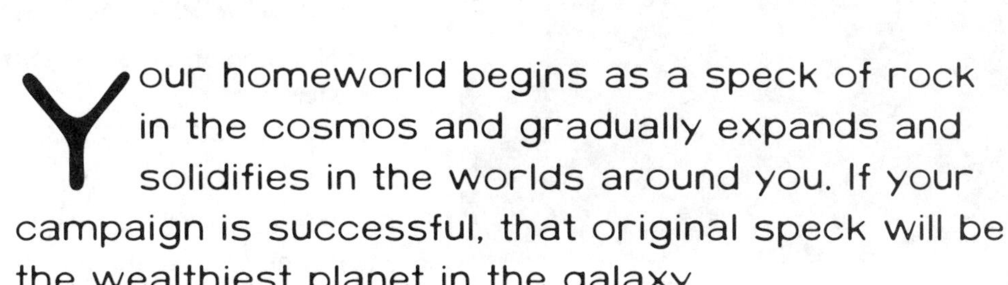

Your homeworld begins as a speck of rock in the cosmos and gradually expands and solidifies in the worlds around you. If your campaign is successful, that original speck will be the wealthiest planet in the galaxy.

From the moment you click on a new game, your task is to grow your homeworld. Taking into consideration all the tips you learned in Chapter 3, your starting planet should flourish and become a spot worthy for the Imperial throne. However, with every rise to power, there are obstacles and setbacks to overcome. Let's look at how to shape the planet Dromos into an economic, technological, and diplomatic juggernaut.

Turn 1

There's a lot of pressure on you. In the first turn, make all the critical decisions so the other races don't get a head start on you. You have to choose the path for your exploration fleets, balance your budgets, handle unrest, entertain diplomats, fund research, train spies . . . and run all the myriad government functions of a prospective emperor. To keep it all straight, you'll need several viceroys.

Where are you in the galaxy? Our homeworld of Dromos sits on the end of the spiral arm, safe from enemies, but away from the potentially lucrative Orion Senate trade.

Exploration

As the Psilon, we're given Dromos as our homeworld. It's located on the rightmost rim of the spiral galaxy. This can be good and bad. It's good if you like to play as an isolationist; you'll be safe from marauding enemies and left on your own to develop your colonies before you have first contact. It's bad because in the center of the galaxy you have access to multiple alien races. These races can become military and economic allies and help you achieve goals you could not reach on your own. We have to discover plenty of space lanes or we'll be stuck in an area with little room for expansion.

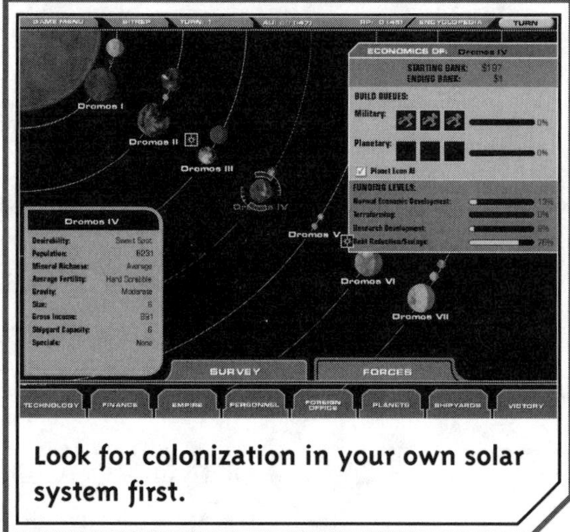

Look for colonization in your own solar system first.

Before we look for conquest elsewhere, let's examine our home system. On the plus side, we have a large system with seven planets, one or two of which may be able to support alternate colonies. Unfortunately, space can be merciless and none of the seven planets are close to supporting Psilon life. Don't quickly spend all your resources terraforming a harsh climate into a barely hospitable environment. We need to look to the stars.

Outside our home system, there are two space lanes. To the left, the Saak star system lies six turns away. To the right, Xolas lies eight turns away. Our home system is a red dwarf, so when we have a choice, we want to search out stars similar to our own. Luck is on our side, as both Saak and Xolas are red dwarves, too.

TIP

While exploring, search out stars similar in temperature to your home sun. Those stars' systems will have the best chance of holding green or "sweet spot" planets.

Which red dwarf do we choose? Both. You want to quickly explore as much of the galaxy as possible. This will give you a better selection of planets to colonize and, especially in your alienated situation, bring you into contact with potential allies and trading partners.

You have three ships orbiting Dromos; send one scout and one colony ship to Saak, and another scout to Xolas. The scout to Xolas will explore that system, then open possible space lanes from Xolas to other systems. However, you're at the outer rim; Xolas might be a dead-end system with no exiting space lanes. Saak, on the other hand, lies toward the heart of the galaxy, where many systems coalesce. You always want to send your colony ship toward the system with the most possible space lands. If Saak doesn't yield a fruitful world, maybe another system connect to Saak will.

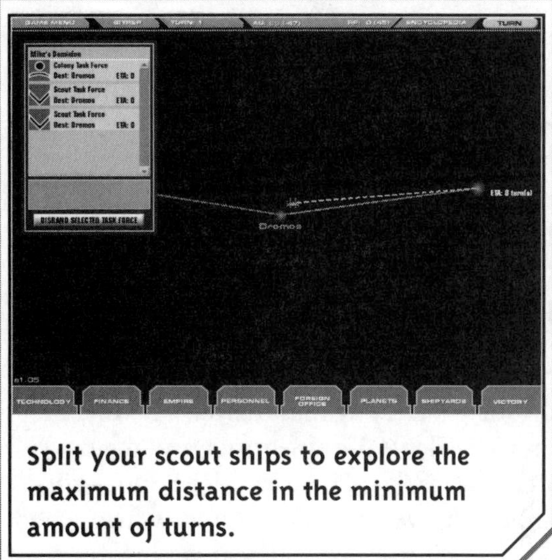

Split your scout ships to explore the maximum distance in the minimum amount of turns.

Technology

We rule in technology. Psilons are the best at Research, plus they have original Creativity, which means they have the best chance of turning a fund-draining overrun into a positive boon for your scientists. Without much effort, your planets produce a plethora of test tubes and Research points to unlock many technological advancements.

Open the Technology menu and briefly scan all your numbers. In the top-left are your six schools and the percentage of Research points you spend on each. To the right, the upcoming possibilities section shows you the next advancements you're poised to discover in that field. At the bottom-left, Research items shows you advancements you've uncovered and how many turns until you'll have a practical application for that advancement. At the bottom, you have total Research points available and Research points expected next turn.

Fiddle with the school percentages, depending on the type of technology you want to press forward with next. In the first turn, those values are locked; wait until your next turn to tweak them.

Upcoming possibilities is a shortcut to show you the next advance in that field, though you'll visit the matrix tab more often to determine where to spend your Research points.

Under Research items, we already have two projects under way: phaser rifle and armor-penetrating mass driver. The rifles aren't available for nine turns, and the mass driver takes five. These are nice bonuses, but shouldn't sway your decision for which schools will benefit from your Research points.

Instead, to help you with your direction, click on the matrix tab to see a listing of schools by what advancements are available at what level. You spend points improving your knowledge in a school and increase slowly level-by-level. You might see a hand blaster at level three, but until you spend money to help your scientists reach level three, you can't turn it into an actual project.

Which technology school will you choose? Look to see which advances are in easy range and invest heavily there. Energy has many early possibilities.

Examine the first few levels in each school. Energy is our clear-cut winner, with phaser rifle at level one, armor-penetrating laser and armor penetrating fighter laser at level two, hand blaster at level three, and autofire laser at level four. It's hard to pass up that many advances in so short a time.

Compare our energy school to biological sciences. We have no advances for the first two levels in biology, only hydroponic farms at level three, and decomposition centers at level four. Unless you have a strong plan for biological sciences, go for advances that will have an immediate impact. It's quantity not quality right now. You don't want to be on the receiving end of an enemy who has more technology at its disposal than you do.

Another school that looks good early on is physical sciences. It emphasizes military and helps defend your empire.

Physical sciences are also strong. The armor-penetrating mass driver is already under development, while level two holds the armor-piercing nuclear warhead. At level three, fighter armor becomes available, and marines show up at level four. Coupled with the energy school, you can help out your military with upgrades and new forces.

Energy and physical sciences look good. You could decide to concentrate in two areas, thus accelerating your growth in those two, but you might want to branch out to another field.

Mathematics is a possibility. You have three advances at level three: advanced policy theory, interchangeable policy structures, and miniaturization I. Tempting as it might be, you really only have two accessible advances. Interchangeable policy structures needs economics level 2 to become available, and you don't want to spread yourself that thin. Skip it until you have extra cash.

To broaden out, we'll opt for social sciences. This violates our principle of going for a lot of early advances, but energy and physical sciences do this for us. Social sciences diversify us and gives us added firepower, such as level four psy-ops that can make our military units up to 30 percent more effective.

Next turn, we'll spend points on these schools. For now, we know where our Research is headed.

Finance

If you have trouble keeping track of where you spent your money, you'll love the Finance menu. Here you can see the complete expenditures for your entire empire. Since Dromos consists of our empire now, it isn't hard. As the turns pile on, you'll want to rely on your planetary viceroy to command the finances. Early on, you can tweak income and expenses to get the planet off to the right start.

Our Imperial Treasury starts at -47 AUs. Not a good start to the empire that will one day rule the galaxy.

On the first turn, set all your financial policies. It's easy to save a few AUs here and there, but if you leave a financial policy on the wrong selection for too long, it could be disastrous.

Click on the budget tab and select military-political economy. There are five different levels: peace and prosperity, peace through strength, limited war, total war, and holy war. The peace and prosperity setting allows you to spend 10 percent on military before you generate unrest throughout the populace. Holy war enables the viceroy to spend 33 to 67 percent on military; if he spends any less or any more, it generates some unrest. In preparation for our military spending in the future, we want to set this to peace through strength. We can now spend up to 20 percent on our military and not alarm the general population.

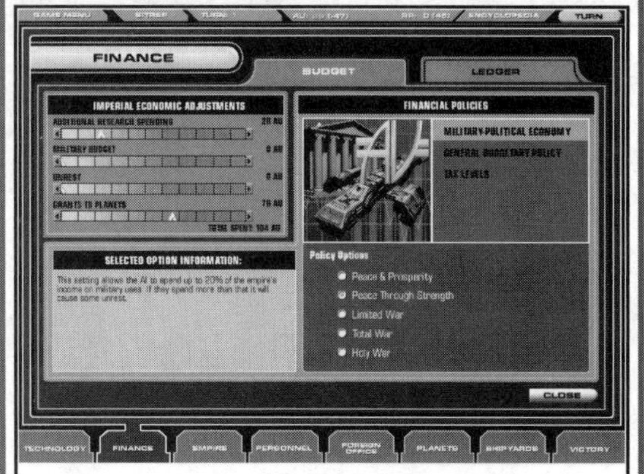

Set your military-political economy at peace through strength so your population doesn't balk at your military spending down the road.

Next, click on general budgetary policy. Set it on balanced, and keep it that way. Balanced means your viceroy will try to spend only the money made that turn. If you need to save money, click on savings; if you want to spend some of your savings, click on spending.

Tax levels are low when you start a game. The trick with any tax system is to get the most out of your population without complaints. Our empire begins with a low three percent system tax and seven percent empire tax. Adjust the numbers to be seven percent system tax and ten percent empire tax. That might be too high, but it's better to set taxes too high and tweak them down. Otherwise, you'll lose out on potential income that could come in handy.

After turn one, if you visit the Finance menu, it will be to tweak the Imperial Economic Adjustments. Because we have so little cash right now, we'll only concentrate on two sliders: additional research spending and grants to planets. We don't have enough AUs to worry about military yet, and there's no unrest on turn one. Grants are applied as floating "petty cash" reserves to be used wherever the viceroy thinks is most appropriate. We'll crank this as high as we can (40 AUs) to help out with the early turns. To balance our budget to zero, that leaves us with 17 AUs for our Research projects.

TIP

Your people become agitated if you make sudden, large changes to things such as tax rates. If you need to increase taxes significantly, it's best to do it over several turns, limiting the change to two percentage points in any direction per turn.

Later in the game, the Imperial Economic Adjustments screen dictates general spending in your empire. On the first turn, apply most of it to planet grants.

Empire

Don't worry about the Empire menu after the first turn. Most of the section deals with general polices for your empire, and they shouldn't change often.

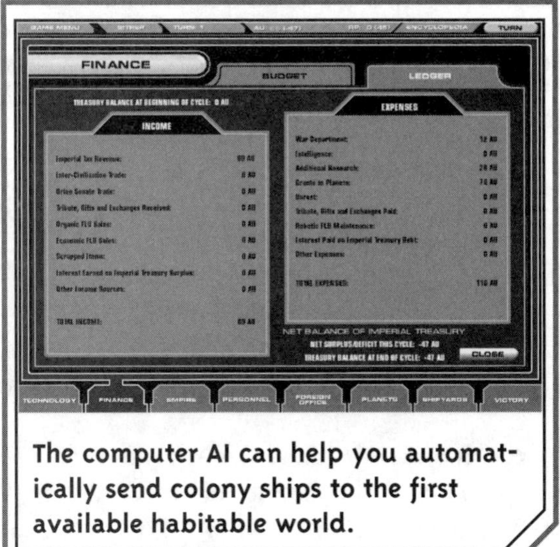

The computer AI can help you automatically send colony ships to the first available habitable world.

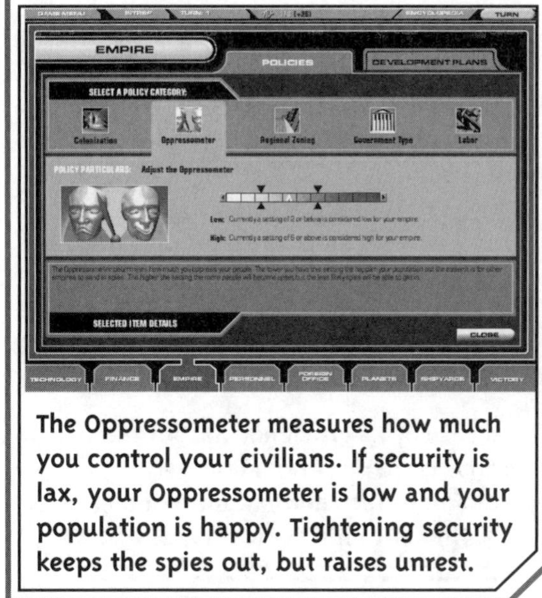

The Oppressometer measures how much you control your civilians. If security is lax, your Oppressometer is low and your population is happy. Tightening security keeps the spies out, but raises unrest.

Under the colonization icon, you have two choices: let the computer AI help you with colonization, or not. The AI automatically launches a colony ship to the nearest available hospitable world, if you've pre-designated it as a colony spot. Don't use this AI recordkeeping if you have multiple colony spots and want to make sure the next colony ship goes to a specific world. Other than that, let the AI do the work.

The Oppressometer is a complete judgment call. It represents your government's control over its citizens. Too low, and enemy spies will infiltrate your empire; too high, and the people will cry for your head. Depending on your race's Citizenship, you might get away with setting it a bit higher. We'll aim for a middle range, around four, and see what happens. If we can get away with it, the planet will be relatively espionage free.

Keep regional zoning on the natural setting. It's too early to specialize your world, and balanced isn't proactive enough. You don't want a world that does a little bit of everything well, but doesn't excel in its strength. We want a natural zoning; your viceroy will concentrate on building what he needs, then switch to what's best suited for the planet.

TIP

Setting the Oppressometer too low is sometimes as bad as setting it too high. If it's too low, you'll get more spies sneaking through and your people will become unhappy because of the disruptions in the empire. If it's too high, people will complain you're running a police state, but at least they'll be safer from attackers.

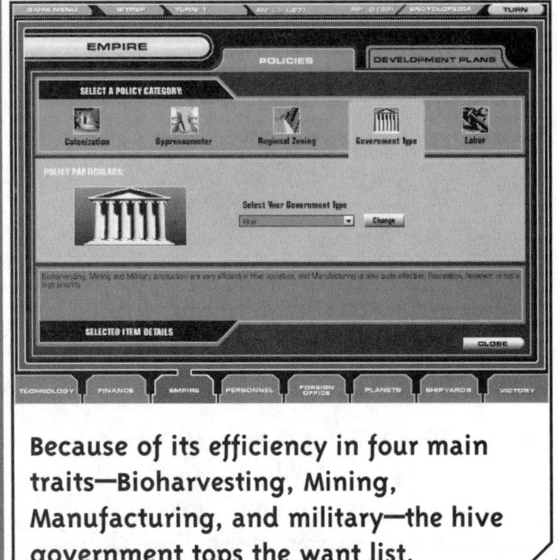

Because of its efficiency in four main traits—Bioharvesting, Mining, Manufacturing, and military—the hive government tops the want list.

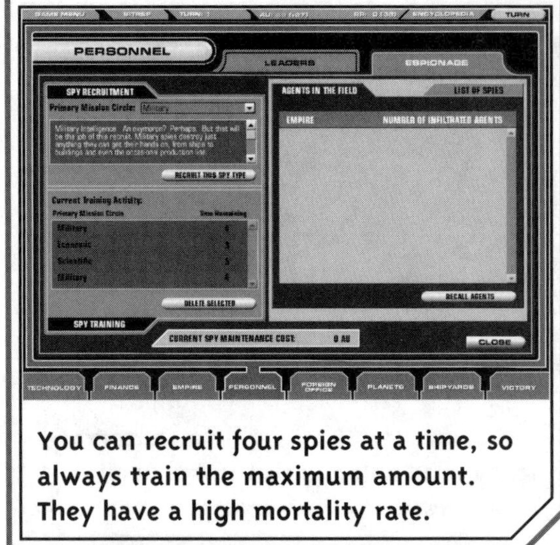

You can recruit four spies at a time, so always train the maximum amount. They have a high mortality rate.

Psilon begins with a Representative government, but it has too many negatives; so switch the Psilon empire to a hive government. With hive, our Bioharvesting, Mining, Manufacturing, and military improve, while our Recreation decreases. It looks like we'll run into problems with unrest in the turns to come.

Lastly, we want to switch forced labor to disallowed. Right now, we don't have any captured aliens to put to work, and hopefully this will be a goodwill gesture to the equal rights activists.

Personnel

The Personnel menu deals with leaders and spies. Our luck hasn't improved here. No leader joined us this turn. Leaders offer bonuses to different aspects of your civilization, some even without penalty. With our high council a big black hole, there's not much to do here.

Under the espionage tab, you can train only one spy at a time. There are various spy types (see Chapter 7 for more details), and we want a pair of military spies, one economic spy, and one scientific spy.

Military spies are the most important, especially if you don't have muscle—the Psilon fall in this category—and that's why we're building two. Hopefully, we'll have dozens ready to undermine the first aggressive enemy that comes our way. Economic spies can slow an enemy who's gaining on us. Scientific spies undermine enemy research. We can use that to our advantage since technology is our strong point. If we win that race, our advances might be too much for the enemy's military to handle.

Foreign Office

Normally, this and the Planet menus are your busiest each turn. However, we're in the middle of nowhere and don't know anyone. When we make first contact with another alien race, we'll come back and negotiate here.

Planets

You'll visit this menu often to fiddle with the finances for all your planets. Change your military spending for a planet, build a few more research centers, devote a chunk of change to terraforming—control of all your planets rests here.

Dromos IV currently collects 197 AUs for you.

When you click on your planet, in our case Dromos IV, all your planetary stats are in front of you. Depending on your concerns for the turn, you'll examine different facets of the economy. Notice that minerals produced and consumed are both 10. For your industry to advance, you have to increase mineral production by building another Mining DEA or two. Everything else looks stable.

> **TIP**
>
> Seldom do you need to monitor every aspect of planetary economy—your viceroys aren't that inept!

Look over your revenue and expenses on the economics tab. Early on, you want to spend all your money. Don't be concerned with a negative ending bank value. The important thing is to grow your planet, not generate a surplus for the bank.

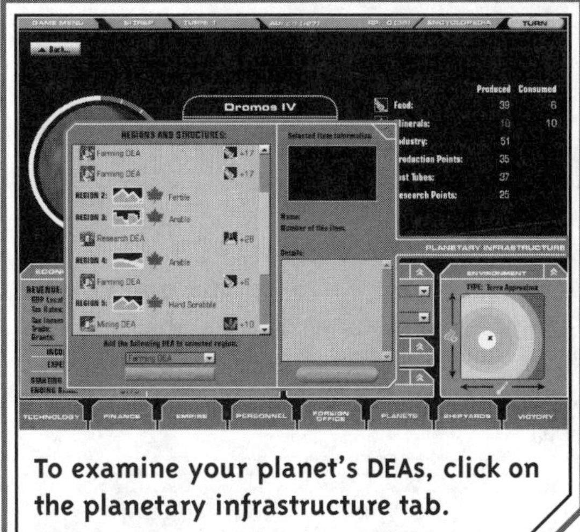

To examine your planet's DEAs, click on the planetary infrastructure tab.

At the bottom of the economics tab, we want to tweak the funding levels. Click on your funds until you hit yellow, then click back one. You want all your funds to be green; that means you're at maximum efficiency. Change your military build queue to 5 percent, and your normal economic development and research development to 14 percent. At this point, spend whatever percentage is left over on terraforming. For us, that's 67 percent. This helps customize the world to our ideal climate and improves our economy.

Do this every turn, then after a few turns, let the viceroy take over and jump in only for an emergency.

Keep all funding levels in the green so you don't waste any money.

Shipyards

We'll return here when we have money to spend. You have to develop a stable economy before you can pour resources into building expensive attack, recon, and colony ships.

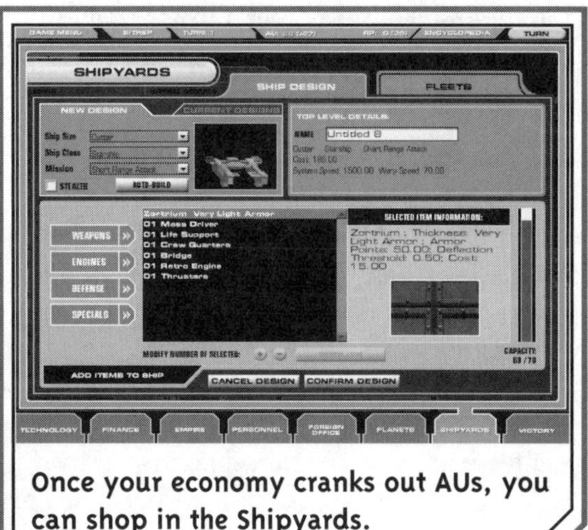

Once your economy cranks out AUs, you can shop in the Shipyards.

Victory

Use the Victory menu for comparing your empire with your allies and enemies. When you want to see who your next target is or you want to weigh whether or not it's wise to ally with a foreign power, this is the place to go.

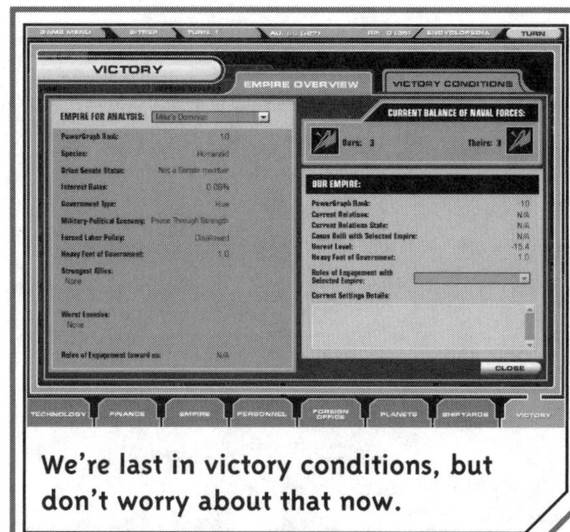

We're last in victory conditions, but don't worry about that now.

Under the empire overview tab, the powergraph rank shows your rank in the race for supreme galactic lord. We're at 10 out of 10, so there's room for improvement. The current relations header measures the diplomatic relations between you and the chosen empire. Similarly, the balance of naval forces section displays your starships versus theirs. Our unrest level clocks in at -15.4, and that's where we want it to be—a negative number means everyone is happy. Under the victory conditions tab, we start with a whopping 17 victory points.

Turn 2

We'll dedicate most of this turn to making sure the plans we started on turn one are headed in the right direction. You won't have to deal with the same level of minutia that we did on the first turn. Even so, check through each menu to ensure the values you thought you wanted are the same.

Exploration

Our opening space screen shows our scout ships split in two. One scout, with the colony ship as company, heads toward the Saak system. The other aims for Xolas. Check back in a few turns after they reach their destinations.

Technology

Last turn, we chose energy and physical sciences as our majors, with a minor in social sciences. Energy and physical sciences offer a ton of advancements that will help our military and conquest capabilities later. Social sciences adds some different skills.

We can't spend points on all six schools or we'd advance slowly. By limiting our spending to three schools, and two primary ones, we'll jumpstart those advances and worry about the rest later. Dump 40 percent into energy, 40 percent into physical sciences, and 20 percent into social sciences.

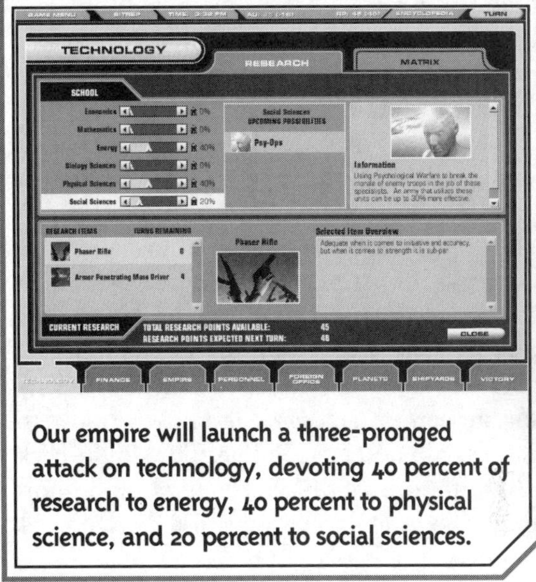

Our empire will launch a three-pronged attack on technology, devoting 40 percent of research to energy, 40 percent to physical science, and 20 percent to social sciences.

Planets

Mineral depletion remains our biggest problem. Our industry will suffer if we can't supply it with the necessary ore. Click on planetary infrastructure and zone regions two

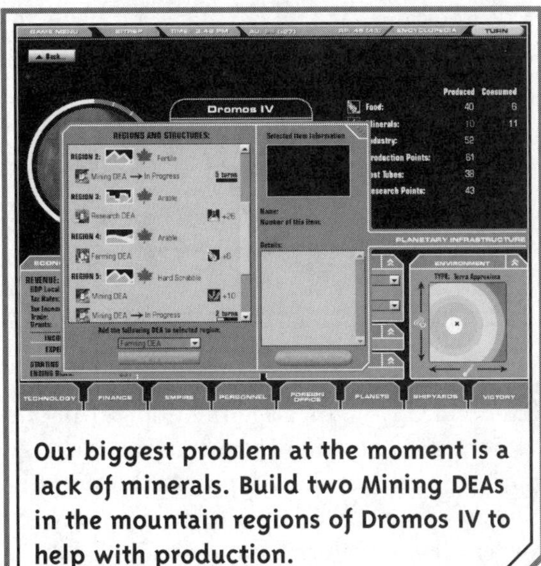

Our biggest problem at the moment is a lack of minerals. Build two Mining DEAs in the mountain regions of Dromos IV to help with production.

and five as mining DEAs. Note that they're both mountainous regions where Mining is most effective. In five turns, our mineral concerns should be over.

Military builds are a long way off; however, we want to build the right things. Your viceroy had a scout, troop transport, and colony ship in the queue. We want the scout to explore new systems and increase our stellar real estate first. We don't want the troop transport next; there's no need for it without troops and we want another colony ship to capture more planets for our empire. Left-click and hold to move the colony ship to the second position. Right-click on the third position, after the troop transport moves there, to cease production on that hunk of junk.

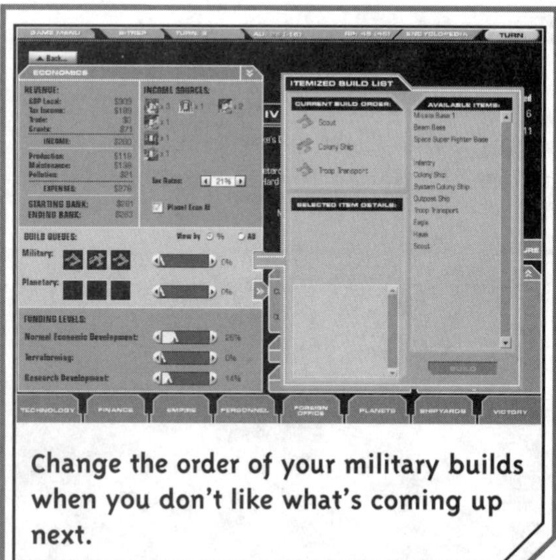

Change the order of your military builds when you don't like what's coming up next.

Below, in the funding levels, our viceroy has decided to go on a spending spree. All our values are in the yellow, which means we're paying double for that output. At this point in time, it's not wise to pressure the economy, so switch all your values back to green.

Turns 3 to 6

Now's the time to let our economy chug along on its own and see how it does. We'll jump in where necessary to avoid potential disasters. At the end of turn six, we should have a good idea of where our planet excels.

Unrest Problem

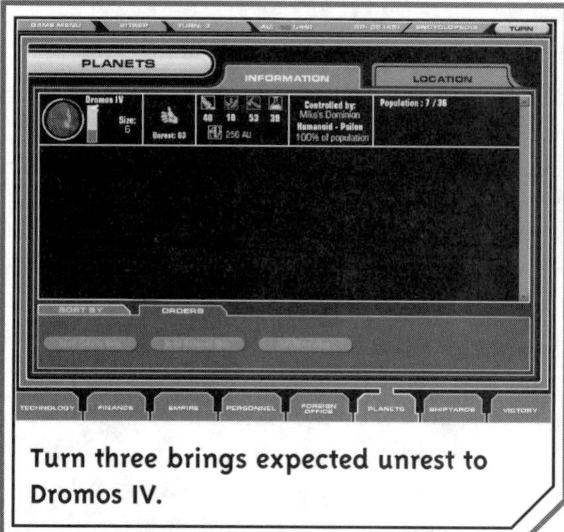

Turn three brings expected unrest to Dromos IV.

Don't be fooled by that green thumbs up on your Planets screen. Dromos IV has 63 unrest; minor revolts will break out soon unless we do something.

Remember, we changed our government and set taxes high at the beginning of the game. To determine what's causing our unrest, click the demographics tab under the Planets menu. The unrest section there claims high taxes are to blame for the people's unhappiness.

That's an easy fix. We want to support the government with as high a tax as we can get away with; this time, however, we may have gone too far. Since a 63 unrest is very high, we significantly drop our taxes—from 20 percent to 16 percent. Also, under Finance's Imperial Economic Adjustments, we slide our unrest funds allotment to the top end of the green. This diverts a portion of our revenue to unrest every turn to help placate the people.

We've identified high taxes as the crux of our unrest problem. It's time to reduce the percentages.

Because of the unrest concerns, we can't push our economy as fast as we'd like. Under the Planets' economics tab, watch that everything is still in the green. Reduce military spending to five percent, and economic and research development to eight percent each. Terraforming could go higher, but we'll raise it to 30 percent and put some savings in the bank to help with the extra drain from unrest.

Situation Report

Our first situation report, or sitrep, comes on turn four. The situation report gives us the key updates that we should be aware of each turn. This turn it tells us that a Mining DEA has been built on Dromos IV. Good news, since we need minerals to increase production and bump up our economy.

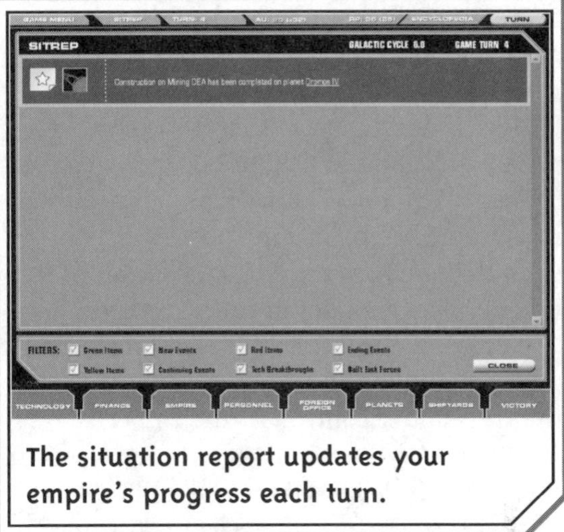

The situation report updates your empire's progress each turn.

Things look better on turn four. Unrest has dropped nearly 50 points. To zoom in on the perfect balance, we'll drop the tax rate one more point to 15 percent, and hope to erode the 16 unrest down to a stable 0.

Spy Factory

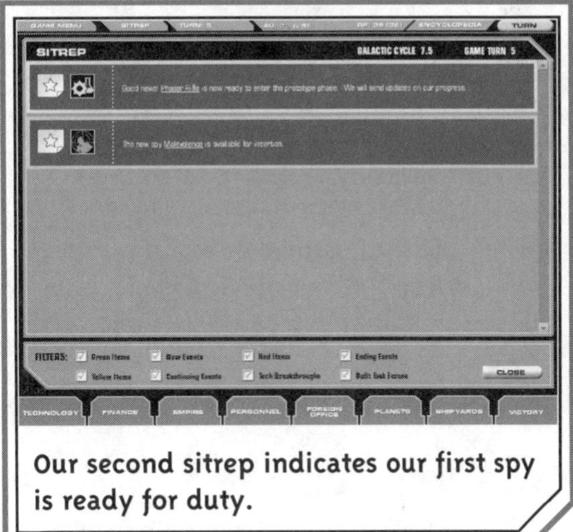

Our second sitrep indicates our first spy is ready for duty.

Turn five brings two revelations: Our phaser rifles are entering a prototype phase and our

first spy, Malevolence, is ready to play secret agent. Go to the Espionage screen to call him up. Malevolence's stats aren't that impressive—8 Cloak, 3 Dagger, 6 Luck, and 95 Loyalty—, but we'll use him to help break up the enemy's money machines when we fight with another race. Immediately start up a new spy; you want a continuous cycle of spies so your force is large when it comes time to use them.

Before we end turn five, we want to adjust our economic numbers now that unrest is under control. At the Imperial Economic Adjustments screen, click research spending up to 30 AUs and give a boost to our race's main trait. Our viceroy dropped the tax rate another percent to 14; we'll go with his suggestion that the populace needs a break. We can always raise it again later. Again, making sure all spending stays in the green, we set military at 5 percent, economic development at 12 percent, terraforming at 30 percent, and research at 9 percent.

TIP

Building spies helps protect you from enemy spies while they're unassigned (any spies which are still in your empire are automatically assigned to counter-espionage duties). This works similar to raising the Oppressometer setting, except that it doesn't raise Unrest. The main constraint is that you can only build one spy at a time, and they don't live forever.

On Our Way

Finally, on turn six, our first technological advance breaks through. With level one energy complete, phaser rifles will help our military's offense . . . once we build a military. Over the course of the next several turns, advances will flourish.

One last check at the Planets screens shows Dromos IV's unrest at zero. Now we can concentrate on increasing profit. In just six turns, our planet makes 35 more AUs per turn than when it started. That'll be nothing when our master plan unfolds.

Like a well-oiled machine, our economy motors along and unrest settles down to zero.

Turns 7 and 8

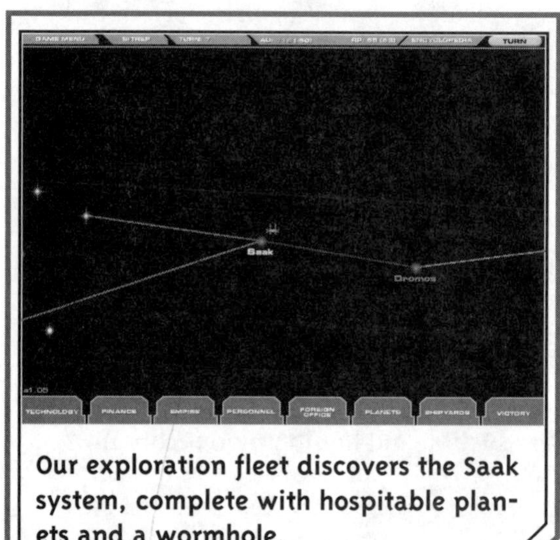

Our exploration fleet discovers the Saak system, complete with hospitable planets and a wormhole.

Turn seven brings a second solar system under our belt. Our exploration fleet has reached Saak, and it's a rich system. Saak contains five worlds and a wormhole to the galaxy's other side. We need to break our scout ship away from the exploration fleet and send it into the wormhole. Eleven turns from now, it'll end up in the Mellas system, and we'll make contact with alien powers on that far side.

Next, we zoom in on the Saak system. Saak III contains an environment nearly identical to our homeworld. That's too good to pass up, so we ask our colony ship to orbit and colonize it next turn. Saak III's sweet spot gives us an advantage over other races that haven't found a near-perfect world.

We've discovered a "sweet spot" world in Saak III.

On turn eight, we establish our second colony. Saak III is ready for economic development. It won't produce much because its population is very small. We need to put in the same care we did with Dromos IV to raise its importance.

Knowing that we have access to a wormhole that opens up the other half of the galaxy, it's wise to increase military spending. Until now, we didn't really care; we were isolated with no neighbors. Now we're several turns away from first contact and a lot more planets to explore. Our military build queue will have a scout ready in four turns, followed by two more colony ships to seize more worlds. Under Planets' economic tab, let's increase military spending to 10 percent, economics to 13 percent, terraforming to 40 percent, and research to 10 percent.

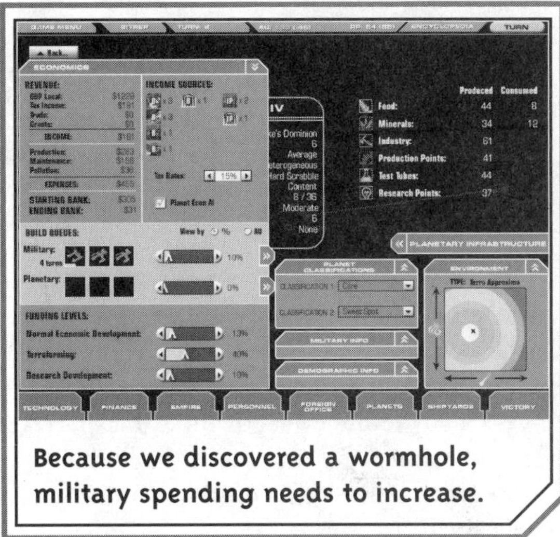

Because we discovered a wormhole, military spending needs to increase.

Turns 9 and 10

On turn nine, our scout ship reports the thorough exploration of the Xolas system. Next turn, the scout will be on its way to explore the rest of spiral rim. Since it can't colonize, we want to set up military building to reach those next two colony ships and improve our planetary holdings.

Examining the Xolas system, we find that Xolas I is another "sweet spot" planet, even better than Saak III. Had we known, we might have sent our first colony ship here instead. Even so, this is a prime target for the next colony ship out of the queue.

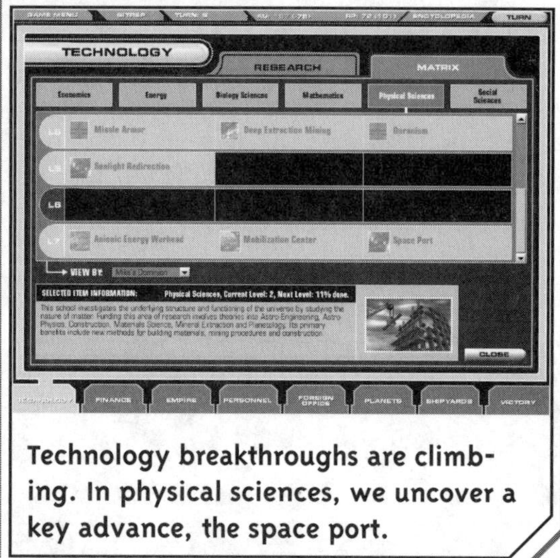

Technology breakthroughs are climbing. In physical sciences, we uncover a key advance, the space port.

As we predicted, Research is rapidly accelerating, even this early in the game. Checking energy, we see six new advances on the horizon at level seven. Physical sciences unveils a key level-seven advance, the space port. When we can build these, they'll help our interplanetary trade and let us build bigger starships.

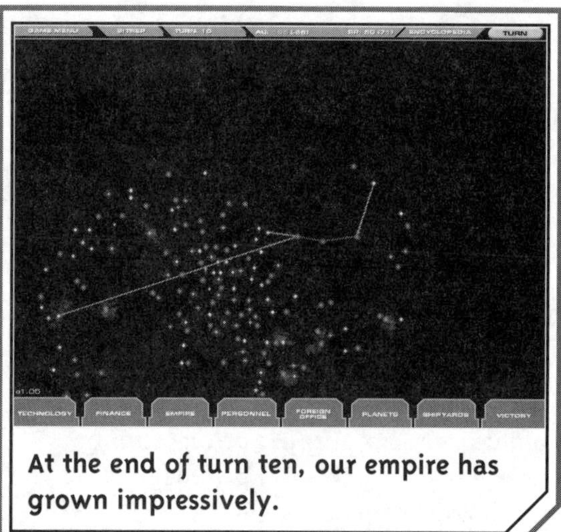

At the end of turn ten, our empire has grown impressively.

Bon Voyage

So there you have it . . . a blueprint for how to develop your homeworld. Every world is slightly different. You need to factor in your species, especially your strengths and weaknesses. The size and regions of your planet also dictate your policies. If you can conquer the continuous run of emergencies that will plague your world, you won't have a problem conquering other races' worlds.

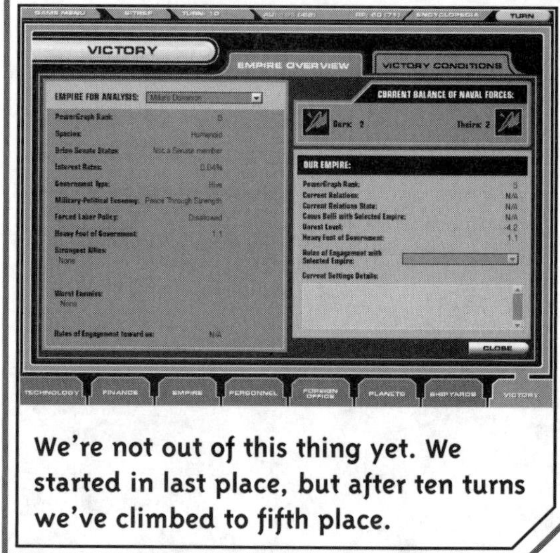

We're not out of this thing yet. We started in last place, but after ten turns we've climbed to fifth place.

TIP

Look closely at the Technology Matrix early in the game and search for technologies to which your empire does not have access. You won't get every tech in every game, so there are some you'll need to trade for. Identify those early, so you can decide which ones to trade for first when you meet another friendly race.

chapter 12

Exploration and Colonization

The popular saying "You've gotta be in it to win it" should be your mantra. Don't sit back on your homeworld and hope everyone else destroys each other or plays nice around you. You have to be careful and build up slowly and strongly, but you can't ignore expansion. If you move too slowly, a more advanced, richer, and tougher race will come along and steal everything you own. Protect what's yours, and then some.

Your starting position can be as a member of the Orion Senate in the heart of the galaxy or isolated in the far reaches of space.

The Basics

Start with your home system. It's the closest source of minerals, food, and possible exotic specials that can boost your colonies. Your best opening position is a system with seven or eight planets, with one or two of those planets ripe with farmland or minerals. If those worlds are green 1 or green 2—compatible with your species—you'll have an advantage. It's as if you're given multiple homeworlds to your enemy's one. If there are no new prospects in your home system, consider restarting the game until you hit a favorable distribution.

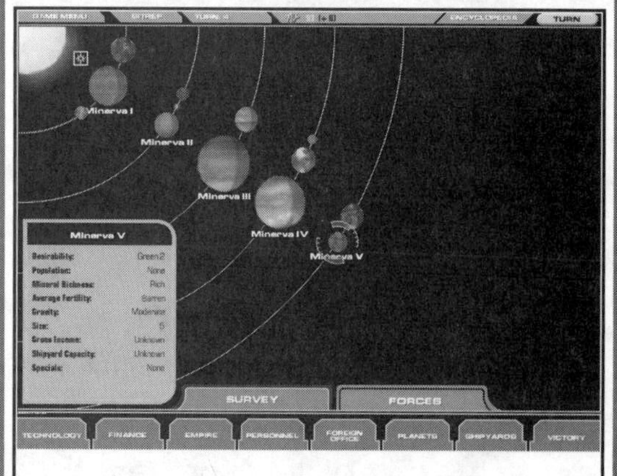

Your first exploration trip is always through your home system.

Early on, work with your race's strengths and weaknesses. High Bioharvesters like the Eoladi should look for planets with better soil. Natural miners like the Silicoids should search out planets rich in minerals. Use common sense: If you have one planet with rich minerals and another with arable soil, and your people are starving, choose the planet where crops will grow.

How do you set up new worlds? With colony ships. It's important to colonize quickly and establish a solid economy empire. With that in mind, your homeworld's military building queue should pump out colony ships early. Two of your starting three builds should be colony ships. One will hopefully head to a planet within your system, and the other will blast off for a recently scouted system.

Speaking of scouts, you start with two, which should immediately head in different directions. Explore as much of the territory around you as quickly as possible. Think of scouting as simultaneously increasing your real estate and filtering military intelligence. Each system opens up new possibilities for colonies and shows you where the enemy is or isn't. Scouts are expendable, so build them often and send them on recon missions deeper and deeper into unknown space.

Depending on where you start in the galaxy, and your race's game plan, explore in a specific fashion. If you don't start on the

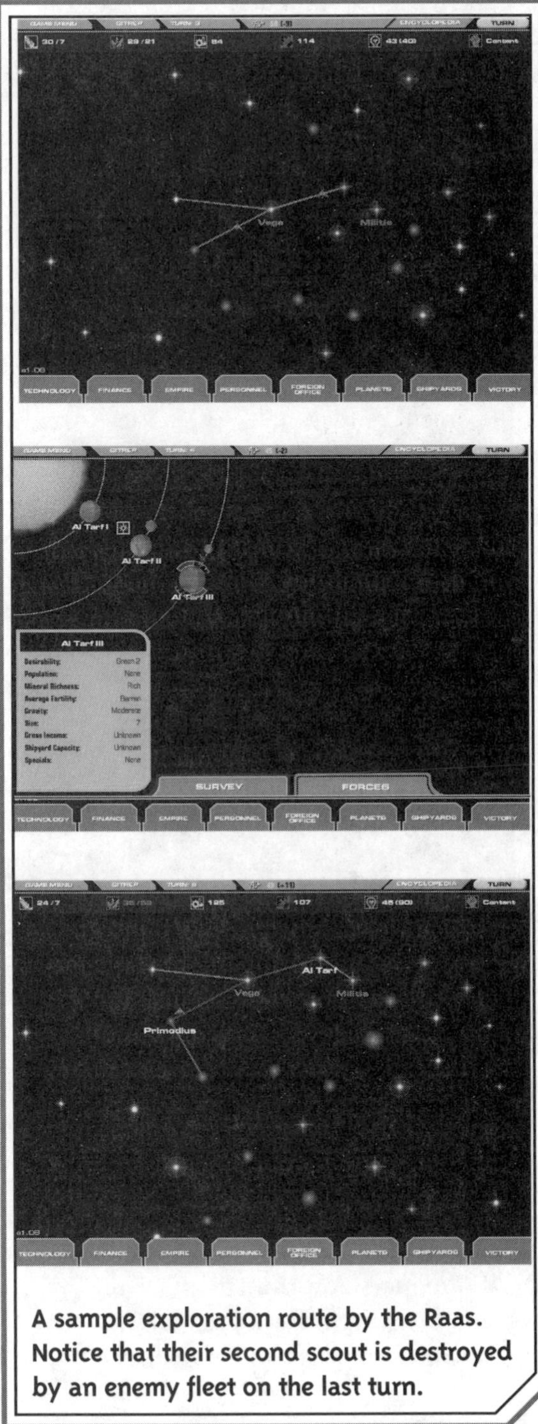

A sample exploration route by the Raas. Notice that their second scout is destroyed by an enemy fleet on the last turn.

Orion Senate and want to trade with other powers, head into the heart of the galaxy. Odds are much better that you'll bump into other races in the more densely star-populated regions. To build slowly and defend before first contact, expand toward one of the spiral arms. As always, look for star systems with a similarly colored star to increase the chances of finding a species-matching world.

Another reason for expanding is to increase your knowledge of the connect-the-dot space lanes. Imagine you're a galactic cab driver and don't want to be driving all over the city and be stuck in traffic. You want to take the fastest, safest route. Same with space lanes. The more you know about them, the better you can navigate your corner of the galaxy. When it's critical that you get a task force to a destination, you'll be able to choose the most direct route. Should you discover a wormhole that shortcuts across the galaxy, so much the better.

Specials

When you explore a system, your ships will report if they find one of the nearly 50 specials on a planet's surface. Specials can have positive or negative effects if you choose to colonize there. It's up to you to decide whether colonizing a sub-par world is worth the extra boost you get from a positive special. Positive specials should be colonized, since their effects are felt right away, whereas a normal world takes a while to develop. Avoid all negative specials unless the world's perfect for your race and you feel you can pay the elimination cost swiftly.

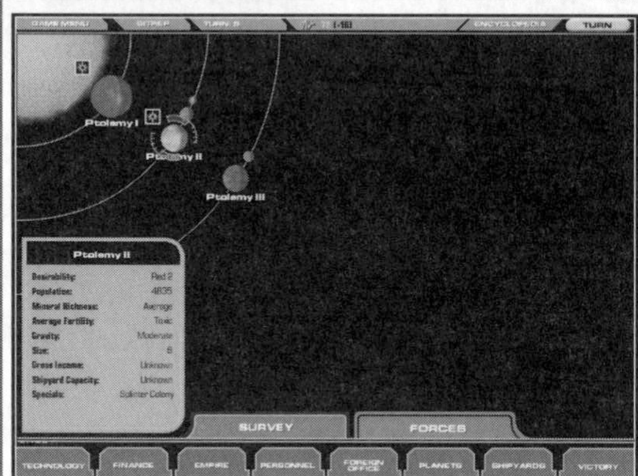

Specials can increase a planet's value. A splinter colony, for example, gives your empire an instant civilization.

Colony Killers

There are two dozen negative specials, none of which you want to deal with. If it's a permanent negative special, forget about the planet. Some specials can be eliminated if you pay a certain cost. For example, the hostile gases special can be removed from the planet if you spend between 600 and 2,200 AUs on terraforming. Certain negative specials can be avoided if they're regional and you don't try to cultivate that particular region.

If the word "hostile" appears in the title, head the other way. The hostile huge animal whacks Bioharvesting for 20 percent and recreation for 15 percent. Even worse, the hostile microbe affects six stats—50 percent to 150 percent increase on military and maintenance costs, 15 percent reduction in Manufacturing, 55 percent reduction in Research, 67 percent drop in population, and a 90 percent reduction in recreation. To get rid of the microbe, you have to spend 900 to 4,000 terraforming AUs—in other words, it'll be a while.

Even your talented leaders can't thwart all events.

Rely on technology to compensate for annoying specials or pay for extra terraforming to remove them permanently from the planet's surface.

You might think a sentient planet could be a boon; it's not. The planet with a mind all its own reduces government efficiency by 20 percent and drops recreation by 75 percent. You could say it doesn't play well with others.

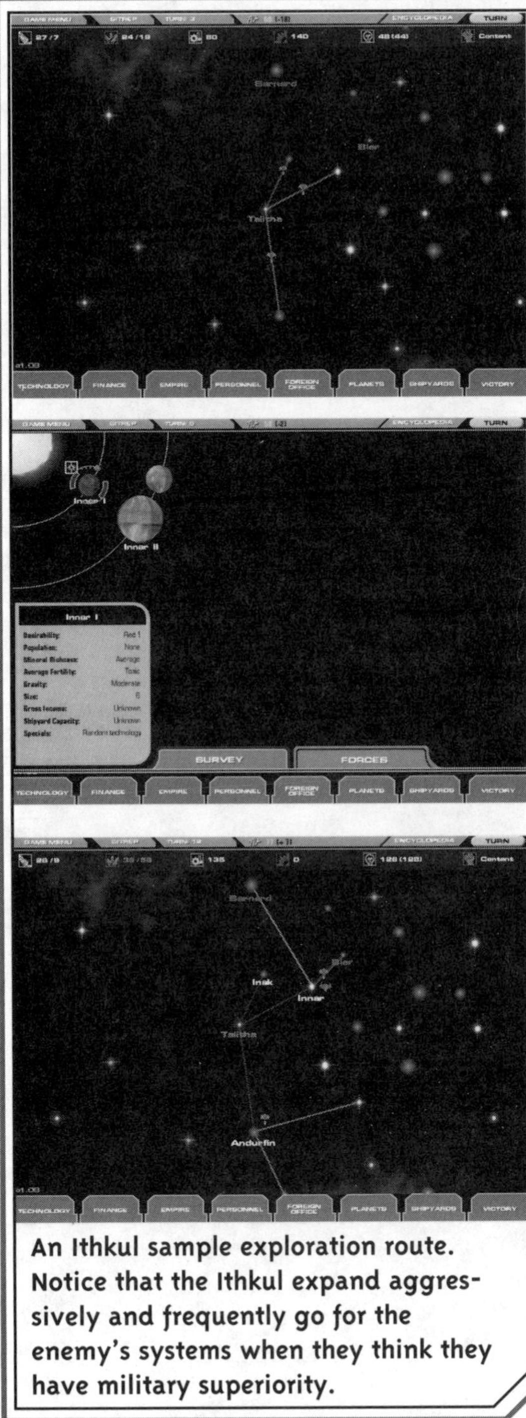

An Ithkul sample exploration route. Notice that the Ithkul expand aggressively and frequently go for the enemy's systems when they think they have military superiority.

Want to capture energy for your generators from the electrical activity planet? Forget it. This negative special knocks down Mining by 15 percent, Bioharvesting by 10 percent, military by 20 percent, and space port activity by 35 percent.

A fun negative special is the booby trap. After you land, you have between 5 and 20 turns before the whole world explodes. Fire up those thrusters and look for shelter elsewhere.

Hidden Treasures

Improve your lot in life through worlds with positive specials. Positive specials can transform an average race into a superior one. Your opponents realize this, too. They'll covet your special worlds, so protect them.

"Rare" specials always benefit you, but don't pop up often. Rare animals, plants, and metals are great for Research, fuels aid space port efficiency, gems boost space port income, and petrochemicals increase Manufacturing. Rare radioactives are a mixed bag. They increase Research and space port by 30 percent and Manufacturing by 25 percent; on the downside, they lower population growth by 50 percent and detract from Bioharvesting.

The pharmacopoeia planet is a colony attractor. It increases Bioharvesting, Research, space port efficiency, and population growth. The stratosphere ring is like a minor version of pharmacopoeia; it increases your Bioharvesting DEA by .75 and pumps up recreation by 15 percent.

Don't pass up random research because it gives you a random advance, which could prove powerful to a beginning race. If you rescue a leader, you get him. His abilities then become permanent for your entire empire. A splinter colony is a starter colony on that world for you that depletes once the population starts to creep over 50 percent of its beginning value.

Several minor positive specials look good. Thriving ecosystem offers +.25 to Bioharvesting. The abandoned colony special nudges up Research 10 percent. A cavernous world sets the maximum population one point higher. Contraband gives you between 5 and 50 AUs each turn, but depletes at a rate of 1 per turn. Natural wells reduce terraforming costs by 5 to 40 percent and boost recreation by 10 percent. Natural wonders only notches your Recreation DEA up by one point.

The best special you can ask for is an Antaran X. You need the five Antaran relics to complete the alternate victory condition. If you're trying to win through this method, an Antaran X special is a godsend.

Planet Specials

Special	Area	Effect	Duration	Status
A Cache	Region	Variable	Variable	Positive
Abandoned Colony	Planet	+10% Research	Permanent	Positive
Active Volcanoes	Planet	+5% to +70% Terraforming Cost	Permanent	Negative
Ancient Battle Damage	Planet	-20% to -90% Hospitable Environment	Permanent	Negative
Antaran X	Region	Victory Condition	Permanent	Positive
Artificial Planet	Planet	Variable	Variable	Positive
Booby Trap	Planet	Destroy Planet in 5 to 20 Turns	Permanent	Negative
Cavernous	Region	Maximum Population +1	Permanent	Positive
Contraband	Region	Add 5 to 50 AUs	Depletes 1 AU per Turn	Positive
Eccentric Orbit	Planet	+20% to +100% Terraforming Cost, -75% Bioharvesting	Permanent	Negative
Electrical Activity	Planet	-15% Mining, -10% Bioharvesting, -20% Military, -35% Space Port	Permanent	Negative
Entrapping Ecosystem	Planet	-15% Government, -95% Recreation, -90% Space Port	Permanent	Negative
FLU Generator	Region	Variable	Variable	Positive
Erratic Weather	Planet	-25% to -75% Bioharvesting	Eliminated after 350 to 900 Terraforming AUs Spent	Negative
HE Geomagnetic Fields	Planet	-1% to -25% Terraforming, +10% Population Growth, -20% Manufacturing, -50% Research, -15% Military	Permanent	Negative

Special	Area	Effect	Duration	Status
HE Huge Storms	Planet	+10% to +200% Maintenance, +10% to +200% Building Cost, -50% Bioharvesting	Permanent	Negative
HE Meteor Showers	Planet	Variable	Variable	Negative
HE Tectonic Instability	Planet	Variable	Permanent	Negative
Hostile Gases	Planet	+50% to 150% Maintenance, +50% to +150% Building Cost, -10% Manufacturing, -10% Research, -30% Population Growth, -5% Military	Eliminated after 600 to 2,200 Terraforming AUs Spent	Negative
Hostile Flora	Region	-30% Bioharvesting, -10% Manufacturing, -15% Research, -15% Recreation, -15% Population Growth	Eliminated after 200 to 2,800 Terraforming AUs Spent	Negative
Hostile Huge Animal	Region	-20% Bioharvesting, +15% Recreation	Eliminated after 600 to 2,200 Military AUs Spent	Negative
Hostile Insect	Region	-10% to -70% Manufacturing and Mining, -40% Bioharvesting, -10% Research, -60% Recreation, -40% Population Growth	Eliminated after 400 to 1,500 Terraforming AUs Spent	Negative
Hostile Large Animal	Region	-15% Bioharvesting	Eliminated after 350 to 1,700 Military AUs Spent	Negative
Hostile Microbe	Region	+50% to +150% Military Build and Maintenance Costs, -15% Manufacturing, -55% Research, -67% Population Growth, -90% Recreation	Eliminated after 900 to 4,000 Terraforming AUs Spent	Negative
Hostile Mineral	Region	-40% Mining, -25% Manufacturing, -20% Research	Eliminated after 1,200 to 4,700 Terraforming AUs Spent	Negative
Hostile Small Animal	Region	-20% Population Growth, -30% Recreation, -10% Bioharvesting	Eliminated after 200 to 700 Terraforming AUs Spent	Negative
Magnate Civilization	Planet	Variable	Permanent	Positive
Natural Wells	Planet	-5% to -40% Terraforming, +10% Recreation	Permanent	Positive
Natural Wonders	Region	+1 Recreation DEA	Permanent	Positive

Special	Area	Effect	Duration	Status
Pharmacopoeia	Planet	+.5 Bioharvesting DEA, +45% Research, +10% Space Port, +25% Population Growth	Permanent	Positive
Polluted	Planet	-20% to -80% Population Growth	Eliminated after 350 to 3,000 Terraforming AUs Spent	Negative
Random Research	Region	Random Advance	Permanent	Positive
Random Tech	Region	Random Military	Permanent	Positive
Rapid Rot	Planet	+20% to +200% Maintenance, +20% to +200% Building Cost	Permanent	Negative
Rare Animals	Region	+25% Space Port, +35% Research, +10% Recreation	Depletes in 100 to 600 Turns	Positive
Rare Fuels	Region	+35% Space Port, +30% Research	Depletes in 20 to 125 Turns	Positive
Rare Gems	Region	+65% Space Port, +5% Research	Depletes in 10 to 75 Turns	Positive
Rare Metals	Region	+20% Space Port, +20% Research	Depletes in 25 to 150 Turns	Positive
Rare Petrochemicals	Region	+40% Space Port, -1 Bioharvesting DEA, +20% Manufacturing, +10% Research	Depletes in 15 to 100 Turns	Positive
Rare Plants	Region	+30% Space Port, +10% Manufacturing, +40% Research	Variable	Positive
Rare Radioactives	Region	+30% Space Port, -1 Bioharvesting DEA, -50% Population Growth, +30% Research, +25% Manufacturing	Depletes in 10 to 150 Turns	Positive
Rescue Leader	Region	Random Leader	Permanent	Positive
Ruins	Region	Variable	Variable	Positive
Sentient Planet	Planet	-20% Government, -75% Recreation	Permanent	Negative
Splinter Colony	Planet	Starter Colony	Depletes after Population Increases by 50% to 200%	Positive
Stratosphere Ring	Planet	+.75 Bioharvesting DEA, +15% Recreation	Permanent	Positive
Thriving Ecosystem	Region	+.25 Bioharvesting DEA	Permanent	Positive

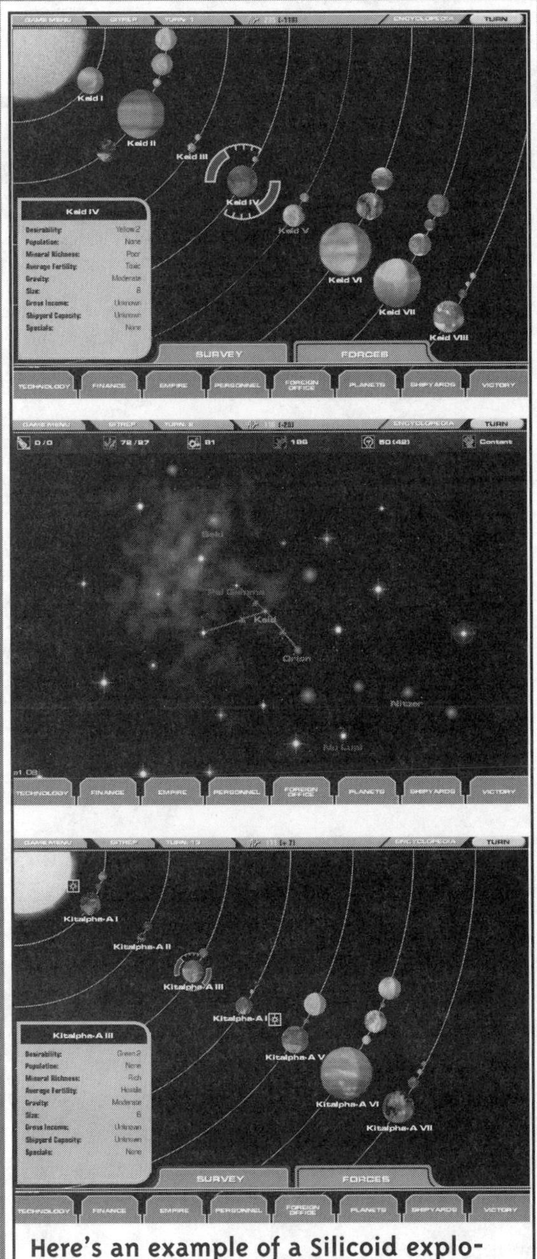

Here's an example of a Silicoid exploration route. Since there is no viable mineral-rich world in their home system, the Silicoid search the galaxy for another substitute.

Advanced Planning

So you think you know how to pilot a ship? Maybe so, but there's an art to expanding your empire. Remember the Romans? They had a great civilization, and then it all fell apart.

Keep It under Control

Colonizing closer to home reduces the risk of outside alien interference.

Don't expand too quickly. Solidify your home system first, and then move on to the next system. Colonize closer to your homeworld. There might be a juicy target five systems away and a decent planet one system away. If they're close, and you don't have a big fleet built up, take the closer planet. You want to be able to protect it. Build colonies methodically and back them up with fleet traffic that will eliminate any small pests that feel like throwing a stone through your window.

Choke Hold

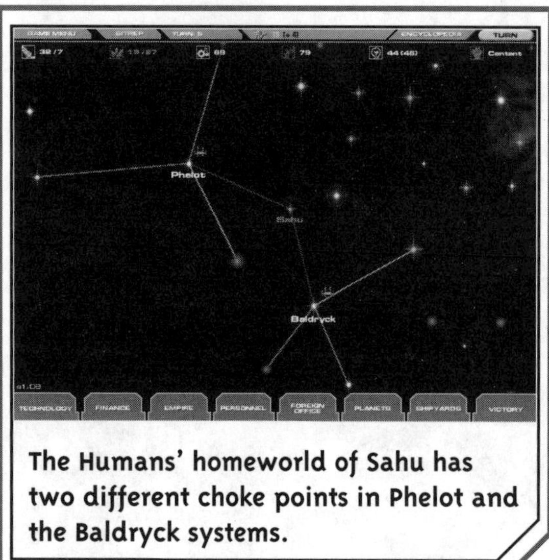

The Humans' homeworld of Sahu has two different choke points in Phelot and the Baldryck systems.

Everyone uses the space lanes, and each system is an intersection for those space lanes. Look around your empire and notice that a few systems are tactically superior—those are the systems where many lanes converge, the systems that, if you defend them, cut off access to the rest of your empire. We'll call these "choke points."

As early as you can identify them, send a task force to defend the choke points. Like guarding the gates to your castle, keep your inner domain safe. Plus, this puts your fleets in the best position to attack if the opportunity arises. Your fleets will be ready at the crossroads for the next declaration of war.

Keep an eye on your diplomatic relationships. If one looks like it's going sour, reinforce the nearest choke point to that power's border. If you launch an attack, either create a new choke point in the contested enemy system or back up the nearest existing choke point in case of counterattack.

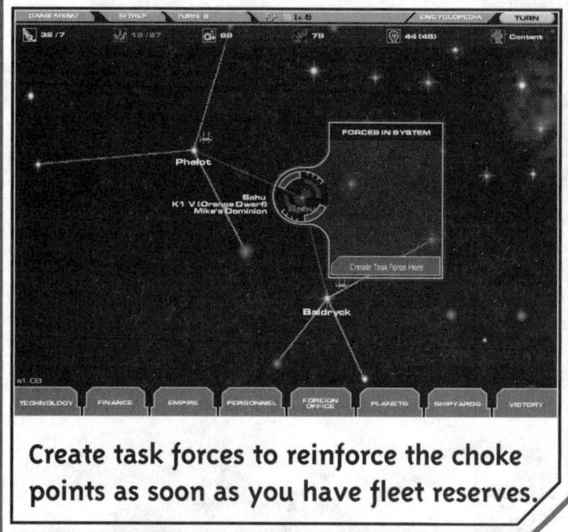

Create task forces to reinforce the choke points as soon as you have fleet reserves.

You can also "force" choke points in valuable systems. Let's say a system has a size 12 planet where you want to design your new ship-building facilities. Even though it's not the strongest military position, you need to defend the area with ships, so convert it into a staging ground for future raids and defense.

TIP

Build system ships at your key choke points. While they can't leave the system they're in, they can provide good defense against intruders. Because they don't need to have large faster-than-light engines, they're more cost-effective than starships for defensive purposes.

Task Force Preparation

React to enemy threats, and they won't be threats any longer—they'll be serious problems. As soon as your ships orbit your planet, design a task force. Need recon of a nearby spiral arm? Send a detachment to scout it out and uncover any hidden mysteries. Worried about an aggressive neighbor? Create a long-range attack force and send it in turns before there's trouble.

It may take dozens of turns to reach your destination, and in space battles that's dozens of turns too many. Prepare for fights before they happen and read situations ahead of time. If you initiate emergency task forces in advance, no enemy can beat you. You'll outthink them every time.

Dealing with Enemies

No matter the situation, always negotiate with your surrounding races. Most of the time, this turns into trade, economic prosperity, and defensive alliances. However, not everyone is going to like you.

Does that mean you cut off discussions? No. If you're not ready for war and the enemy has you beat militarily, your only hope might be peace talks. Even if you mean to attack, you want the upper hand that comes with the element of surprise. Lull your foe into a sense of safety, then take advantage of his weakened position. Just watch that your actions don't upset the Orion Senate.

If you're thinking ahead, you will have an alliance in place when the enemy power declares war on you. Why an alliance? Two powers on one power should equal victory, unless your forces are so far separated that it's an agreement only in principle.

Your enemy might have a larger armada, but you can destroy double what they can with sound tactics. Using all the tools at your disposal, identify your toughest competition and keep an eye on them. Anyone else won't stand a chance.

TIP

You can negotiate with anyone, but the Ithkul are not worth the trouble. If they're on your border, build that fleet right away, because it's likely you'll be at war shortly after you meet. There's a reason other races don't like them, and it's not just because they consider your colonies to be edible.

chapter 13

Combat

After you've spent all those AUs on eagles, transports, and infantry, they have to go somewhere and do something. Unless you win through the Orion Senate or get lucky with an Antaran expedition, you'll have to fight

Be prepared—an alien power will declare war on you.

your way to the top. This chapter fills you in on task force management, space battles, planetary bombardment, and ground assaults. When you're tired of sliding economic bars and clicking advances in the tech tree, it's time to blow stuff up.

Task Force Creation

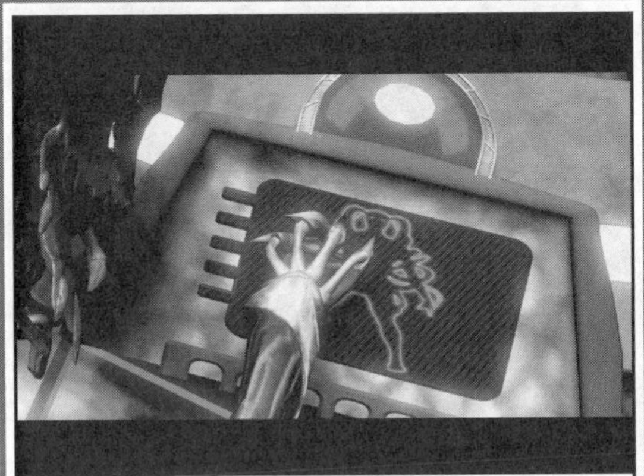

The genetically engineered Ithkul are the best fighters.

You'll build mostly fleets. *Master of Orion* combat revolves around fleets and space battles, with ground forces doing the cleanup work. A task force is defined by what ships you include in it or, more specifically, what kind of equipment that ship carries.

There are different types of ships, depending on your tech level and money in the bank. For this example, let's assume your planet can build a destroyer-class ship and you have an advance you'd like to jam on that vessel.

To build a starship that can travel outside our home system, we need stardrives. We choose warp factor X and transwarp drive for

To leave your home system, you need to build a stardrive, but it's a dangerous universe out there.

their top-of-the-line speed. You also want the best defenses you have space for. In this case, all our ships will run adamantium light armor and a damper field shield. Go with the most effective armor and shields so your ships last longer. Your crews have basic survival needs, which leads to life support, crew quarters, and a bridge being installed. Whatever space is leftover goes to the primary piece of equipment tied into the task force mission.

On attack missions, your weapons are the focus. A destroyer sent on a short-range attack would build a plasma cannon for maximum damage and have a particle beam as a backup weapon. The same ship for a long-range mission would pack a phaser beam to hit from farther away and keep the particle beam as backup. A planet destroyer, despite the name, stocks up on defense. You don't need a weapon to assault a planet—once you win any space battles around the enemy planet, you can commit to planetary bombardment. The armor-heavy planet destroyer makes sure it's around after the battle to unload on the world's surface.

Long-range craft rely on beam weapons, while indirect-fire ships use missiles.

Other combat missions include indirect-fire ships. These vessels aren't armed with a beam weapon, but have a projectile missile. The ionic pulsar warhead works best. Carriers should bolt in a space control fighter chassis and pack it full of fighters, mini-warships that spray out and pester the enemy. For a point-defense ship, run a particle beam to clean up those incoming enemy missiles.

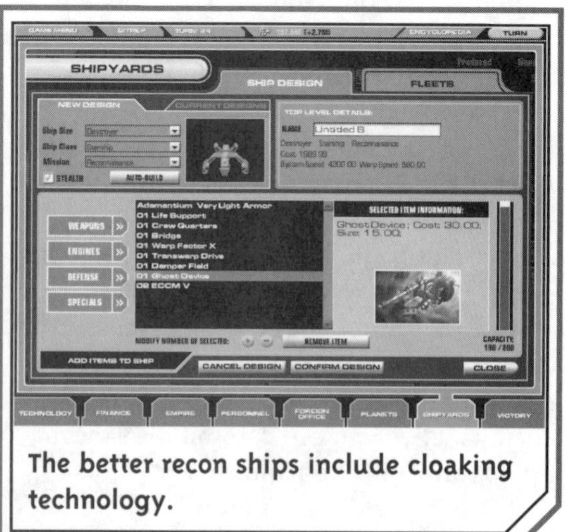

The better recon ships include cloaking technology.

As for non-combat vessels, the transport ship hasn't much room except for the troop pod to carry infantry and the like. The same applies to colony ships with their colony bays and outpost ships with their outpost modules. On recon, you want the best cloaking device and electronic countermeasures; try the ghost device (if you can support it with all the schools it needs) and ECCM V.

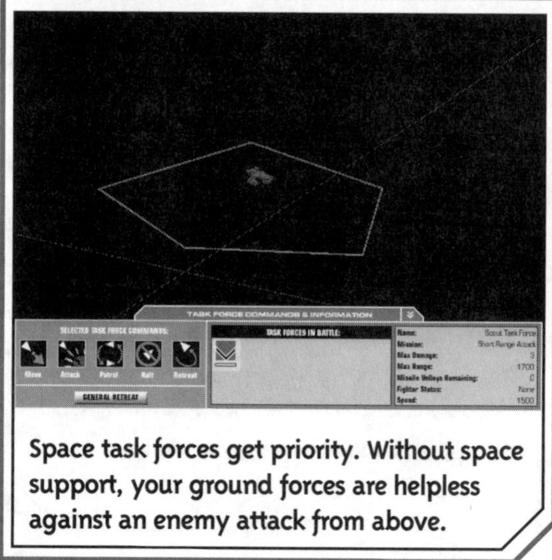

Space task forces get priority. Without space support, your ground forces are helpless against an enemy attack from above.

When planning missions, first set your space-combat vessels in order. The most important parts of MOO combat are the firefights inside systems. Control a system with your ships and you can have your way with the planets therein. Ground units are great for the killing blow and seizing planets, but on their own they only stall the inevitable—if you don't get a fleet to their side, an enemy ship will bombard them or overrun them with superior ground forces. Analyze your enemy's ships when you encounter them. If you see they have a weakness—all shields, say, and no defense against missiles—build a couple of task forces that exploit their vulnerability.

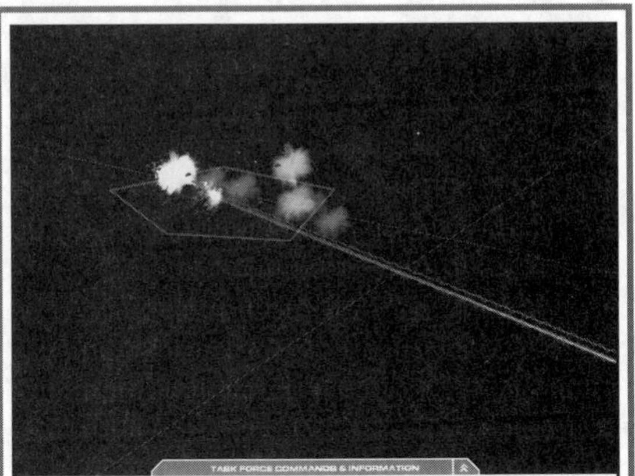

Analyze your opponent's ships for a weakness, like short-range weapons to your long-range ones, then exploit that vulnerability.

Finally, build your system defense. Set up space task forces to patrol the system, build some missile and beam bases for added measure, then recruit infantry and armor units to fortify the surface. Once you don't fear losing your own planets, you can move on to winning alien worlds.

Space Combat

If you don't have sound task forces, you won't win space battles. It helps to have superior technology and bigger ships, but it all comes down to which ships are better prepared. For example, if you outmatch your opponent with long-range attackers to his short-range strikers, you win.

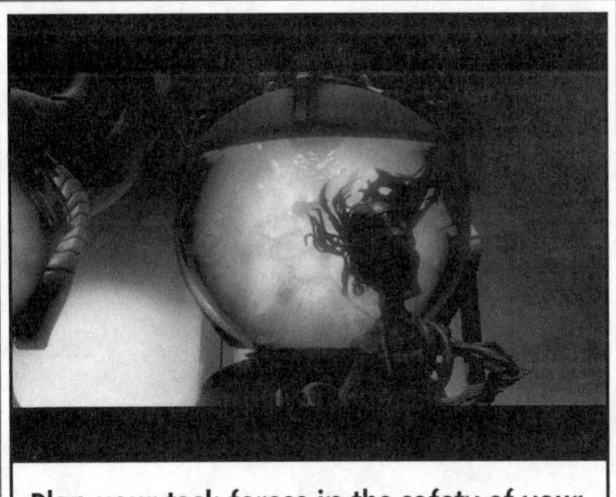

Plan your task forces in the safety of your home before attacks force your hand.

Unfortunately, it's never that simple. In the example above with long-range attackers, what happens if your opponent's ships have tough armor that can absorb your blasts? When they get in tight, they'll eat you alive. When creating big, warfare-worthy fleets, it's best to mix things up. Primarily, you want long-range attackers with powerful weapons (like the plasma series), backed by indirect-fire ships to launch missiles, and point-defense ships to patrol the perimeter and suck up damage. You also want two to four speedy task forces that can outflank the enemy and get in a bunch of cheap shots.

In a sample battle scenario, let's assume we have the layout suggested above. In an evenly matched contest, we'd send expendable ships and the ones with shorter range directly at the enemy. Sometimes these will be point-defense ships or ships with longer-range scanners to track the enemy. When we know the enemy's location—not just a single ship, but the bulk of the enemy's ships—we loop our faster ships around the sides and rear to barrage the enemy from all directions.

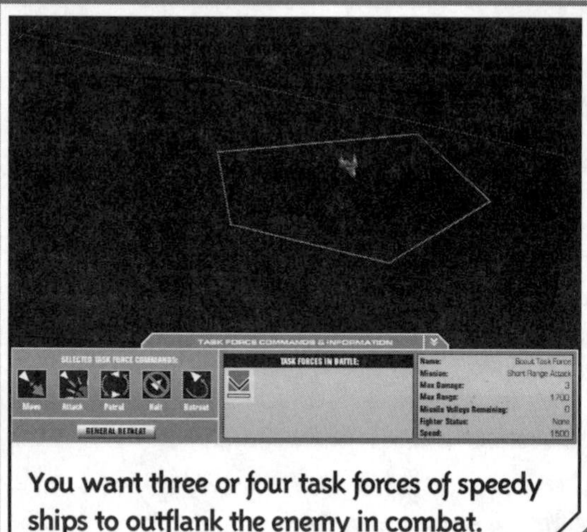

You want three or four task forces of speedy ships to outflank the enemy in combat.

If you can break through your opponent's system defenses, you can bombard any colonies there.

While our shorter-range vessels are engaged, the main part of our fleet, the long-range attackers, unload from a safe distance. Where possible, our ships concentrate fire on the nearest enemies so they can't damage our long-range attackers. Pull any ships back that are double-teamed and gang up on your opponent's out-of-position task forces. Don't worry—in any battle, you'll lose ships; it's the price you pay for glory.

Send your scouts out to find the enemy, then engage with your pricier ships.

If you win the system battle and there are any enemy planets, you have a chance to conduct planetary bombardment. It's a good practice if you need to eliminate an enemy's ground forces before you engage, or if you want to wipe out a colony so your opponent can't recover it later. Should you decide to keep the enemy colony for yourself, don't unload all your ordnance at once. This will cause severe population and infrastructure damage. Instead, shoot in increments of 25 percent and stop after you destroy enemy resistance. Then send in the ground troops for some action.

Ground Assaults

Battleoids will beat marines any day. As in space combat, ground battles can be won with technological superiority. Fill your armies with battleoids and combots and let them rip.

Assuming you're not that wealthy or tech-advanced, even engagements can be won through tactics. When you enter a ground battle, order your troops to adapt a battle tactic. It can be anything from massed assault

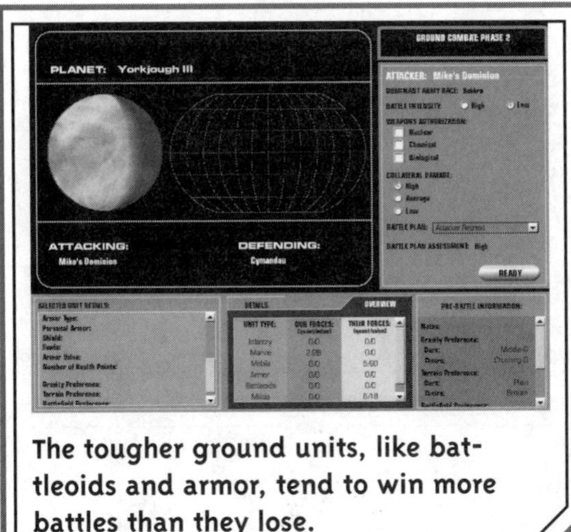

The tougher ground units, like battleoids and armor, tend to win more battles than they lose.

to sweep to trap, or even vertical envelopment if you have flying units. The defender also chooses a tactic, and the maneuvers are compared on a battle matrix that determines how effective the tactics are against each other. The battle matrix number is a percentage. If it is 115, the attacking army's strength, defense, and other values are multiplied by 115 percent and the defending army's strength, defense, and other values are multiplied by 85 percent. Refer to the battle matrix chart at the end of this chapter for all the match-up results.

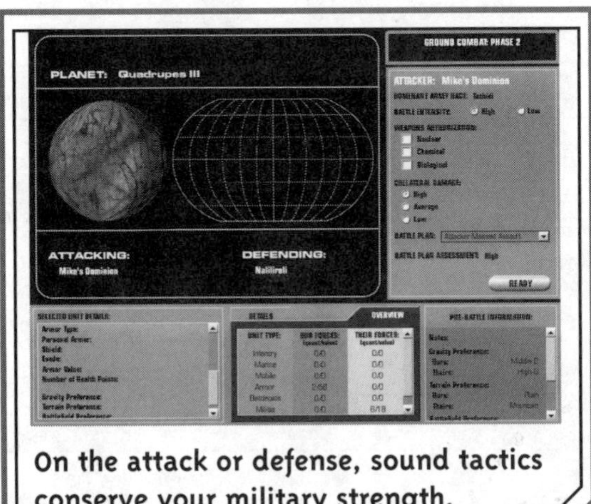

On the attack or defense, sound tactics conserve your military strength.

If you thought your opponent erred on the side of caution and was to launch a defensive probe, you'd want to call a pronged attack. This match-up nets you a 123, or a 23 percent bonus for you and penalty for them. Your pronged attack would not, however, want to run into a ruse or surprise; you'd be penalized severely and probably lose the battle. You also could try an attacking divide and hope your opponent defends with a massed assault. That match-up yields +40 percent for you and -40 percent for your opponent's army.

The best offensive moves are the attacking ruse and attacking surprise. You can gain up to 12 positive results, and the worst you can do is a 100 percent, which is an even split between both forces. If you don't have to gamble because you have troop superiority, choose one of these two maneuvers.

Stay away from flesh and blood when constructing your army. Infantry and space marines are cheap, but don't match up well with battleoids, combots, and armor units. Go in with numbers, choose a sound ground strategy, and you'll be fine. As the saying goes, you might lose a battle, but you'll win the war.

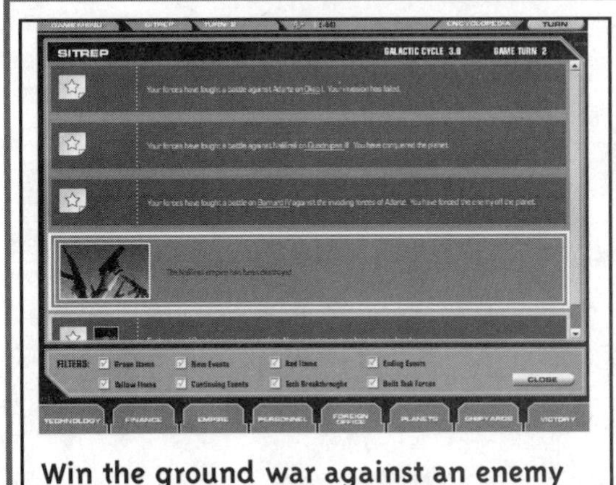

Win the ground war against an enemy homeworld to receive this report—their empire has been destroyed!

Battle Matrix

Maneuver Match-up	A_Maneuver Failed	A_Surrender	A_Massed Assault	A_Vertical Envelopment	A_Pronged Attack	A_Sweep	A_Probe	A_Harass	A_Echelon	A_Attrition	A_Flank
D_Maneuver Failed	100	170	170	170	170	170	170	170	170	170	170
D_Surrender	30	100	190	190	190	190	190	190	190	190	190
D_Massed Assault	30	10	100	100	95	80	70	70	70	70	80
D_Pronged Attack	30	10	102	102	100	92	83	83	83	83	87
D_Sweep	30	10	115	110	107	100	85	85	85	85	85
D_Probe	30	10	115	120	123	115	100	100	100	100	120
D_Harass	30	10	115	120	117	115	100	100	100	100	120
D_Echelon	30	10	115	120	117	115	100	100	100	100	120
D_Attrition	30	10	115	120	117	115	100	100	100	100	120
D_Flank	30	10	110	115	112	115	80	80	80	80	100
D_Maneuver	30	10	112	117	115	117	83	83	83	83	102
D_Limited Resistance	30	10	115	120	117	120	85	85	85	85	105
D_Feint	30	10	70	80	77	75	105	105	105	105	80
D_Ruse	30	10	65	75	73	70	100	100	100	100	75
D_Surprise	30	10	65	75	72	70	100	100	100	100	75
D_Trap	30	10	72	83	80	77	107	107	107	107	83
D_Divide	30	10	80	90	87	85	115	115	115	115	90
D_Single Line	30	10	95	100	97	95	120	120	120	120	120
D_Spread Defense	30	10	105	110	107	105	110	110	110	110	120
D_FOR	30	10	100	105	102	100	115	115	115	115	120
D_Retreat	30	10	85	90	87	85	100	100	100	100	105
D_Fighting Withdraw	30	10	85	90	87	85	100	100	100	100	105
D_Ambush	30	10	77	82	80	77	92	92	92	92	97

A_Maneuver	A_Limited Resistance	A_Feint	A_Ruse	A_Surprise	A_Trap	A_Divide	A_Single Line	A_Spread Defense	A_Retreat	A_Fighting Withdraw	A_Ambush
170	170	170	170	170	170	170	170	170	170	170	170
190	190	190	190	190	190	190	190	190	190	190	190
75	70	160	170	170	155	140	90	110	130	130	145
85	83	122	132	132	120	112	93	102	112	112	120
83	80	125	130	130	122	115	95	105	115	115	123
117	115	95	100	100	93	85	90	80	100	100	107
117	115	95	100	100	93	85	90	80	100	100	107
117	115	95	100	100	93	85	90	80	100	100	107
117	115	95	100	100	93	85	90	80	100	100	107
97	95	120	125	125	117	110	80	80	95	95	102
100	97	122	127	127	120	112	83	83	97	97	105
102	100	125	130	130	122	115	85	85	100	100	107
77	75	100	105	105	97	90	105	105	90	90	97
73	70	95	100	100	93	85	100	100	85	85	85
72	70	95	100	100	93	85	100	100	85	85	93
80	77	102	107	107	100	93	107	107	93	92	100
115	115	110	115	115	107	100	115	115	100	100	107
117	115	95	100	100	93	85	100	100	85	85	87
117	115	95	100	100	92	85	100	100	85	85	92
117	115	95	100	100	92	85	100	100	85	85	92
105	100	110	115	115	107	100	115	115	100	100	107
102	100	110	115	115	107	100	115	115	100	100	107
95	93	102	107	107	100	93	93	93	93	93	100

chapter 14

Dealing with Emergencies

Run a government, run a business, run a school—emergencies consume the unprepared. To avoid suffering losses because you didn't know how to face a revolt, undermine sabotage, deal with an economic depression, or recognize a random

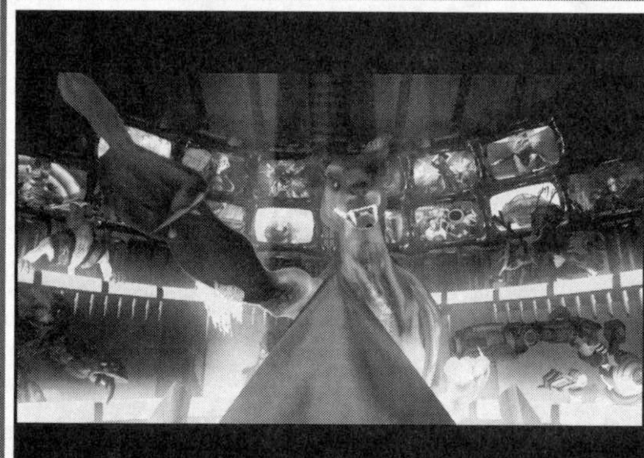

As emperor, deal with emergencies as soon as the next turn rolls around—unless you want your planetary viceroys yelling at you.

event, this chapter is your crash course in emergency services. Other than aliens knocking down your door, these helpful hints will prevent disasters from rocking your civilization back into the Stone Age.

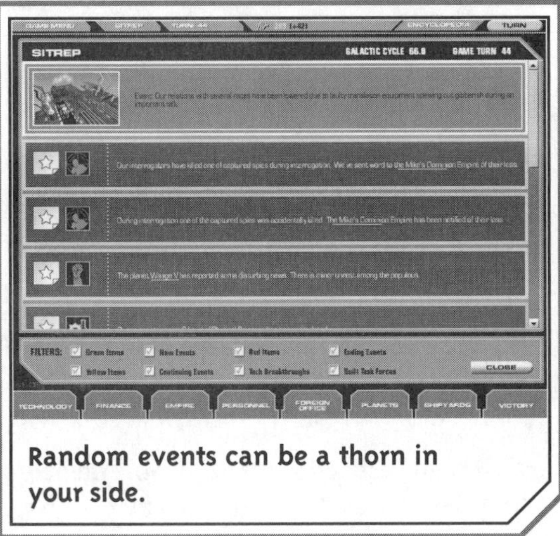

Random events can be a thorn in your side.

Unrest and Revolt

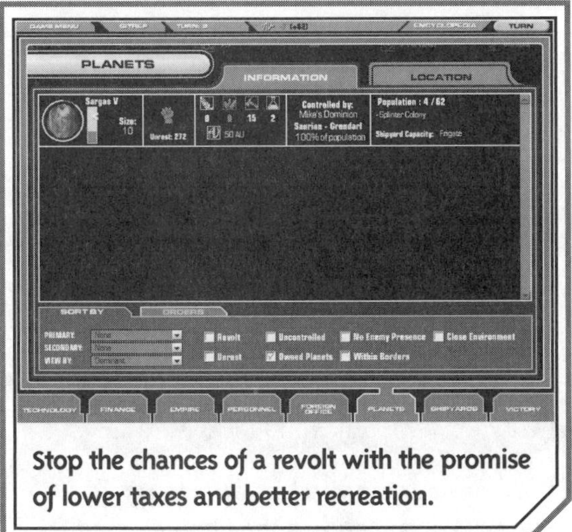

Stop the chances of a revolt with the promise of lower taxes and better recreation.

Unrest is the most common problem and is the easiest to fix. Some races increase unrest, some decrease it, while some governments control it better than others. No matter where you fit into the equation, don't let unrest escalate into a rebellion or you'll lose the world completely.

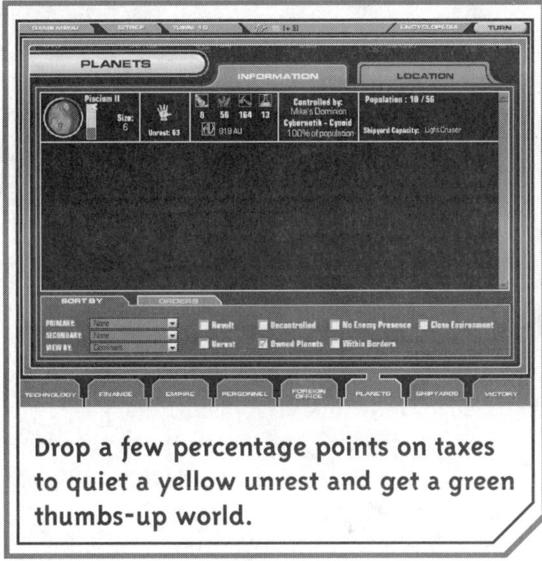

Drop a few percentage points on taxes to quiet a yellow unrest and get a green thumbs-up world.

The most effective way to silence unrest is with a tax drop. Check the demographics tab on a planet to see what's causing the unrest. If it's not a random event or enemy espionage, it's the Oppressometer or high taxes. Either situation is alleviated with a tax break. Drop the tax percentage one or two points a turn until everything stabilizes. If the situation is dire—the world's about to fracture and ignite a revolution—then drop taxes by 10 percent or more. After a time, work up to an acceptable threshold. If you're watchful, unrest won't become an issue.

Sabotage

Someone out there doesn't like us. Enemy spies invade with plans of sabotage.

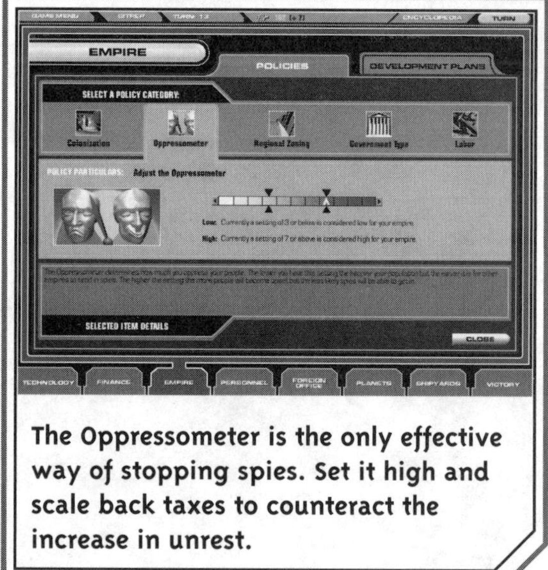

The Oppressometer is the only effective way of stopping spies. Set it high and scale back taxes to counteract the increase in unrest.

Espionage is the unseen killer. Military spies destroy installations and cut supply lines. Scientific spies steal research and technological advances. Political spies can slay a leader or blow up an important government building. You don't know who they are. You don't know what they're up to. Who can you trust?

When an enemy, or enemies, invade with espionage, you only have one recourse—the Oppressometer. It's the only way to shut down terrorist spies, other than wiping the entire enemy off the map. It's not life-threatening if one or two spies trickle in. Simply click the Oppressometer up one notch and call it a day.

A spy infestation is another matter. Crank the Oppressometer to your race's comfortable limit. If that doesn't work, each turn click the Oppressometer one notch higher. Eventually, the spies quiet down. Keeping unassigned spies in your system is a second way to reduce enemy spies' effectiveness.

The price you pay for order is unrest. Your people will be unhappy with government restrictions that inconvenience their normal lives. Make amends by dropping your taxes two or three percent. You want to keep everyone safe, after all.

Financial Disaster

When your empire hits an economic depression, head to the Finance menu.

Spending habits, random events, and sudden enemy attacks all contribute to an economic depression. If your empire coasts in the red for a few turns, it's no big deal. When it plummets deeper and deeper without any spending from your end, then you have a situation.

By turn seven of our example depression, we're 960 AUs in the hole. At one point over the next few turns, we'll drop as low as 1,400 AUs. How do we reverse this runaway train?

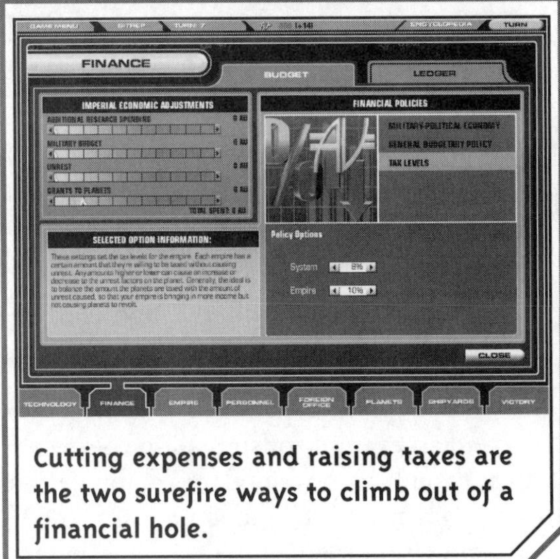

Cutting expenses and raising taxes are the two surefire ways to climb out of a financial hole.

Head to the Finance menu first. Switch your general budgetary policy to "savings." Now's not the time to spend on everything we see. Next, head to tax levels and push them as high as your people will allow. You can always drop them down a percentage point or two later. The extra generated income helps.

Don't forget about the planetary spending. It may take you going into each of your world's economic screens and adjusting the spending bars. Don't stop production completely. Spend on your main industrial activities to keep the economy moving. For the foreseeable future, cut back on military, terraforming, and research, and concentrate on economic development.

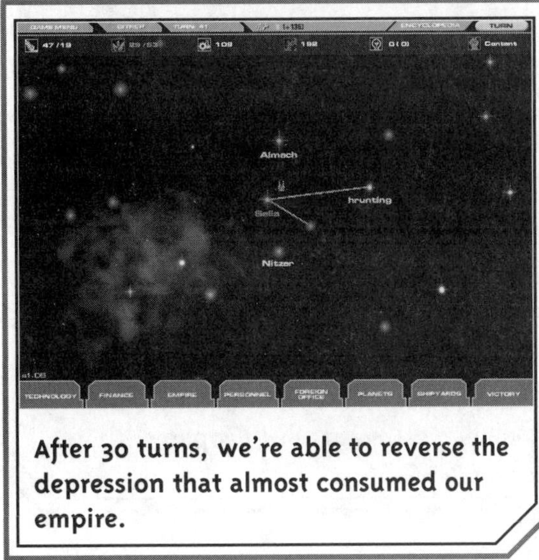

After 30 turns, we're able to reverse the depression that almost consumed our empire.

Be patient. As long as you see a positive gain each turn, it means you're heading in the right direction. Cut unnecessary spending, such as paying spies to sit around when there's no enemy. In our sample, it took us until turn 41 to reverse the depression. It's a lot of number tweaking, but it's the only way to stay in the game.

Starvation

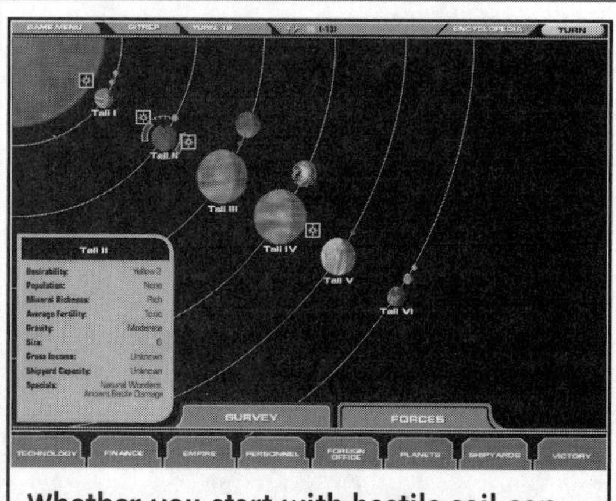

Whether you start with hostile soil conditions or you lose worlds to enemy attack, your food production will one day suffer. Know how to jump start Bioharvesting or your people will starve.

It's easy to get distracted in this game. You have finances to consider, diplomatic treaties to negotiate, military campaigns to plan. The planetary viceroys are there for the everyday needs of the planet, right?

Yes, and no. A viceroy usually runs the planet smoothly, but he's not as smart as you. If you see a problem creep up, step in and disarm it immediately. In the case of starvation, watch your food supply at all times. If the "need" approaches the "produced" number, you have to plan for more food. The red food number is also a dead giveaway.

Superior Bioharvesting ekes more out of the fields and a poor skill level. Even so, you have to gauge your population growth and how much food will be needed. Each planet gets two DEAs per region, so don't stockpile on industry only to realize you didn't build a single farm. A good rule is one Bioharvesting DEA for small worlds, two for average-sized worlds like your homeworld, and three or more for the giants. If your main skill is Bioharvesting, you want more so you can make a huge surplus and sell it.

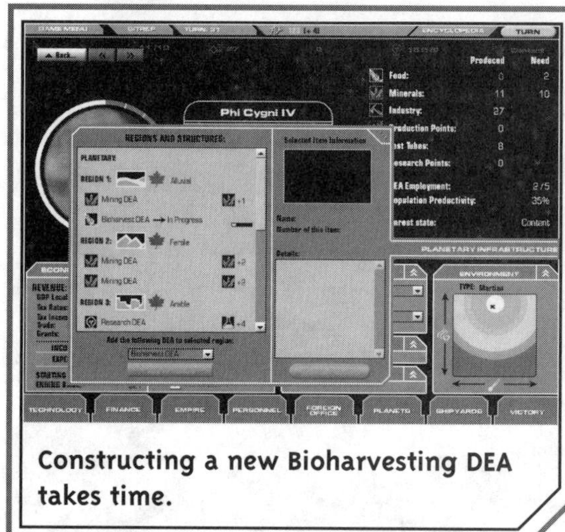

Constructing a new Bioharvesting DEA takes time.

Need an example of starvation control? Let's say you have zero food and a population of two. Your need is two food per turn, and your population is going to die unless you up the food quota. Head into planetary infrastructure and scan the regions. Find one that isn't full, preferably in a fertile lowlands, and construct a Bioharvesting DEA. In an extreme emergency where there's no space, delete the least important DEA and construct a Bioharvesting DEA over it. It's more important to feed your people than anything else. Without a population, you'll lose control of the planet.

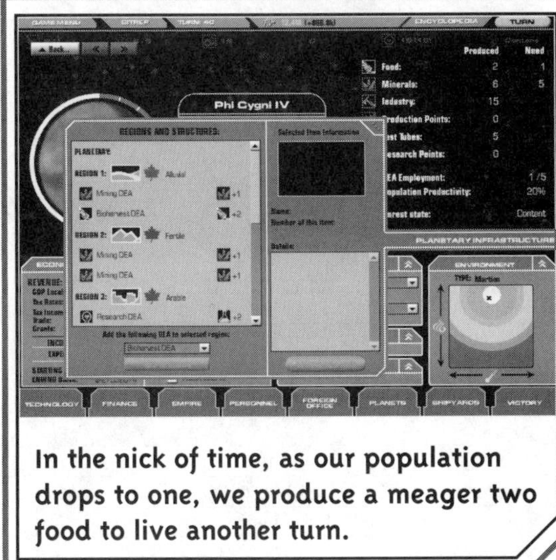

In the nick of time, as our population drops to one, we produce a meager two food to live another turn.

The next turn, the Bioharvesting DEA should be in the planning stages. Crank up the economic development spending as high as you can afford. In our current starvation example, we lost another population point in the nine turns it took us to build the new DEA. If we lost one more, we would have lost the planet. As it stands, we're now producing two food for one population point, and should be well fed from here on out.

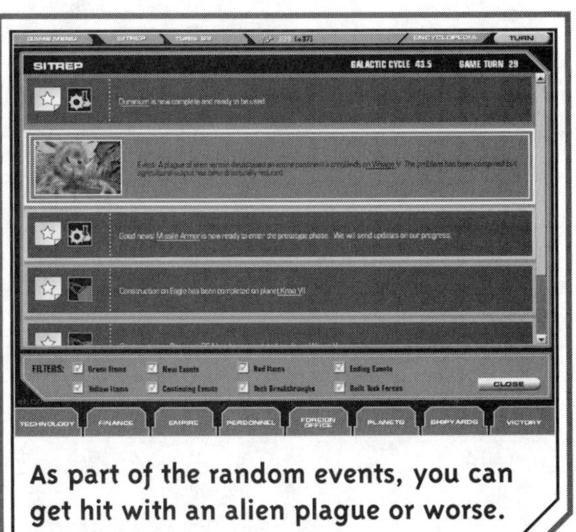

As part of the random events, you can get hit with an alien plague or worse.

Random Events

There's no way to stop a random event from occurring. The situation report pops up, and some devastation or another slams you. You can't stop it, but you can patch the wound. If you know what the event is doing to your empire, you might be able to rectify the situation.

A void crystal event helps space ports for a few turns.

If an AI goes wild on you and attacks your research center, expect a five percent reduction on test tubes for two to six turns. During that stretch, flip over to your Imperial economic sliders and bump up Research spending to counteract the effect. That's what a treasury is for. For the same length of time, pirates can cause unrest in your empire. When it strikes for a 35 percent increase, cut those taxes or your citizens might cut your throat.

Respond to the disasters swiftly, or those small problems can snowball into empire-ending calamities.

Random Events

Event	Status	Duration	Result
AI Glitch	Negative	2–6 Turns	-5% Test Tubes
Ancient Orion Relic	Positive	1 Turn	Random Advance
Crackpot	Negative	1–5 Turns	-5% Test Tubes
Devastating Earthquake	Negative	1 Turn	-200 Infrastructure
Dramatic	Negative	1 Turn	Variable
Drifting Debris	Positive	1 Turn	Variable
Earthquake	Negative	1 Turn	-10 Infrastructure
Exotic Animal I	Negative	1–5 Turns	-5% Bioharvesting
Exotic Animal II	Negative	2–6 Turns	-75% Bioharvesting
Exotic Animal III	Negative	2–6 Turns	-35% Bioharvesting
Exotic Animal IV	Negative	2–6 Turns	-15% Bioharvesting
Foreign Language Innovation	Positive	2–6 Turns	+1 to +10 Diplomacy
Foreign Language Reform	Positive	2–6 Turns	+1 to +6 Diplomacy
Foreign Language Revolution	Positive	2–6 Turns	+2 to +16 Diplomacy
Government Cleaning	Positive	1–5 Turns	-1 Heavy Foot of Government
Government Laundering	Positive	1–5 Turns	-7 Heavy Foot of Government
Government Scrubbing	Positive	1–5 Turns	-5 Heavy Foot of Government
Government Washing	Positive	1–5 Turns	-3 Heavy Foot of Government
Insurrection	Negative	2–6 Turns	-60% Test Tubes
Leader Killed	Negative	1 Turn	Leader Killed
Local Entertainment Star	Positive	1–5 Turns	-3% Unrest
Loon	Negative	1–5 Turns	-10% Test Tubes
Mechanical Transportation Disaster	Negative	2–6 Turns	-4 to -16 Diplomacy
Mechanical Transportation Failure	Negative	2–6 Turns	-2 to -8 Diplomacy
Mechanical Transportation Glitch	Negative	2–6 Turns	-1 to -4 Diplomacy
Miner Revolt	Negative	2–6 Turns	-65% Mining
Miner Uprising	Negative	2–6 Turns	-40% Mining
Mining Agitation	Negative	1–5 Turns	-5% Mining
Mining Unrest	Negative	2–6 Turns	-25% Mining
Minor Earthquake	Negative	1 Turn	-5 Infrastructure
Murmurs of Pirates	Negative	2–6 Turns	+15% Unrest
Planetary Nanite Release	Negative	1 Turn	-60 Infrastructure
Psionic	Negative	1 Turn	+15 Unrest
Raving Madman	Negative	2–6 Turns	-20% Test Tubes
Research Failure	Negative	1 Turn	Delay Random Advance
Research Success	Positive	1 Turn	Random Advance
Revolt	Negative	2–6 Turns	-25% Test Tubes
Rumors of Pirates	Negative	2–6 Turns	+35% Unrest
Scath Hive Attacks	Negative	1 Turn	-10 Infrastructure
Scientific Congress	Positive	2–6 Turns	+20% Test Tubes
Scientific Gathering	Positive	1–5 Turns	+4% Test Tubes
Scientific Symposium	Positive	1–5 Turns	+10% Test Tubes
Strong Earthquake	Negative	1 Turn	-100 Infrastructure
System Entertainment Star	Positive	1–5 Turns	-5% Unrest
System Entertainment Star II	Positive	2–6 Turns	-20% Unrest
Uprising	Negative	2–6 Turns	-10% Test Tubes
Void Crystal	Positive	1–5 Turns	+10% Space Port
Whispers of Pirates	Negative	2–6 Turns	+5% Unrest

SAMPLE SCENARIOS

Playing the Humans

Just because you live and breathe the human experience doesn't mean you're equipped to triumph with them in *Master of Orion III*. Humans are not balanced; they're on the bottom end of the gene pool. They can trade, invest money soundly, and research well; they can't fight or save the environment if their lives depend on it, and they do. You'll have to be fast on your feet with the Humans and adapt to whatever the galaxy throws your direction.

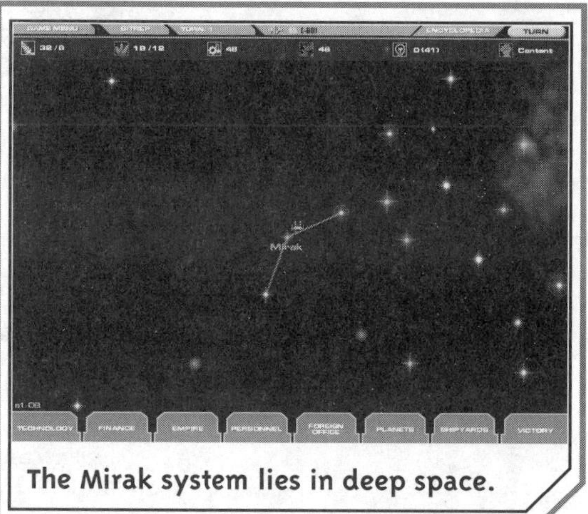

The Mirak system lies in deep space.

Your Homeworld

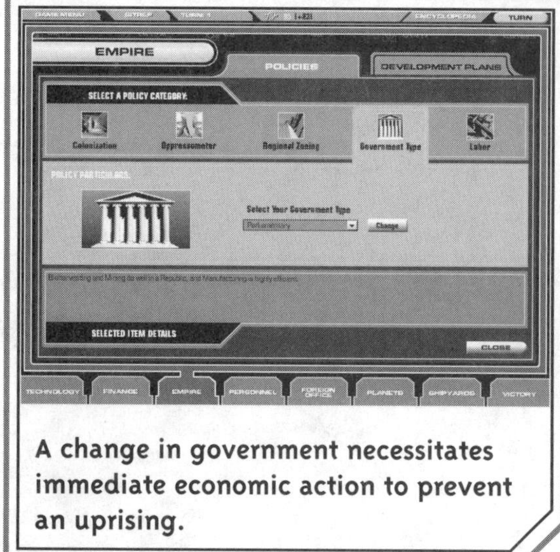

A change in government necessitates immediate economic action to prevent an uprising.

You might be happy with a democratic system. Our Humans aren't. A democratic government provides money for Bioharvesting, Mining, and Manufacturing, but holds back on military. In the long run, this will hurt us when it comes time to engage other alien powers. On the other hand, parliamentary governments increase Bioharvesting and Mining, with a big push for Manufacturing. Parliaments don't have the same drawback against military as do democracies.

With all that in mind, we change our government from democracy to parliamentary. We also alter our Oppressometer. Humans start at the lowest setting, which means spies can nest themselves in our society. We push the Oppressometer up two notches in anticipation of foreign spies.

These two moves will stir up unrest. If we're not careful, our society will collapse into a revolution and we'll be out of a job. Our top priority will be ensure peace in the next few turns.

We have no neighbors. It might be rash to create a team of spies, but we want to take advantage of our dangerous-level espionage. The upkeep won't break us one way or the other. If we hit a foe early, we'll be able to respond without fleet power.

Inside our home system of Mirak, two potential colony worlds flank our homeworld.

Twin colony possibilities flank our homeworld, Mirak VI. Mirak V holds a splinter colony, so it'll develop into a Human-controlled world on its own. Mirak V lies in the yellow ecosystem range, and has poor minerals and hostile soil. It looks like more trouble than it's worth. Still, it's early so we'll give it a chance. Mirak VII is better. It's a "sweet spot" world with poor minerals and hard scrabble soil. Never pass up a sweet spot world. We can always use the extra farming from Mirak VII.

Galactic Expansion

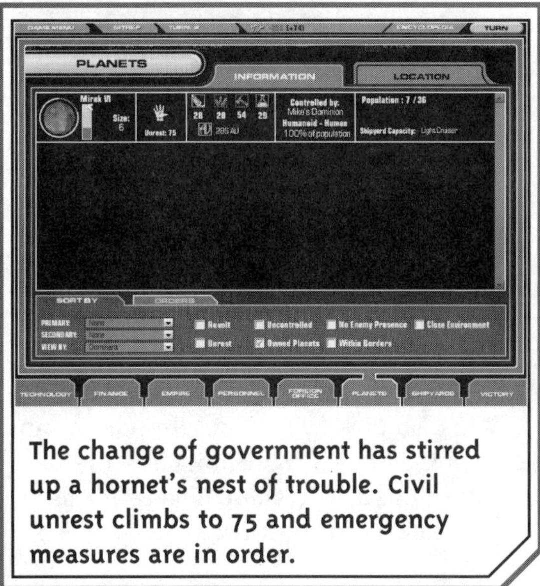

The change of government has stirred up a hornet's nest of trouble. Civil unrest climbs to 75 and emergency measures are in order.

On turn two, civil unrest erupts. One or two more turns of this, and we'll have a revolt. The first thing we do is open up Mirak VI's Planetary Economics screen and cut taxes by five percent. We might be able to raise them later; it's more important now to calm everyone down. Next, we examine the imperial economic sliders in the Finance section. We can't afford to spend much on research and military. Instead, we leave planetary gifts where they are and raise the expenditure on unrest. Combined with the lower taxes, this will do the trick.

Our tactics work to quell unrest, even as the Mirak VII colony joins the empire.

On turn three, unrest has dropped to an acceptable 22. All this turmoil has sent our economy into a depression. Luckily for us, we have no neighbors to worry about.

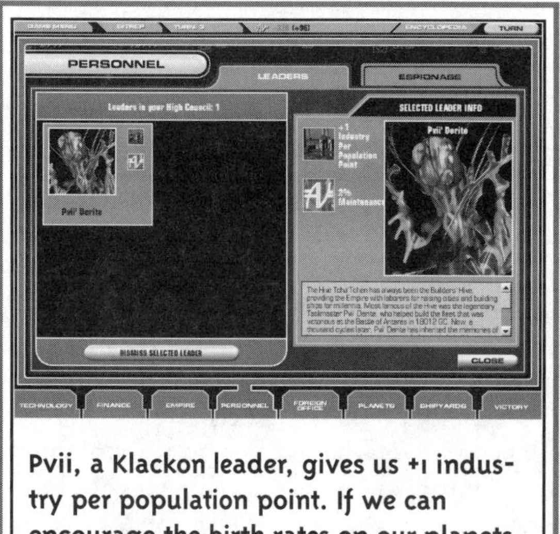

Pvii, a Klackon leader, gives us +1 industry per population point. If we can encourage the birth rates on our planets, the Imperial Treasury will swell.

A Klackon leader asks to come on board. Considering that he increases industry, which will be a boon after our economy gets rolling, we accept. It's up to our colonization plans to increase our population to get full value from our leader.

There is nothing in the Pherkad or Mekbuta systems. Looks like we're trapped in a dead-end sector of space.

On turn four, we're in a dead-end part of space. The only avenue out is a single space lane departing from the Mekbuta system. Consequently, expansion will be slow. We'll take it, as you couldn't ask for a better defensive position.

On turn five, a malicious AI throws our research endeavors into chaos. If we were in a race with other powers militarily, this could be deadly. It's not, and we weed out the AI without trouble.

On turn seven, we recover from our initial downward economic spiral. We cut back on spending and waited for the finances to climb out of the red. We monitored spending during those turns, though we had other activities to keep our government busy.

Taking Command

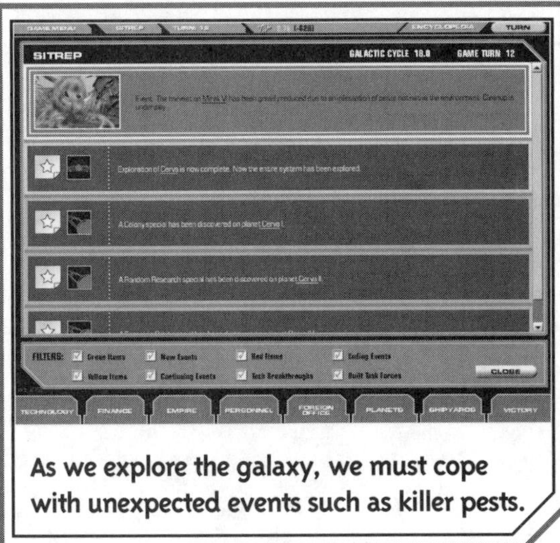

As we explore the galaxy, we must cope with unexpected events such as killer pests.

There's no need for military yet, so our money will go into building more colony ships for exploration and colonization.

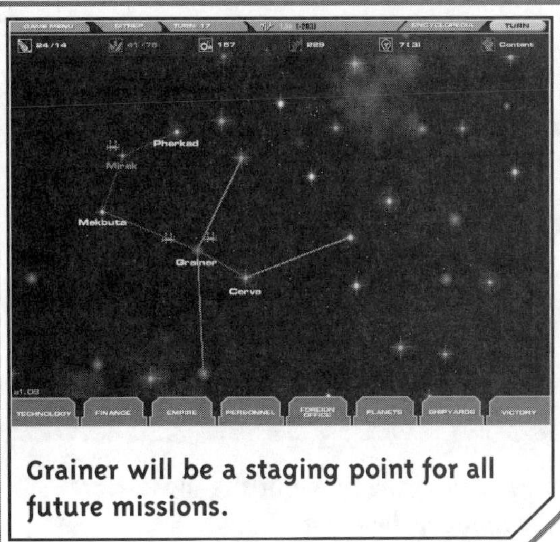

Grainer will be a staging point for all future missions.

The next system we explore, Granier, becomes our biggest find. Strategically, it intersects three other systems and is the only way out into the rest of the galaxy. All our ships will dock in the Granier system before heading out on exploration and conquest missions. Right now, there isn't a world to colonize in Granier. After we build up cash, we will colonize one of the larger planets into a military base.

On turn 17, there are no aliens in sight. This gives us a moment to catch our breath and concentrate on solid exploration. Money that might otherwise go into warships goes into colony ships. The idea is to build up an infrastructure that one or two setbacks can't topple. Look over your worlds and set up development plans under the Empire screen. Those worlds that can specialize should do so.

From Grainer, the rest of the universe is up for grabs. We won't quickly expand. We'll pick a direction and head down one space lane at a time. If we meet an alien, we'll charm them through diplomatic channels; otherwise, it's all-out war and heaven help them if they have an enemy on their tail.

The trick is not exposing ourselves to the hidden enemy too early. One alien race is fine, but stumbling into several could hurt.

Every step of the way, especially in colonization systems, we need to reinforce with military task forces. By the time an enemy counteracts, we'll be strong.

Playing the Evon

If you like spy movies, you'll like the Evon. Masters of espionage, the Evon can destroy empires without leaving their home system. Their other race traits flat line, so they need time to develop. If they get into a military tussle, they're fairly tough. Should trouble rear up, there's always those special wristwatches the Evon agents carry around . . . .

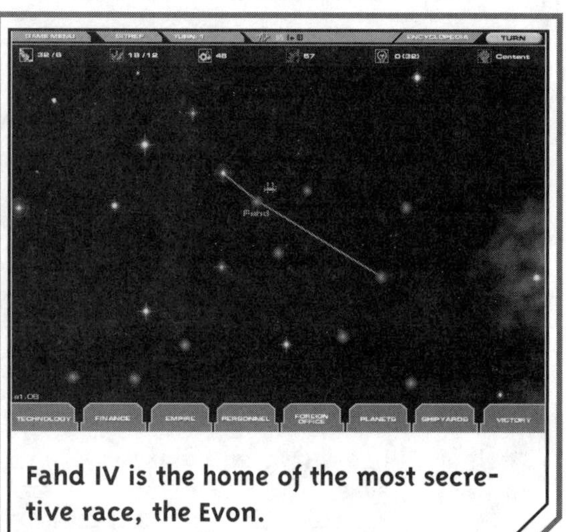

Fahd IV is the home of the most secretive race, the Evon.

Your Homeworld

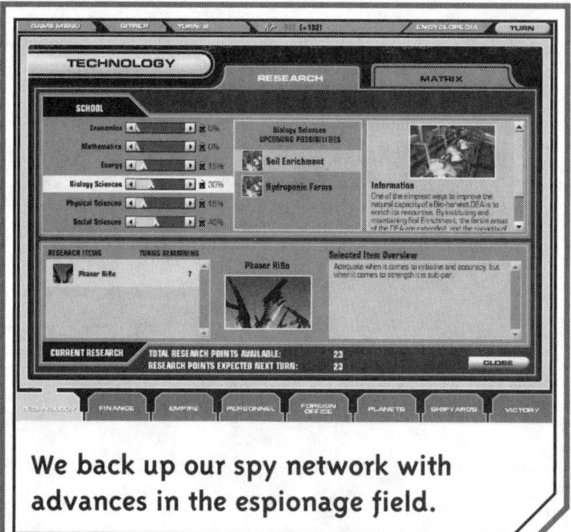

We back up our spy network with advances in the espionage field.

We have an obligation as the Evon to keep spies employed. Our dangerous Cunning trait makes it natural for us to undercut the enemy with a barrage of secret agents. The idea is to train as many agents as possible—10, 20, 30 at a time—and blanket the targeted enemy. Many of the spies will be caught at the border or captured before they complete their mission. Many others will be interrogated, tortured, and executed. A hefty percentage, though, will slip through the defenses and blow up people and things. Five or six key incursions put the enemy at a severe disadvantage if you time your military attack at that exact moment.

The three best agent types are military, political, and scientific. They have the best chance of doing the most damage against the enemy. We start with two military spies and one each of the other two types. We follow with four more military spies in five turns. By the time a serious attack is launched against us, we'll have a supply of two dozen spies to mess with them.

A leader, Onasasi of the Psilon, decides he's better off with us than his own people. He doesn't do us any immediate good, but down the road, he'll help our ground forces improve by 20 percent. We have to keep him around until war time.

The first world we discover, Oatka I, falls in the red with two specials.

Decisions are never easy. Our first explored system uncovers a world, Oatka I, with two positive specials. The downside? It's in the red range, meaning it'll take a ton of time and money to terraform it into Evon-friendly terrain. We'll wait for a better proposition.

Our first batch of spies shows up on turns five and six. Given that we have no enemy yet, they'll just sit around costing us AUs. It's worth it, though, to be prepared for future hostilities—they always happen in this game.

Galactic Expansion

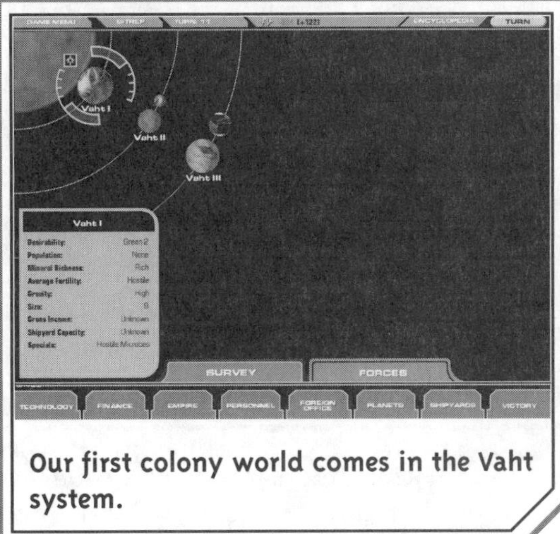

Our first colony world comes in the Vaht system.

Our colonization is slow and deliberate. We don't want to get too stretched out, since we don't plan on having any sort of military for a while. The Vaht system provides a green world, except it's full of hostile microbes. We haven't had luck elsewhere, so we dispatch a colony ship there. Terraforming is paramount on Vaht I to wipe out the microbes and get our world up to speed. All this money puts us in the red with our treasury. We'll have to watch the problem so we don't dip too far into a deficit.

Like a blessing from the sky, Aonahi from the Imsaeis, arrives as a leader of espionage. He offers 10 percent to spy Cloaking and Luck, and he has no penalty associated with the bonuses. Our spies are now considered the best agents in the universe.

Another world joins our fold. A splinter colony, Asterion VII provides more industry

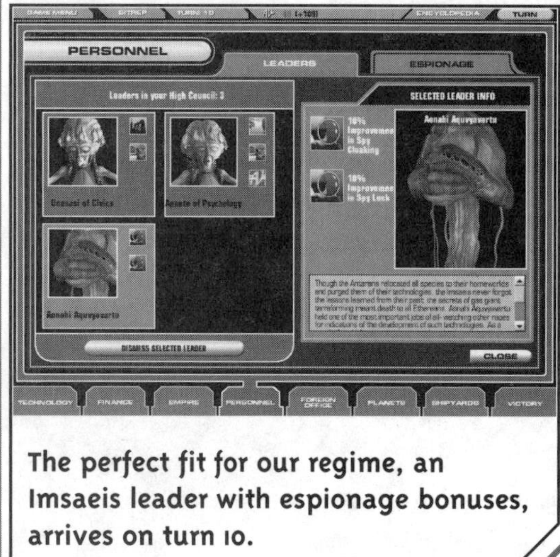

The perfect fit for our regime, an Imsaeis leader with espionage bonuses, arrives on turn 10.

for us and, hence, more money in the long run. Even with slow expansion, we have three worlds producing for us.

The Imsaeis show up on our radar. Before they can solidify ties elsewhere, we offer an economic deal that will aid both worlds. Meanwhile, our agents continue to train and hone their stealth skills.

If only the Imsaeis race were more like our Imsaeis leader, Aonahi, then we might get along. Instead, the Imsaeis try to race us for the better planets in the systems we've already explored. In the Indu San system, the fourth planet shows sweet-spot green and will give us another fast-growing world.

As you might guess, our stance of claiming the worlds in nearby systems angers the Imsaeis. They declare war as their ships gather on the border. We now have a target for our spies.

The Imsaeis go to war over border disputes.

Taking Command

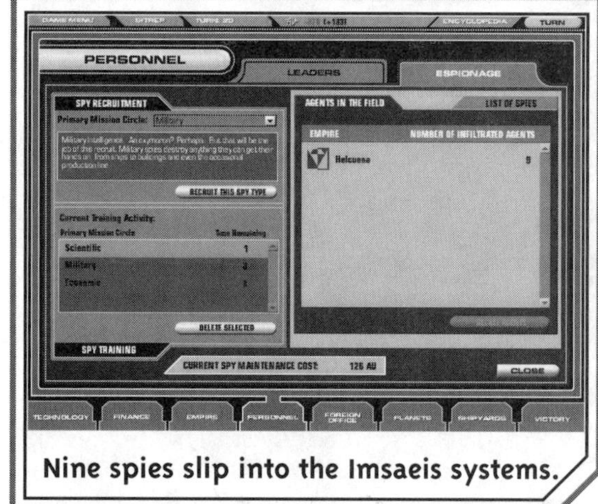

Nine spies slip into the Imsaeis systems.

Our first nine spies invade the Imsaeis empire. One spy dies during insertion; the rest are delayed or make it through the guarded border. On turn 21, the results are spectacular—we assassinate a leader, damage ships in the Imsaeis repair yard, slow down two research centers, and blow up a building. These terrorist acts would have anyone cowering in fear.

Our spies deliver with spectacular results. The Imsaeis beg us for a treaty a turn after our spies eliminate one of their leaders.

On turn 22, the Imsaeis effectively surrender. They quiet their military saber-rattling and retreat. Our agents' sabotage has pushed them to beg for an economic trade agreement as a peace offering. We accept. There's no need to get in a prolonged war that will hurt both nations. Maybe they'll feel obligated to us in the future.

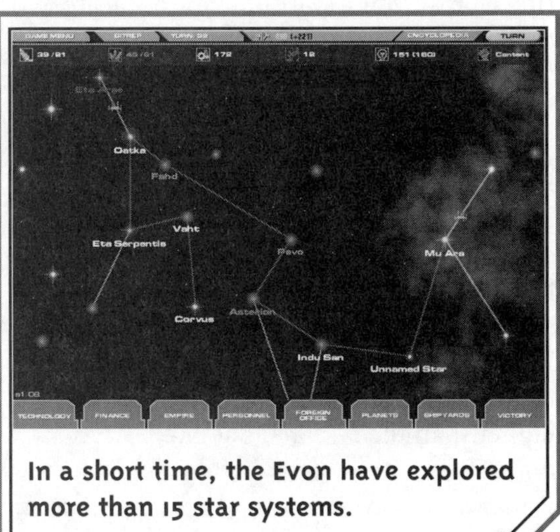

In a short time, the Evon have explored more than 15 star systems.

Our plan is based on expansion, colonization, and economic saving. We beat the deficit problem earlier by cutting the budget until we had spending under control. Now we can tweak the economic development values back up and save for an inevitable military campaign. Will the Imsaeis be our first target? Not if they stay in line. In fact, we'll continue to work on them for an alliance. If anything goes wrong, we still have our agents deep in their homeworld.

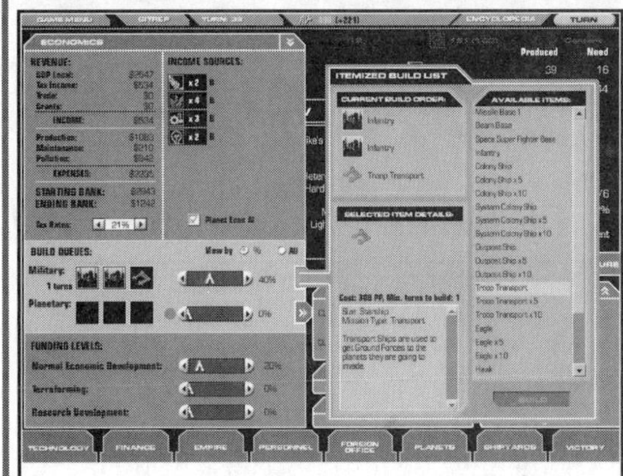

It's time to build the military. We opt for infantry with troop transports to carry the ground fight to enemy worlds.

Unlike other races, the Evon have the luxury of either expanding heavily or sitting at home. In the "turtle" state, the Evon can throw spies out at a neighbor and weaken the alien power to the point of submission. They don't have to expend great amounts of money on extra military. When a spy network weakens an enemy, the Evon military seems twice as strong. Whenever the Evon play a part in the galaxy, the natural state of things becomes paranoia.

Playing the Psilon

The Psilon land on Nasak VI, in the middle of nowhere.

It's a killer combination: superior Diplomacy and Technology. If the Psilon can't invent a gizmo to help their empire flourish, they just ask someone else for it. Because of their physical handicap, they're the second-worst military race, though the fleets and the troops that they do build are usually technologically advantaged. They have trouble dealing with basic economy—Bioharvesting and Mining—so stay on top of planetary economics to bring them to the next level.

Your Homeworld

Because the Psilon have no neighbors, we can take certain liberties with the economy. To earn extra income, we reduce military grants to zero.

Is it fortune or folly to be stuck away from everyone? It's fortunate that you don't have to worry about attack for the early part of the game. On the other hand, your Diplomacy is superior, so you'll want to communicate with others. We'll just have to deal with this setback and direct the economy to take advantage of our isolation.

Under the Finance screen, cut military funding to zero. No neighbors means no attacks. Until we get established, we won't spend any money on military. Set research in the high green area of the bar. Our second specialty, other than Diplomacy, is Research. We want to spend as much as possible on our tech schools. Set the planetary grant bar higher than the research bar. We'll have difficulties with our food and minerals—the Psilon don't have a strong work force—so the surplus treasury goes to smoothing over these problems.

The Trilarian leader, Aeneerala, starts on our homeworld. Normally, we'd send this loser packing. He grants a 10 percent bonus to recreation—no big deal—yet he subtracts seven percent from military effectiveness and adds two percent to maintenance. Those are serious drawbacks for a minor reward. We keep him, though, since we don't have any military and don't plan to have any in the near future. Later, he hits the road.

Without military, we have more to spend on economic development and research.

Under the Planets tab, we knock military down to zero, raise economic development to 51 percent and research to 26 percent. Both these values are still in the yellow, so we aren't overspending much. Hopefully, the economic development score will bolster our lackluster Bioharvesting and Mining skills. If we can get the industry rolling, we can hold out until we find colony worlds to strengthen our soil and ore situation. Note that this spending will most likely bring us into the red financially, but it's worth the heavy early output to finetune our economy.

We'll invest in energy technology for better warp drives.

Our focus will be Research. At the start, we're still generating over 60 research points a turn, so we can advance quickly. We could learn about economics, but without alien interference, our planets' economies should do fine. Energy is definitely a possibility, as well as physical sciences, for the future military value. In the case of energy, we can also develop our warp drive technology with level four's improved thrusters, allowing us to quickly zip around the galaxy.

Hydroponic farms and enriched soil are a must for a race that can't grow a weed. Biological sciences looks good, as does mathematics with its upcoming interchangeable policy structures and advanced policy theories. We leave out the much-maligned social sciences; we don't need recreational help right now.

Galactic Expansion

When we finally meet up with an alien power, they could be hostile. Instead of military, let's pursue the cheaper alternative—spies. We'll hire four military spies to infiltrate the first hostile we run into and throw them into chaos. We don't want to spend too much on spies—just enough to give us a sting—since they require turn-by-turn upkeep costs.

After a few turns, we're able to raise our economic development to 62 percent and research to 38 percent. Our economy is steadily getting better. Though we still aren't spending an AU on military, we have two colony ships queued for construction when we're ready to expand our empire.

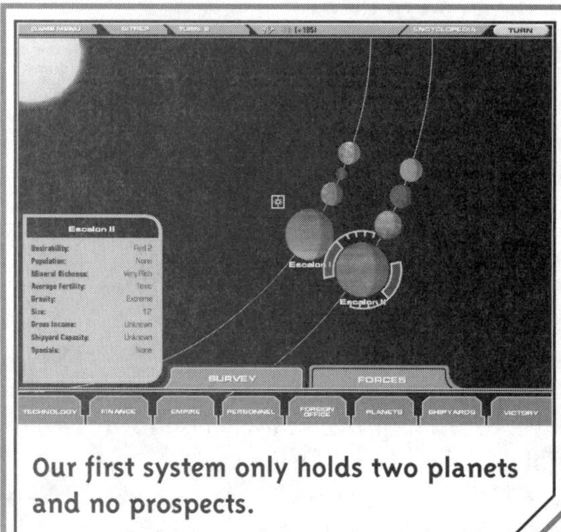

Our first system only holds two planets and no prospects.

Our goal is to explore slowly. We'll take an alien relationship if it comes, but it could be hostile and we've got our economy headed into independent mode. The Escalon system holds nothing. Two planets, both in the red, don't offer more than inhospitable rock. Maybe our next system . . . .

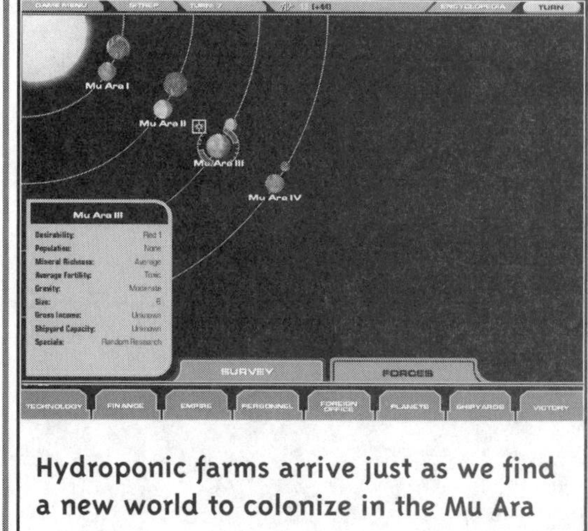

Hydroponic farms arrive just as we find a new world to colonize in the Mu Ara system.

Finally, our research pays off when we discover hydroponic farms. Our population won't starve any time soon. We also discover the Mu Ara system, which contains two notable planets. Mu Ara I holds average minerals and lies in the green for Psilons. Mu Ara III holds a random research. The extra research boost could help tremendously, but the world's red and would need severe terraforming. We'll skip Mu Ara III and colonize I.

We need more minerals, so we build a new Mining DEA.

To continue with our economic development, we need more minerals. Our planetary viceroy is one step ahead of us. When we check our homeworld's infrastructure, the viceroy has already built a Mining DEA. It'll be ready next turn and will increase our ability to create productive industry.

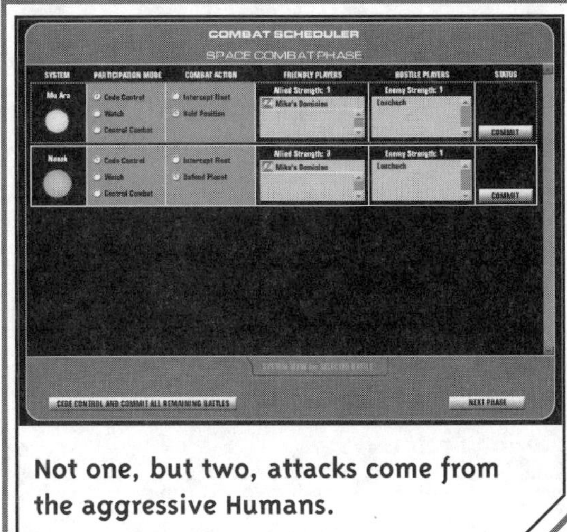

Not one, but two, attacks come from the aggressive Humans.

Ironically, we get invaded at the same time in two separate systems. A Human warship enters our home system, undetected till this point. In the Mu Ara system, a second warship opens fire. We beat the fleet in the Mu Ara system in a close one; the battle above our home planet isn't even close. Our first military encounter is a success, no doubt due to our technological superiority.

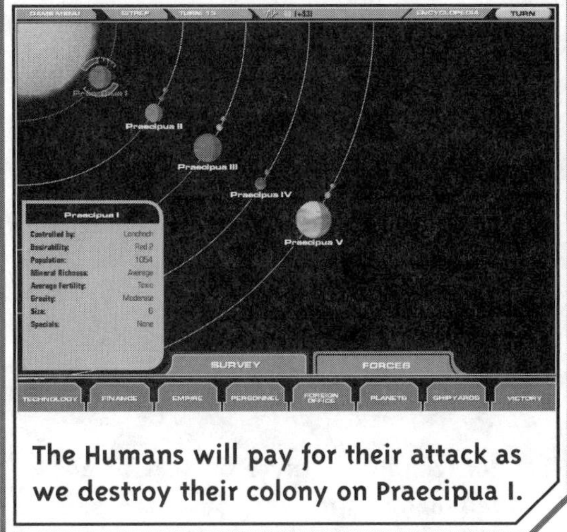

The Humans will pay for their attack as we destroy their colony on Praecipua I.

The following turn we move into the Praecipua system. Now we know why the Humans were so touchy—there's a Human colony on the first planet. To further our edge against the Humans, we'll steal the colony or destroy it trying.

Taking Command

Psilon should stay the course at this point. Our technology can't be stopped. Energy advances on the fourth level are in production, while we can see all the way up to level ten in mathematics. In our main school, the biology advances automated biocare and bio-organic monitoring station have revealed themselves. If the run-in with the Humans is any indication, we have nothing to fear from inferior races that can't hold a candle to our armor-penetrating laser.

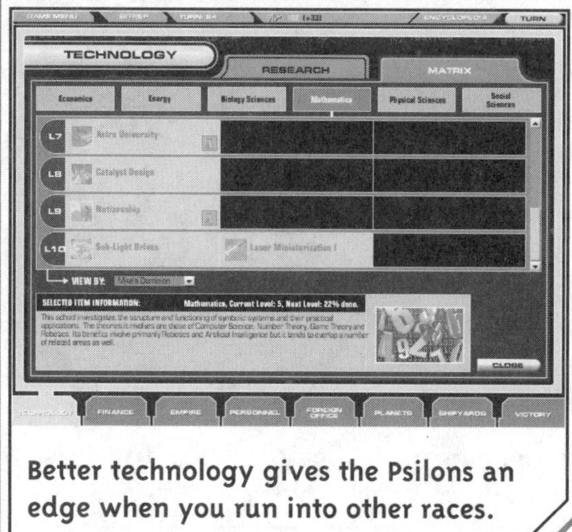

Better technology gives the Psilons an edge when you run into other races.

Playing the Meklar

The mechanical Meklar are always living in the shadow of their cyborg brothers, the Cynoid. They fall short in Mining, Manufacturing, and Trade. The only thing the Meklar do better than the Cynoid is communicate. For a mechanical inorganic race, the Meklar can wheel and deal with the best of them.

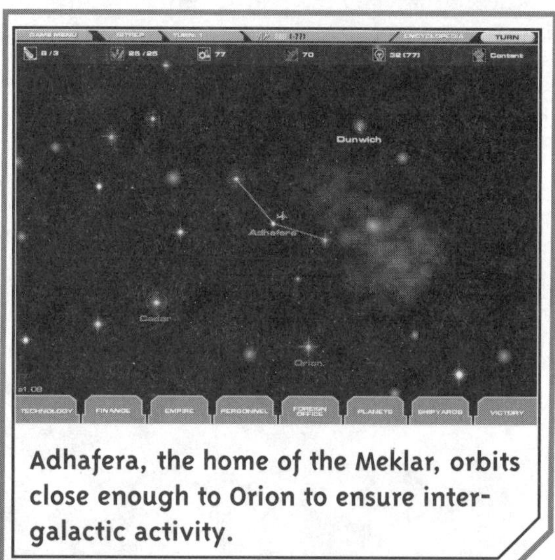

Adhafera, the home of the Meklar, orbits close enough to Orion to ensure inter-galactic activity.

Your Homeworld

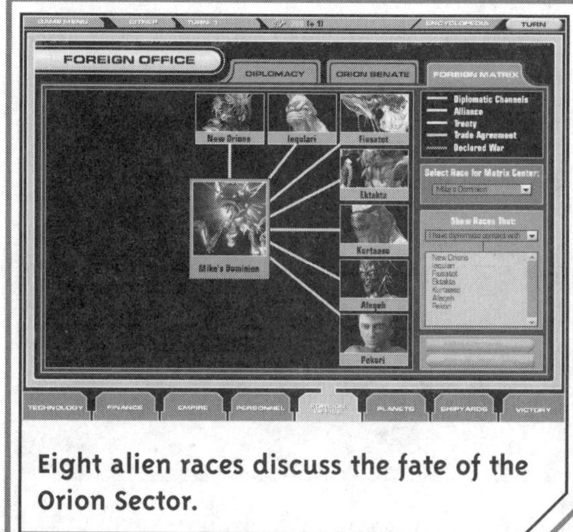

Eight alien races discuss the fate of the Orion Sector.

Not counting the Meklar, there are seven other races gathered together at the heart of the galaxy. We have our work cut out to conduct some serious diplomacy. It's the only

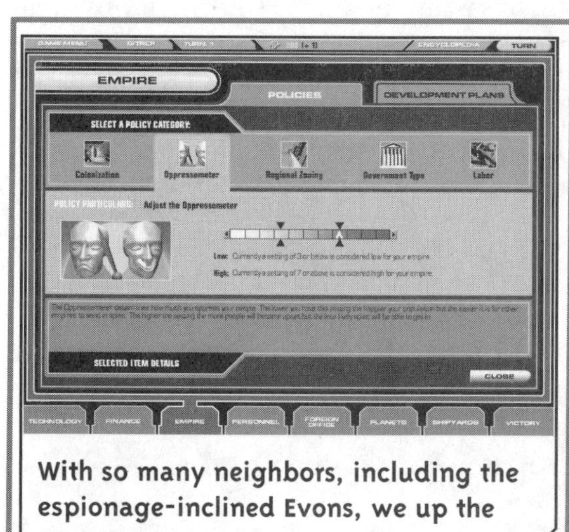

With so many neighbors, including the espionage-inclined Evons, we up the Oppressometer.

way to get what we want, with so many other needs trying to override ours.

The New Orions run the Orion Senate and could be useful allies, since they own every technological advance in the tech trees. Of course, that's if they respond to you. They usually play the ultimate neutrals, and prefer to stay out of other races' affairs. The Tachidi, too, won't have any feeling, good or bad, for us at the outset.

Based on our race, the Eoladi, Humans, and Evons will initially dislike us. We have to overcome this prejudice with smooth talking and gifts at the beginning of the game. If we initiate economic trade offers, we will be required to send them a percentage of our profits first. This should get them to trust us faster.

If past history has anything to say, the Trilarian are the only ones who will respond favorably to us at the start. We'll pay extra care to them, so we have at least one ally in the diplomatic free-for-all.

Contrary to our potential diplomacy woes, our home system looks like a paradise. Three planets fall in the instantly habitable range. Adhafera II and VII contain exactly the same makeup—rich minerals and subsistence soil. Adhafera V takes it a step higher with rich mineral, arable soil, *and* rare gems. With this setup, we don't have to leave the safety of our home system. In fact, most of our efforts will be to turn this into the most dominant system out there.

So many neighbors, so little space . . . . Eventually, there will be showdown in the space lanes around our home system. Considering that and the fact that our military strength isn't half bad at a base of six, we choose to study energy and physical sciences in the tech tree. The weapons and ground forces the schools generate will be immensely useful should we be attacked.

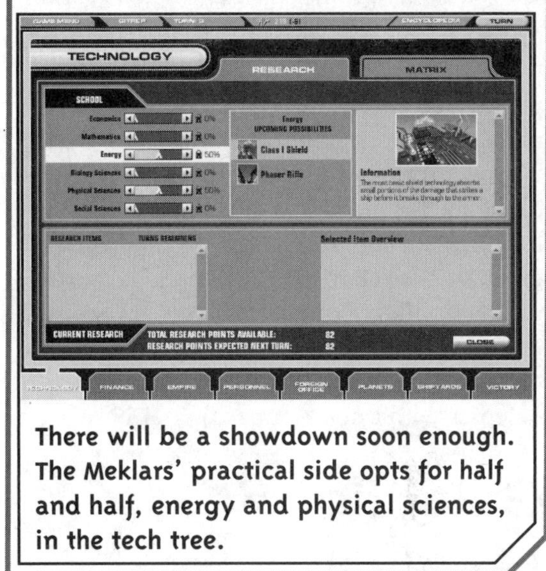

There will be a showdown soon enough. The Meklars' practical side opts for half and half, energy and physical sciences, in the tech tree.

On turn three, we come up zero percent on diplomatic treaties. No one wants to talk trade. It's frustrating. We grit our mechanized teeth and send another round of messages. Maybe our honorable intentions will come through with persistence.

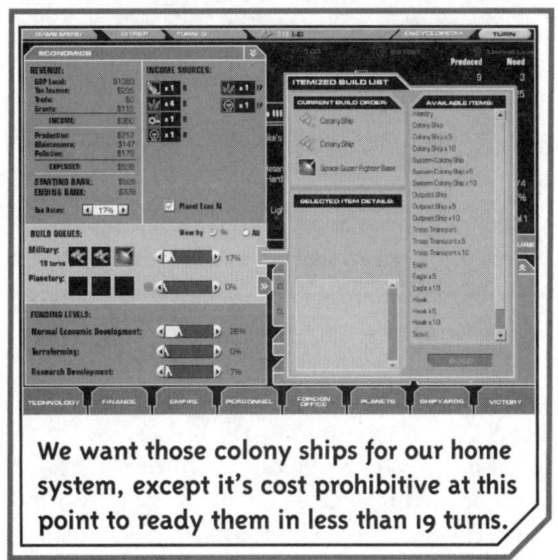

We want those colony ships for our home system, except it's cost prohibitive at this point to ready them in less than 19 turns.

Early on, it's difficult to do much with our economy. We push our meager resources to the maximum and increase military to 17 percent, economic development to 28 percent, and research to seven percent. Since it's our sweet spot homeworld, we don't need to do any terraforming. We'll save those AUs for the planets in the yellow or just in the green that we choose to colonize. In the military building queues, two colony ships await missions in our home system. Once those are built, we'll fortify our homeworld defenses with a space super fighter base.

Galactic Expansion

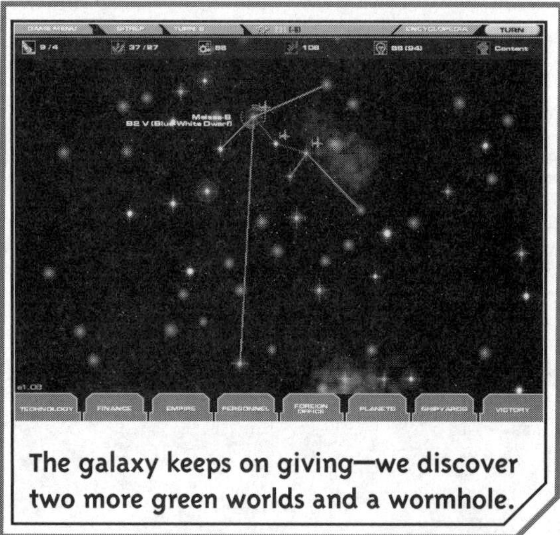

The galaxy keeps on giving—we discover two more green worlds and a wormhole.

Just because we have a fantastic home system doesn't mean we sit idly by and let others claim territory all around us. We don't want to spread ourselves too thin, either, so it's a balancing act. We decide to head out until we run into a neighbor, then pull back. This philosophy nets us three new systems, two of which have habitable worlds. Samenia I could be colonized if we weren't picky. We are, and don't want its average ratings. The white dwarf system of Meissa-B contains a wormhole and a green world. We'll take the access the wormhole offers—we might need to expand outside of this congested space soon—but don't need the world.

Our hard work breaks through on the diplomatic front and a potential ally, the Evon, step forward.

On turn six, our diplomacy succeeds with races we weren't sure would accept us. The Trilarian we thought would respond, but it's an unexpected surprise to see the Eoladi and Evons agree to hear us out. It could be a ruse; they could need an ally to suck resources from. For now, we'll work with them to see where it leads.

On turn seven, the Silicoids enter the Meissa-B system through the wormhole. Like us, they have ideas of using the wormhole to expand, except they don't realize they've just warped into the most populated part of the galaxy. In prompt fashion, they destroy our scout and take

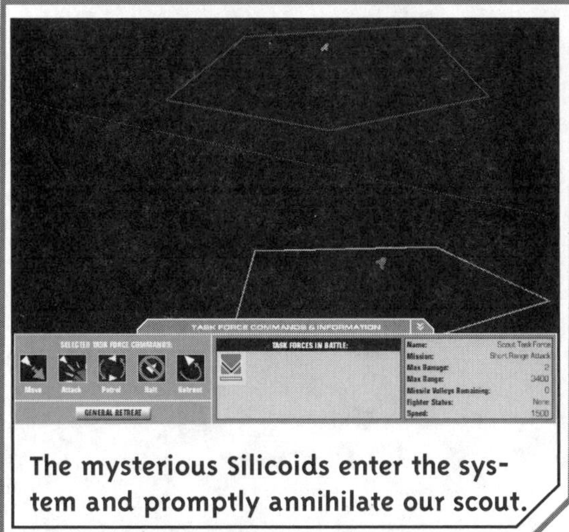

The mysterious Silicoids enter the system and promptly annihilate our scout.

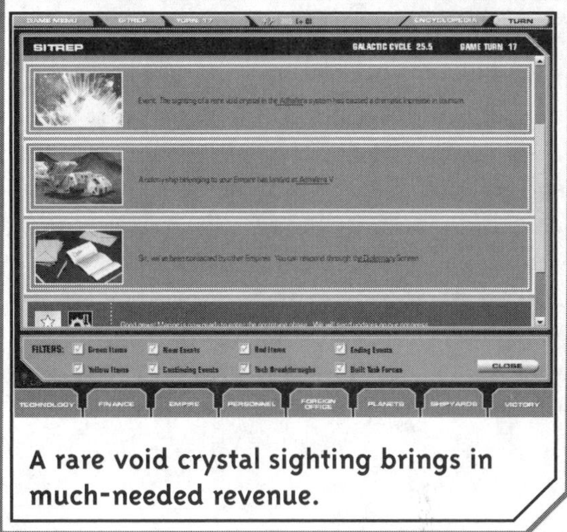

A rare void crystal sighting brings in much-needed revenue.

control of the wormhole. If this were a normal setup, we could be in for grief from the Silicoids. It's not. There are too many races around here for them to make much noise. They'll most likely retreat back the way they came, and we don't care enough about the wormhole to fight over it. The Silicoids will have a lot of battles to wage if they continue their current course.

Taking Command

Back in our home system, we push our economy a little harder. We've built up treasury reserve, which enables us to push into the orange on the sliders and spend 50 percent on military, 27 percent on economic development, and 11 percent on research. If we can maintain this pace, we'll have our two colony ships in four turns.

On turn 17, we get our wish and more. The first colony sets up tents on Adhafera V and should be a contributing member of the team in no time. We're also blessed with a rare void crystal sighting that increases tourism in our system and nets us extra revenue.

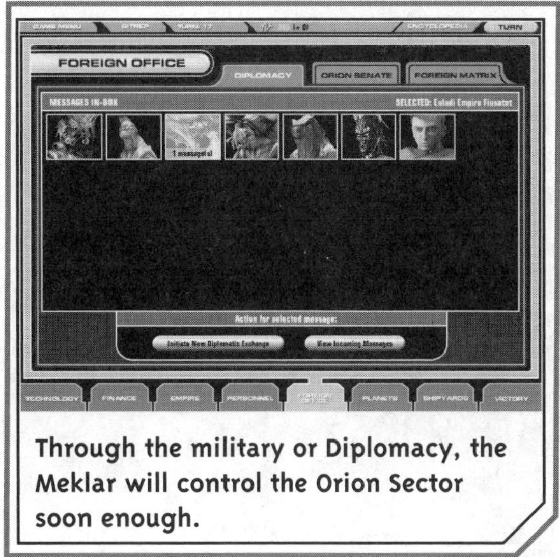

Through the military or Diplomacy, the Meklar will control the Orion Sector soon enough.

Our plan seems to have worked. On the Diplomacy front, we currently have four allies and no enemies. The Silicoids took a chunk out of us, but we never heard a peep from them afterward. Developing our home system should give us more income than other races have in their entire empire. From the protection of our home, we'll reach out and absorb systems—or other races—one by one. Any race that once thought of the Meklar as toys might want to reconsider the cyborgs as the new weapons of mass destruction.

Playing the Cynoid

These guys are loaded. You can exploit Mining and Manufacturing for large sums of cash, and if you broker any deals, your superior Trade skill magnifies profits. As machines, you don't care for the natural environment, so your Bioharvesting and Environmental traits suffer. You don't have many worries when it comes to combat—you're as strong or stronger than most races. The Cynoids are a complete package, but that doesn't mean you'll have an easy go of it in the beginning.

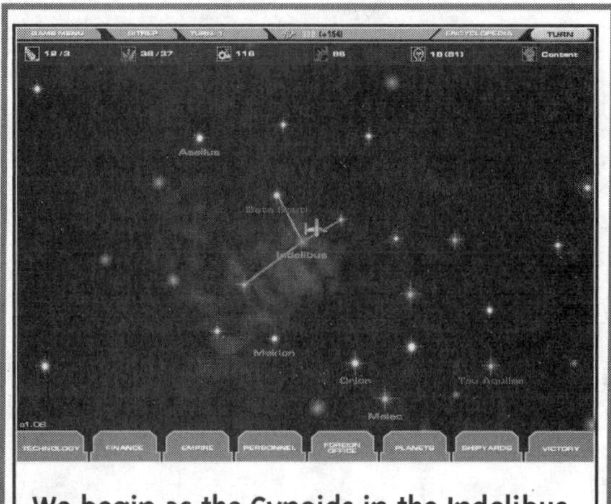

We begin as the Cynoids in the Indelibus system at the center of the galaxy.

Your Homeworld

We're surrounded by seven neighbors, so the Orion Senate will require much of our attention.

At the center of the galaxy, surrounded by a ton of bordering aliens, we've been given the toughest position for a Cynoid. The Cynoids can out-produce anyone; our big downfall is Diplomacy. The fewer neighbors you have at the beginning, the better. Sure, you want to trade with many of them; unfortunately, a lot of times those neighbors won't listen despite your best efforts. Let's see how we can turn this galaxy position to our advantage.

Checking out our homeworld, Indelibus III, our first conscious decision is to downplay military. Until we get into a potential military skirmish, we'll concentrate on growing our industry. Cutting military spending to zero, we bump economic development up to 26 percent, terraforming to 20 percent (to help perfect our world's environment), and research development to 5 percent. Our imperial economic sliders in the

Finance section help out with planetary grants and research spending.

On the tech side, we'll choose four schools at 25 percent each. We probably don't need any more help with economics and we're not going to employ spies yet, so we need to concentrate on the other four schools—energy, mathematics, biological sciences, and physical sciences. Later, we can choose to scale one back and zoom up the other three.

On turn two, a Grendarl leader, Pukashor, joins our cause. He increases factory output by 5 percent, but reduces fleet production by 15 percent and lowers tax collection by 4 percent. He's not that good, but we'll use him in the beginning to help out our industry, then dump him when we're ready to build military.

With so many aliens cramming the Foreign Office, we're forced to spend our time there. If you blow someone off and don't answer, that race will treat your brush off as a negative action. You want as many allies as possible, so don't *alienate* the aliens. Our first attempt at conversations with everyone yields one negative and two positives. The Eoladi impose sanctions on us for suggesting economic trade talks, while the Psilons want to trade research, and the Trilarians think about a non-aggression treaty.

The Eoladi impose sanctions on us early. However, the Trilarians enter into a non-aggression agreement with us.

We need more minerals, so it's time to build a Mining DEA.

The Eoladi don't want to listen to any sort of reason. Fortunately for us, a Cynoid leader joins us and increases our diplomatic relations by 15 percent. It doesn't help sway the Eoladi, but it gives us better lines of communication with the rest of the galaxy. In retaliation for the war declaration, we head to the Orion Senate and propose an official condemnation against the Eoladi. If passed, it would drop the Eoladi's standings with all Senate members by 1 to 20 diplomatic points. Unfortunately, no one seconds the proposal. We'll just have to keep trying.

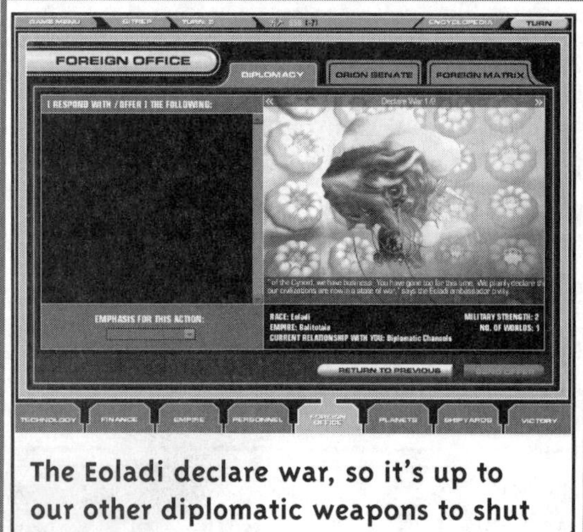

The Eoladi declare war, so it's up to our other diplomatic weapons to shut them down.

Galactic Expansion

We strike pay dirt with our exploration of the Tiam system. The third world in the system is a green 2 with moderate resources. More importantly, the Tiam system contains a wormhole to the other side of the galaxy. We can now use this portal to get away from the overcrowded situation we're in now. If no other aliens are out there, it'll be a wealthy place to colonize.

On turn 10, Tiam III joins the team. We'll leverage its decent resources into a stable economy and the beginnings of our first military ships. It might later become an important staging area for our trips into the wormhole.

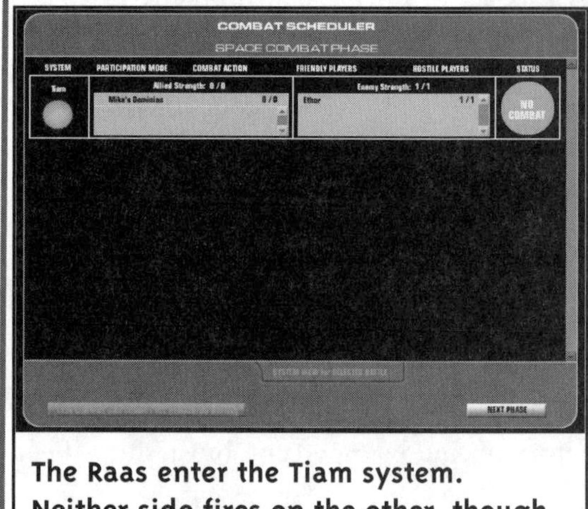

The Raas enter the Tiam system. Neither side fires on the other, though we'll have to watch that they don't try to steal our planet.

The following turn, the Raas come knocking on our door. There's a standoff in the Tiam system, where we just colonized a world. Neither side backs down, but neither opens fire on the other. We'll need to reinforce that system as soon as possible. We don't want the Raas stealing our world or taking control of the wormhole.

Taking Command

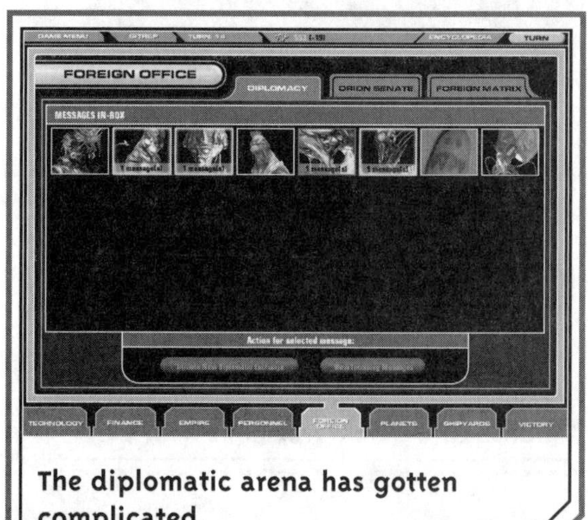

The diplomatic arena has gotten complicated.

As our economy gets rolling, another race, the Ithkul, have entered the political arena to further complicate matters. We're looking good. We currently have three trade agreements (with the Raas, Psilons, and Klackons), one non-aggression pact with the Trilarians, and one full alliance with the Nommo. The Eoladi still want our mechanical heads, and the Ithkul could be a problem down the road. All in all, we can't complain about the progress in our toughest area. If we keep following up on every conversation—and throwing some well-timed gifts in there—we should have more friends than enemies when it comes war time.

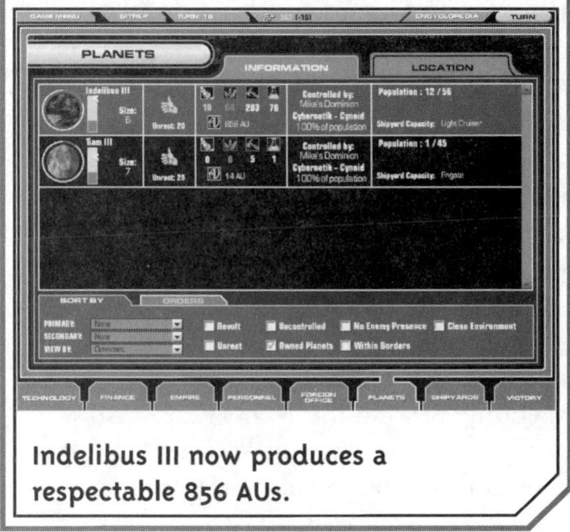

Indelibus III now produces a respectable 856 AUs.

Our starter colony on Tiam III still has a long time to develop, but our homeworld on Indelibus is flourishing. It now produces 856 AUs per turn and isn't having trouble spitting out what we desire.

With the Raas parked in our system, the Eoladi in a state of war, and the Ithkul hovering nearby, it's time to step up our military. For the foreseeable future, raise military to 50 percent, then set economic development at 20 percent and research at 8 percent. As you gain momentum, these numbers can be incrementally increased. We want to win the military race in the next dozen or so turns in case of attack. After that, we'll fortify our home system and the Tiam system, then head into the wormhole for greener pastures.

In the Technology realm, we need to specialize more. Lose mathematics for the time being to increase the war skills, energy, and physical sciences. Since we're close to three more advances in biology, we'll leave the push there until we get them. At that point, depending on our diplomatic situation, we might swap out points to energy or physical sciences.

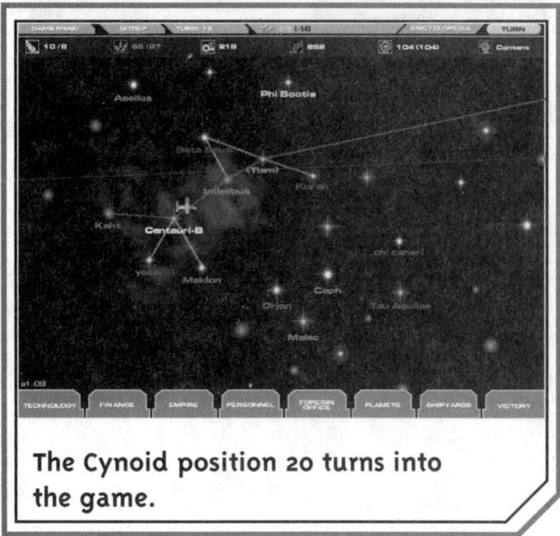

The Cynoid position 20 turns into the game.

Given space and no more than one enemy attacking you at the same time, the Cynoids are in position to steamroll the competition. Our economy is solid and will improve with the prospects on the far side of the wormhole. Defend what is yours with your very tough military units, and machine will triumph over flesh.

Playing the Sakkra

An insult is praise to the Sakkra. They are a demanding race and expect respect, and if they don't get it, they'll arrive in force to ask why. The Sakkra treat the military with almost religious fervor. It should be your primary focus, especially since you aren't that good in Bioharvesting, Diplomacy, and Trade.

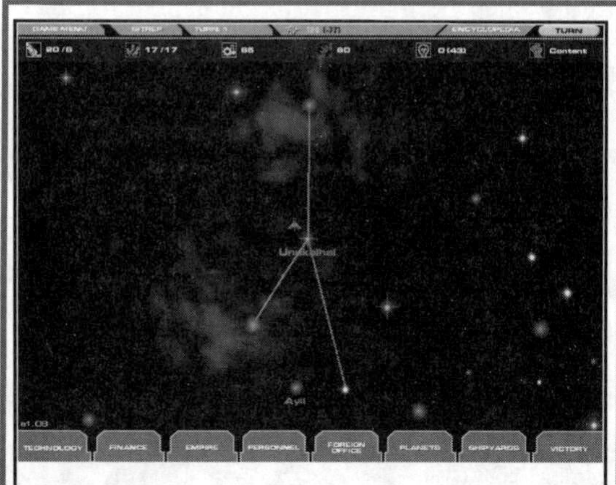

The Sakkra's home planet, Unukalhai VII, neighbors with one other race.

Your Homeworld

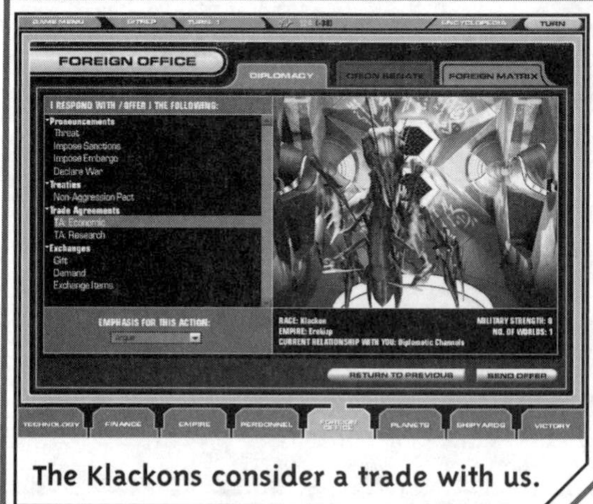

The Klackons consider a trade with us.

We only have one neighbor to worry about, the Klackons, so we should try a trade offer. The bugs aren't strong militarily. We'll offer them a trade, and if they don't take it, we'll give them something else to think about in the form of a gauss cannon.

Immediately our attention turns to military. We can't spend as much as we'd like—we don't want to tax our system with spending beyond the yellow range—so we settle for 10 percent military and 34 percent economic development. In our military building queues, we have two colony ships and a beam base. The colony ships will head out to new worlds to build up our infrastructure, and the beam base provides extra protection for our homeworld in case we have unexpected visitors.

Two problems keep us busy: mineral deficiency and unrest. Our planetary viceroy comes to the rescue and builds a Mining DEA to funnel more minerals into our industry. Unrest seems to come from our high taxes.

Under the Planets tab, we find our homeworld and tick down the tax rate two percent. It's important to bring our citizens in line now. We don't want a riot on our hands when we increase our Oppressometer later in response to an enemy using concentrated espionage against us.

The Klackons turn out not to be enemies. They respond favorably to our economic proposal, though they don't accept at this point. We can't complain if it keeps the bugs off our back.

The Klackon diplomat politely asks for more time to consider our economic proposal.

Urenean, an Imsaeis espionage trainer, joins our team. He offers a 10 percent improvement in spy Cloak rating and a 10 percent improvement in spy Luck. Since he has no drawbacks, let's keep him around until we dip into our spies later in the game.

Galactic Expansion

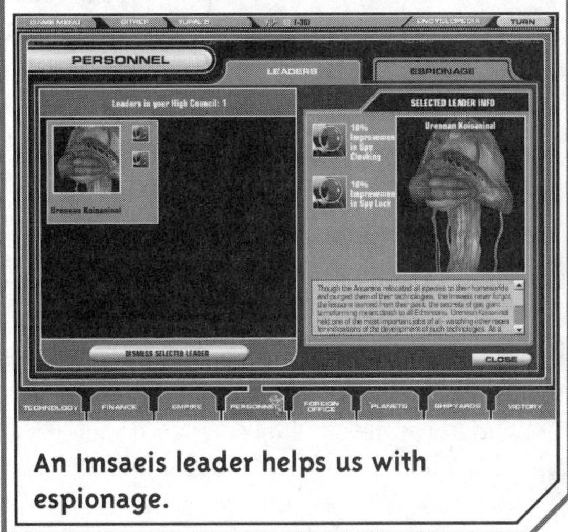

An Imsaeis leader helps us with espionage.

On turn six, we explore our first system that yields two barren planets. Our second system, a turn later, doesn't have hospitable planets, but it does have a wormhole. It becomes a valuable system to protect and watch in case of surprise attacks.

We've been thinking about military and exploration, and have neglected some of our other areas. A level four mathematics advance grants us free mass driver miniaturization technology, which reminds us to set our technology growth rates with the research sliders. As any good military race is apt to do, we set the sliders to 50 percent energy and 50 percent physical sciences. Our fleets and ground forces will appreciate the extra hardware.

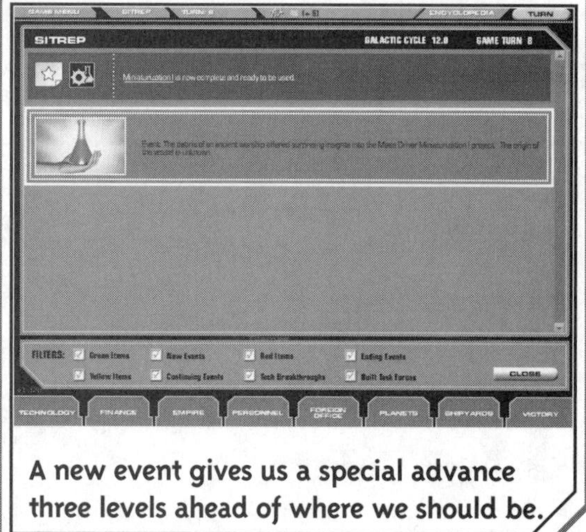

A new event gives us a special advance three levels ahead of where we should be.

Rumors of an Antaran Star Killer dip into our Imperial Treasury.

The Antarans, an elder civilization capable of technology we could only dream of, leave behind a technology cache on Ishi I. It's also a green world, so we'll colonize it and reap the rewards.

Ironically, the Antarans come back to bite us on turn 14. A random event claims pirates have gotten a hold of an Antaran Star Killer, a warship capable of destroying entire systems. If it's true, we're in trouble. Most likely, it's just a rumor and only stirs up panic. As a result, we drop taxes again to lighten up the citizens.

On turn 15, we decide minerals are a serious problem for us. Our industry can't be stopped, except by the lack of ore. We finally break down and colonize inside our system on Unukalhai I. It's rich in minerals, even if we have to deal with pollution and a yellow environment that will take moderate terraforming to make it suitable for Sakkra life.

We've gotta hand it to the bugs—they're slow but steady. It takes them 15 turns to finally respond to our economic trade. They agree, so we can both generate extra income from trade. It also means we can ignore that area of space and look to conquer the star systems around the wormhole.

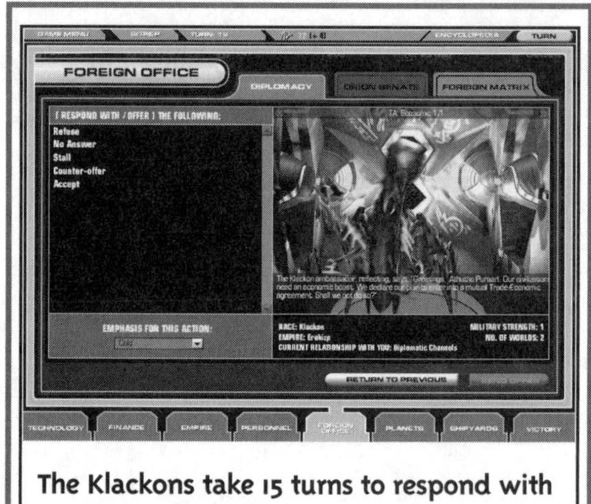

The Klackons take 15 turns to respond with a simple "yes" to our trade proposal.

Taking Command

A splinter colony in Phaet collects us our fifth world.

Our military has been hovering for a while, but now it's ready to soar. After collecting our fifth world, we have the assets to crank out two or three military units per turn. With five or six hawks and eagles ready, we design one long-range and one short-range task force. These task forces will lead the charge through the wormhole. Our conquest plan is to lay siege to everyone on that side. If things get nasty, we can always retreat and fortify at the Tilamas system, our designated chokepoint to hold off alien penetration into our sacred space.

It's time to design task forces and go on a conquest tour.

In the following turns, we'll increase the military until it's 60 percent of our spending. We don't have to worry about the Klackons, even if they choose to break our treaty. We can continue to expand our empire around the homeworld, until we run into a new neighbor. Then, we either have a new ally or, more likely, a new target. If left alone for another 20 or 30 turns, there's no telling how much military we can pile up.

If we advance wisely, many of the other races will have wiped each other out by the time we reach them. One to one, no one should be able to withstand our firepower. We have to be careful about running into a powerful alliance, but that's why we're keeping the Klackons in tow. We'll let them advance slowly on their own and, if things get dangerous, they'll have no choice but to join us against alien invaders. We might not be smart diplomats, but the Sakkra are cunning survivalists.

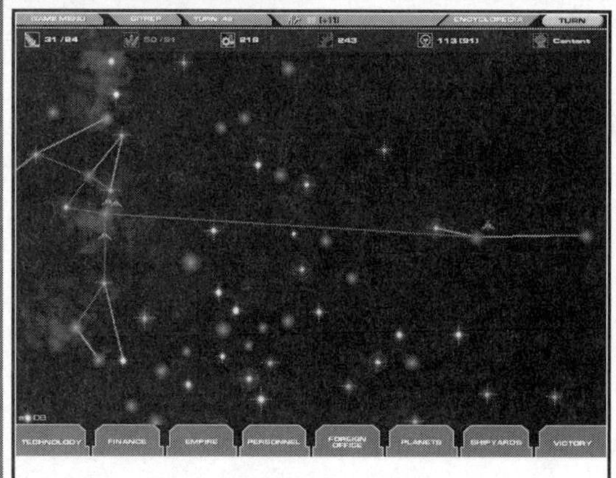

With a military juggernaut in place, we take our attack through the wormhole and into the unknown.

Playing the Raas

The Raas are the politically incorrect of the bunch. They don't treat their environment kindly, abusing it with all methods of industry and pollution. They excel in Manufacturing and Trade, raking in the money, and when they've used a planet's potential, they move on to the next disposable planet. They're never wanting for trade opportunities because of their strong ties with the other races.

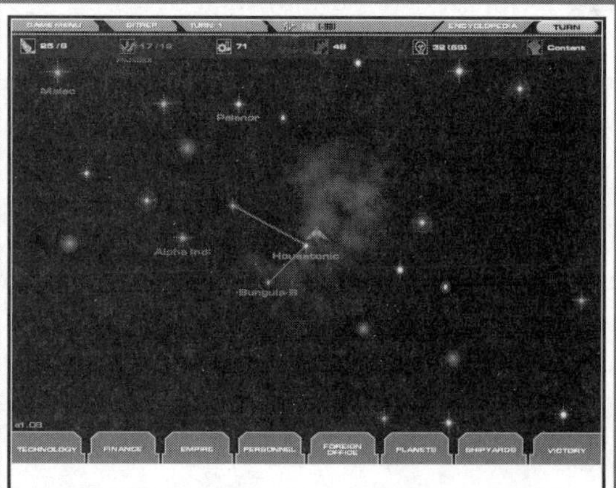

The Raas begin in the Housatonic system, near the heart of the galaxy. They have nine neighbors!

Your Homeworld

We're surrounded. The Raas start on Housatonic I, but there's not much room with nine neighbors. Good thing we have decent Diplomacy skills or we'd be space junk.

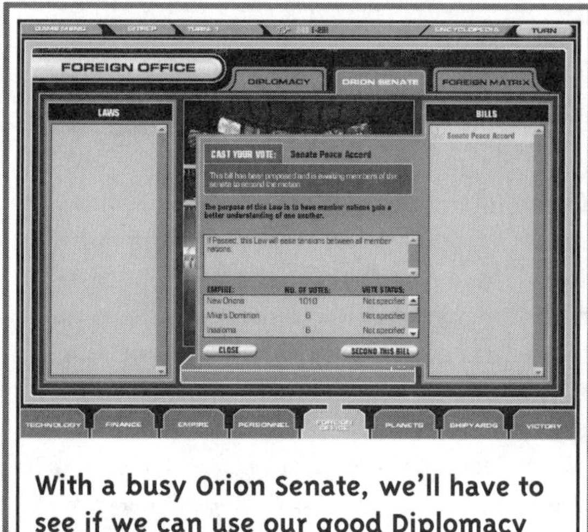

With a busy Orion Senate, we'll have to see if we can use our good Diplomacy skills to get ahead.

The Orion Senate is key. We can rally support for ourselves here and get assistance from like-minded powers. If someone decides to act out against an ally, we can reduce their political standing so that every move will be a violation of a treaty. The economic and political ramifications will ruin them.

We don't want war—at least not when we aren't prepared for it—so we second the Senate peace proposal. This proposal, if passed, reduces tension among all members and attempts to keep the peace. We'll push for this to become a law to buy us more time.

Our first setback comes from the Nommo. Without provocation, they hit us with economic sanctions. Still, we won't give up on our talks with them or the others. We start out trying to get economic negotiations going with all the races. Any boost to our economy is a big plus when we only have a couple hundred AUs to work with. Later, we'll look to strengthen our military situation with alliances. One exception to that rule is the New Orions. They own all the technological advances at the start of the game, so we want to trade with them in a technological capacity. Strike a deal like that and you'll bump your society ahead by 100 turns.

We can only pump up our economic slider to 29 percent before we leave the yellow and start paying too much. Even so, that's where we keep it, with zero percent in military, for now. It's important to get your economic infrastructure in shape, even at the expense of military early on.

Galactic Expansion

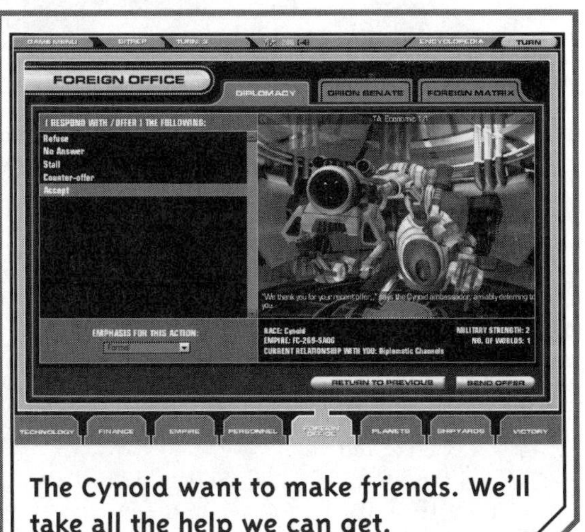

The Cynoid want to make friends. We'll take all the help we can get.

An expedition into the Bungula-B system meets with disaster. The Ithkul are lying in wait and destroy our ship shortly after it transmits a warning. No one wants to be one system away from the Ithkul homeworld, so this game is going to require all the skill and planning we can muster to survive.

Bad luck. Our immediate neighbors are the militaristic Ithkul.

In the Senate, the peace accord comes up and we vote yes. Fortunately, it does pass the next turn and cools everyone's tempers . . . for the time being.

Our second scout fleet could have met with disaster if the Tachidi didn't get along with us. We discover their homeworld on Altair I and, miraculously, we don't get shot out of the sky. As a thank you, we don't linger and set out for home on the next turn.

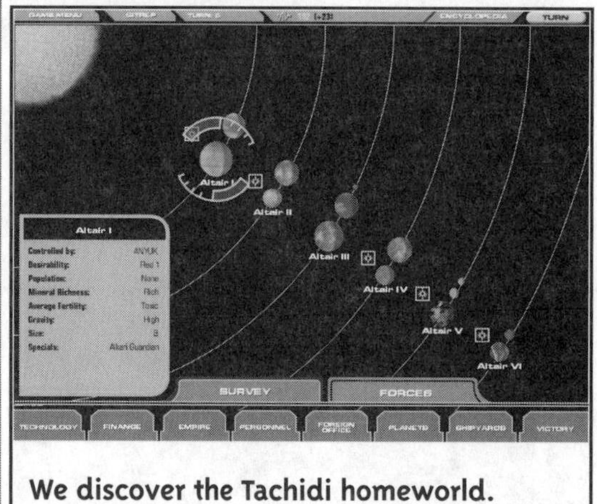

We discover the Tachidi homeworld. Luckily, they don't mind that we examine the system, and no fighting takes place.

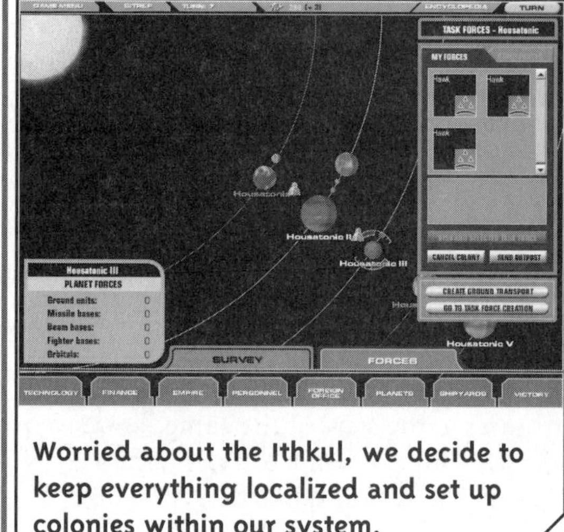

Worried about the Ithkul, we decide to keep everything localized and set up colonies within our system.

Our first colony finally settles its roots on Housatonic IV. It's very rich in mineral content, has fertile soil, and hits in the green. We couldn't ask for more, but we get it anyway. Two of the other worlds in our own system are in the green, too, so there are possibilities for rapid economic growth in our backyard.

Instead of the usual "expand and conquer" theory, the Raas think smaller. The Ithkul could strike at any moment, and there isn't room to move safely around here, so we're going to build only in our home system. Normally, you couldn't do it because there wouldn't be enough hospitable worlds, and the cost to terraform planets in the yellow or red would be enormous. With four out of five Housatonic worlds being green, we get decent colonies that we can keep under the protection of one massive fleet.

The only question is: Can we build up fast enough to challenge the mighty Ithkul? Diplomacy becomes more critical than ever to get others involved in our fight.

Taking Command

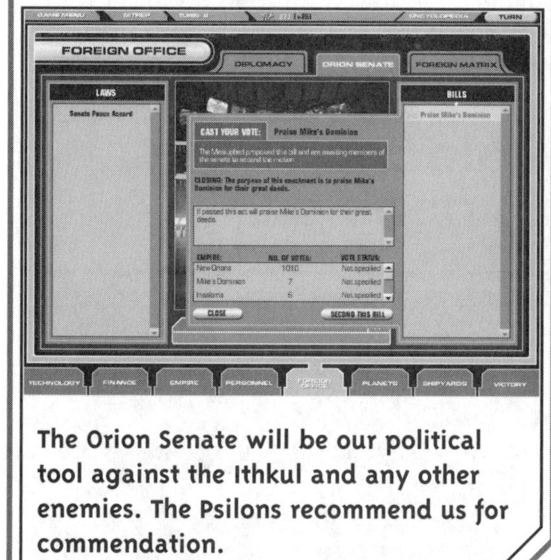

The Orion Senate will be our political tool against the Ithkul and any other enemies. The Psilons recommend us for commendation.

Diplomatic relations are coming along fine. The Psilons vote for a Raas commendation—always a positive sign. The Cynoids and the Grendarls, two military powerhouses, have active trade routes open with us. A little more convincing and we can share a defensive alliance with at least one of them.

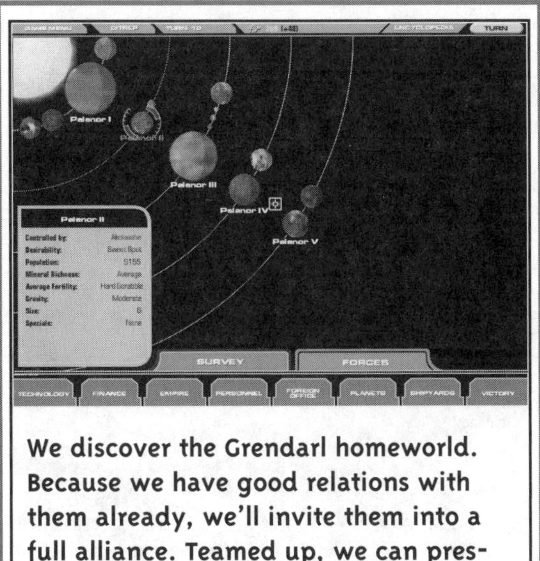

We discover the Grendarl homeworld. Because we have good relations with them already, we'll invite them into a full alliance. Teamed up, we can present a united front against common enemies.

As predicted, the Ithkul attack in force. They go for the throat, sending three warships after our homeworld. We're ready. We've kept all our new fleets at home and designed a special eagle task force to blast them at long range. The combat comes down to five Raas ships against three Ithkul ships and it's not even close. Our faster ships can outflank and deal significant damage to the Ithkul's tougher ships and slow them down. Like piranha, we strip them apart bulkhead by bulkhead.

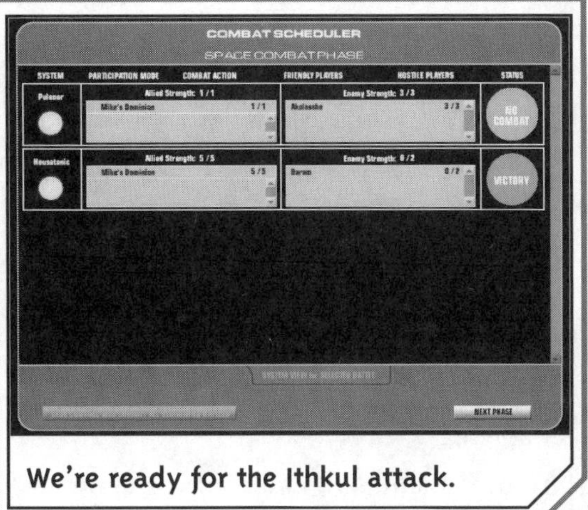

We're ready for the Ithkul attack.

That's just the beginning. The Ithkul are already rebuilding; they live for war and death. We didn't take any losses, but that doesn't mean the next fight won't devastate us. We need to beef up the defenses, and we do so by turning all four of our Housatonic colonies into war machines. Now, our focus has flip-flopped. We want military on full power to protect our assets. After we have an ample amount, we'll switch back to economic development and hope to enter a more peaceful time in which we can dominate through our top-ranked Manufacturing and Trade skills.

With so many major powers on top of each other, the winner will be the one with the most friends. When you enter into larger battles, your odds of success increase exponentially if you add your allies' fleets to the total. As the Raas, we want to ensure that no matter what, the Grendarls, Psilons, and Tachidi stay happy. Together we can wipe out the scourge that is the Ithkul.

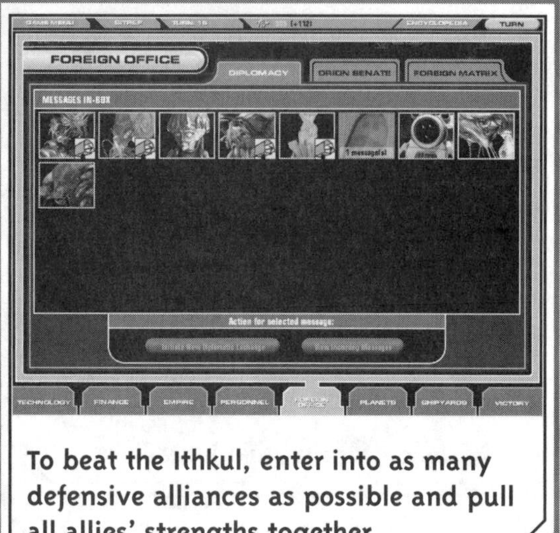

To beat the Ithkul, enter into as many defensive alliances as possible and pull all allies' strengths together.

Playing the Grendarl

The Grendarls and the Sakkras rival the Ithkul for raw military power. Collect those planets, pump up that Manufacturing, and throw in a little Trade skill for good measure and the Grendarls become a fearsome force in the middle to late game. They don't deal well with the other races—mostly because they get taken advantage of so often—so keep a safe distance away from anyone you don't trust.

Alshain-A, the Grendarl homeworld, lies next to the Orion system in the galaxy's heart.

Your Homeworld

An immediate splinter colony doubles your starting worlds and kicks off our Grendarl game.

If you could ask for one way to start a game, it would be like this. We're given a gift in an instant splinter colony. Instead of one homeworld, we actually begin with two. The first, Alshain-A VII, holds most of our economic power. It needs to gain a Mining DEA or two to keep up with demand, but other than that it looks productive. The second world, Alshain-A V, has nothing going for it yet but a population of three and a blank slate to build anything you want.

Our home system isn't done giving yet. Alshain-A II is a sweet-spot world *and* it has rich minerals and rare gems. A veritable gold mine . . . if we dare set foot on the surface.

Rapid rot consumes the planet and that means building and maintenance costs are increased by 20 to 200 percent. It's a toss-up whether it's worth it or not. You don't know how much the rapid rot will cost you until you start to colonize there. Still, there are tangible rewards just sitting there, so we'll take a chance and colonize our third world in-system.

As a precaution against enemy espionage, we click the Oppressometer up two notches. If you can get away with it, set the Oppressometer higher than the norm. You'll have to cut the tax rate back but you'll gain the peace of mind that random espionage events won't spoil your plans. The more aliens nearby, the more imperative it is to follow this course of action.

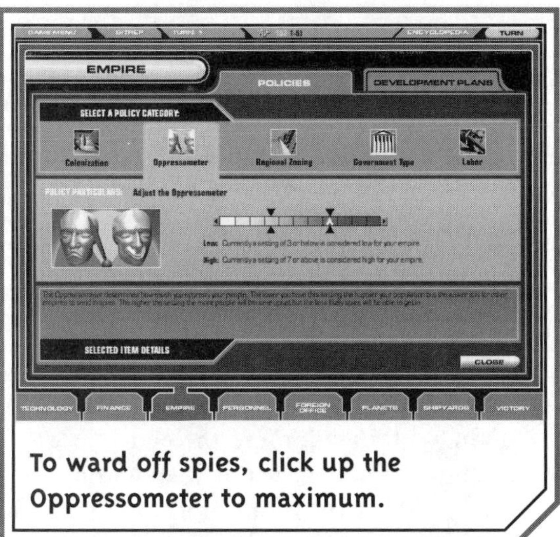

To ward off spies, click up the Oppressometer to maximum.

On turn two, the Nommo sanction us. We'll ignore them for now and focus on Technology. Just in case of early war and because the Grendarls excel in military, energy and physical sciences get 50 percent each. We can always spend in other schools later.

The Grendarls have four neighbors, and one of them, the Nommo, immediately sanction us.

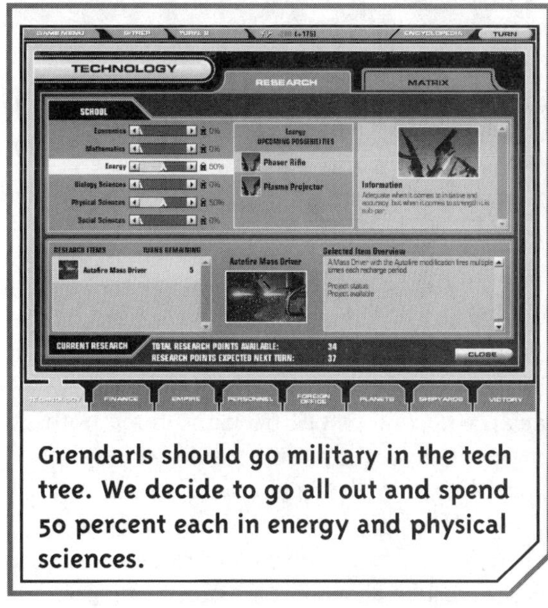

Grendarls should go military in the tech tree. We decide to go all out and spend 50 percent each in energy and physical sciences.

Under the Planets screen, we need to make some alterations. On Alshain-A VII, we raise military spending to 20 percent and economic development to 30 percent. To avoid the Oppressometer backlash, we lower taxes by two percent. On Alshain-A V, we do similar adjustments, except we pour 76 percent into terraforming. The splinter colony, though in the green, isn't in the sweet spot. To increase future production, we'll spend a little money on perfecting the environment.

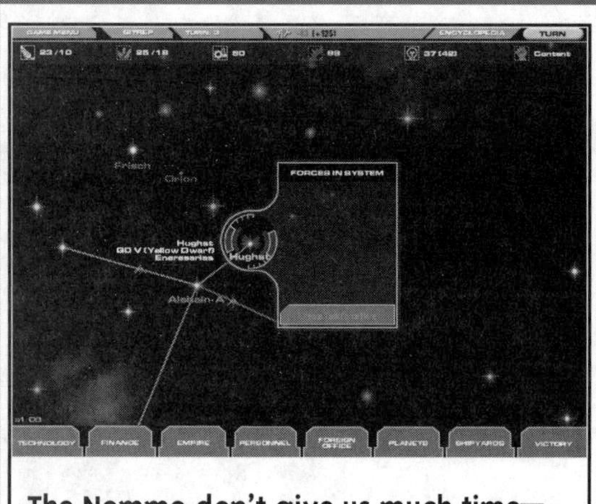

The Nommo don't give us much time—they declare war on turn three. Because their homeworld borders ours, it's a serious problem.

On turn three, we're already at war. The squids don't like us. This can be a serious problem because their homeworld borders on ours. When a threat is a single space lane away, you can't just sit back and hope nothing happens. Expect the worst and plan accordingly. With the Nommo, we know they're the worst-ranked military race, so if we can keep even with them in the arms race, we should be all right. As a precaution, we'll beef up military more.

And it's not just the Nommo who are on the warpath. A "declare total war" proposal hits the Orion Senate floor. If voted for, the Imsaeis and a race not on our map will erupt into galactic war. We're caught in the middle of major turmoil.

Galactic Expansion

The Nommo force us to spend more than we want on military.

Our spies are ready for insertion on turn five. When you don't have a lot of military, especially at the beginning of the game, espionage can be an effective substitute. Pay for four spies at the start and rotate more into the mix as the current ones get trained. We buy two military, one political, and one scientific spy. Anyone want to guess which spineless race they'll be heading for first?

While we send our spies out, we talk cease fire with the Nommo through diplomatic channels. Even if we plan on attacking, there's no reason not to quiet them down and hopefully delay an attack.

At the Nommo border, one of our military spies is caught. He doesn't crack under interrogation—if he did, the Nommo would know we'd sent him and probably launch an attack before we were ready. The Nommo do execute him, however, so we need to create more.

While our spies infiltrate the Nommo, we try to lull them to sleep with a "cease fire" proposition.

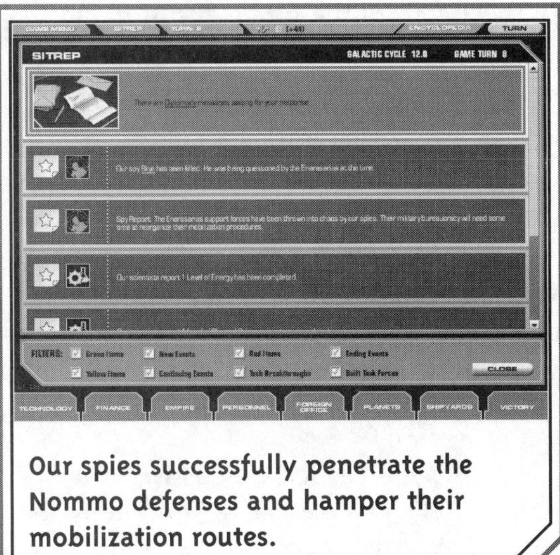

Our spies successfully penetrate the Nommo defenses and hamper their mobilization routes.

We have success on the next turn. Our second military spy blew up mobilization stations so they can't maneuver their troops as well. If we keep this up, the Nommo won't muster any respectable force whatsoever.

Taking Command

In the future, our first priority is to wipe out the Nommo. The rest of our immediate neighbors seem to be fine; the squids won't be calmed down, though. Our three active colonies will produce as much military as possible. Alshain-A II and Alshain-A V can only build slowly. Alshain-A VII can safely spend 60 percent or more on military, even at the expense of whatever the planetary viceroy had planned. We can't waste time. A strike now could cripple the Nommo.

If we launch a powerful fleet now, we can bombard their homeworld and absorb its remaining assets into our empire. With a big boost like that early, we should be the dominant power in our sector. By the time another threat rolls around, we'll be a military juggernaut.

Our attack fleet launches toward the Nommo's Hughst home system.

Playing the Trilarian

The pressure of the deep is, apparently, good for the brain. An underwater race, the Trilarian excel at Research, and their Bioharvesting and Environmental skills rank good. Unfortunately, when it comes to military, they fail miserably. Better that they stay hidden under the seas, than face a Grendarl armada. Hopping from water planet to water planet, the Trilarian meet up with other races while in space, a position not entirely comfortable for the fish people.

The Trilarian home system of Inari has great access to an uncharted region of space.

Your Homeworld

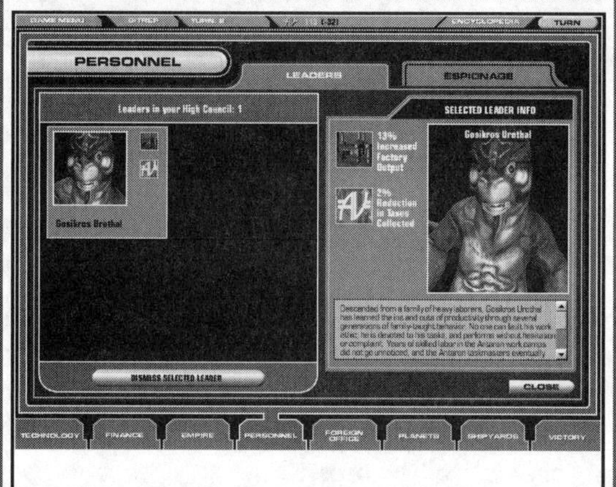

Nothing develops inside the Trilarian home system. The only productive encounter for the turn is the introduction of a new Raas leader.

There's no place like home, except in the Inari system. Inari II is the only possible colonization spot. It's green, and well, that's the only thing it has going for it. It also has active volcanoes and poor mineral richness, so we won't land there any time soon. To find the minerals needed for a higher level of industry and Research, we'll have to journey out of system.

A Raas leader, Gosikros, arrives and immediately increases factory output by 13 percent. We lose two percent taxes to him as a fee, but it is well worth the industrial advantage.

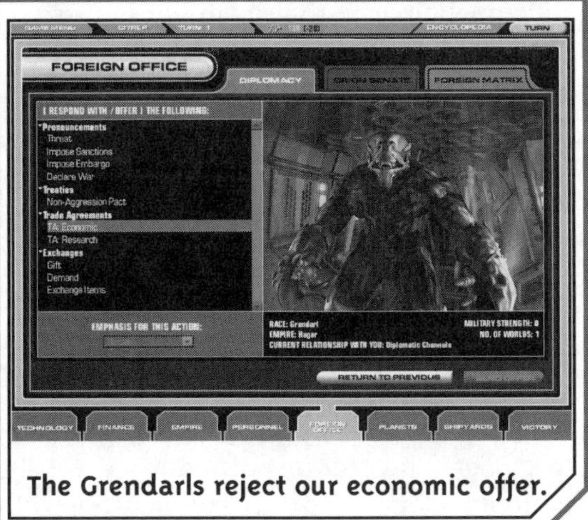

The Grendarls reject our economic offer.

The Grendarls are going to be a problem. Combat comes naturally to them, so they'll strike out at anything that moves. Even so, it's Diplomacy time, and we choose the least offensive proposal we can think of—economic trade. We figure that both our races will benefit from some interstellar trade. The Grendarls obviously don't see it that way since the offer comes back rejected on the following turn. Judging from the Grendarl ambassador's dismissal, it could mean war in the near future.

Technology is the Trilarian strongpoint. One approach to tech development, especially if you can excel quickly and have lots of time, is to spread out in many areas and wait to see what the first few levels reveal. If a key advance shows up—for example, the space port in the physical sciences—devote a higher percentage to that school and climb to the advance in a hurry. We'll try this and watch carefully for what advances are revealed first.

Galactic Expansion

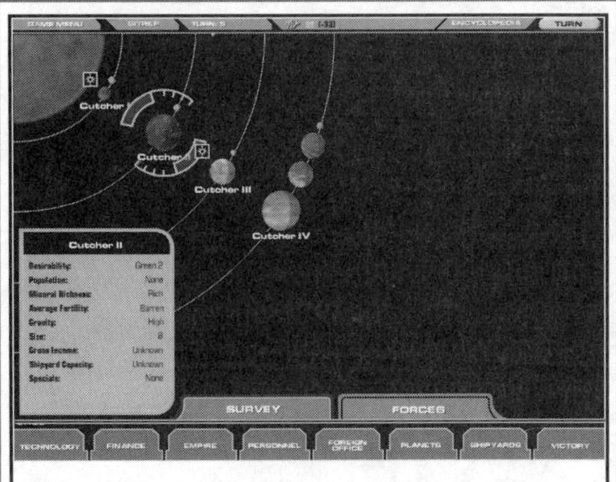

Our exploration fleets head away from the Grendarl. The Cutcher system has the minerals we need.

Common sense tells us not to send our scouts toward the Grendarl. There are three new systems in the other direction, and they're probably in better locations because they're on the fringe of populated space.

One by one we explore them. The Crux system holds a planet with a technology special. It could be promising. As usual though, the planet lies in the red range—hostile to our species—and can't be colonized without great effort. The second system, Cutcher, is a winner. The system's second planet lies in the green and has rich minerals. Our homeworld has been deficient in minerals from the start, and this could be the missing piece in our financial puzzle. The third system holds another tech special without hope of colonization.

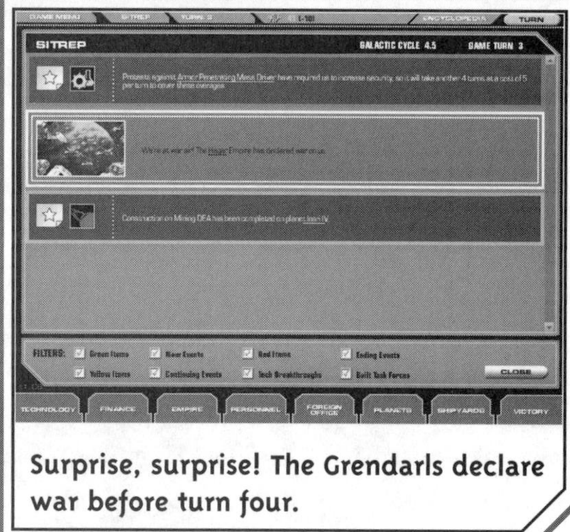

Surprise, surprise! The Grendarls declare war before turn four.

We don't think the Grendarl even listened to our economic proposal. They've eyed us from the beginning as a juicy target. Well, we won't go down lightly. Their declaration of war is just the excuse we need to mobilize our military. We have the tech advantage, they have the size advantage—let's see who wins . . . .

Cutcher II comes onboard as the second world under our influence. If we can mine it fast enough, we can transform our industry into a real machine and crank out more AUs than ants at an Imperial picnic.

On turn eight, we step up the military builds. There's a colony ship still in the queue and rather than waste the money already spent on it, we continue with its construction. After that, we switch to eagles. Once those ships are ready, we'll design some task forces just for the Grendarls.

All this military activity pushes us into the red as far as economic spending goes. Dropping 40 percent on economic development and 40 percent on military will dry up our Imperial Treasury in a dozen turns. Yes, it's all worth it to get the jump on the Grendarls.

Despite the drain on our finances, it's time to construct a formidable military.

Our scout stops at Pelenor, an ideal chokepoint for watching a second avenue into the galactic core.

After exploring the Crux system, our scout stops in Pelenor. We don't want to stretch too thin. Pelenor is the perfect chokepoint, as it contains two space lanes to the galactic core and one to a splinter system. Our scout stays put to identify any trouble heading from that direction.

To recover from an earthquake on our homeworld, we colonize Iras IV.

On turn 11, an earthquake rips apart our homeworld. Thousands of lives are lost, and the center of our economic infrastructure crumbles as we lose key buildings. If we didn't have the backup colony on Cutcher II, this could be game over for us.

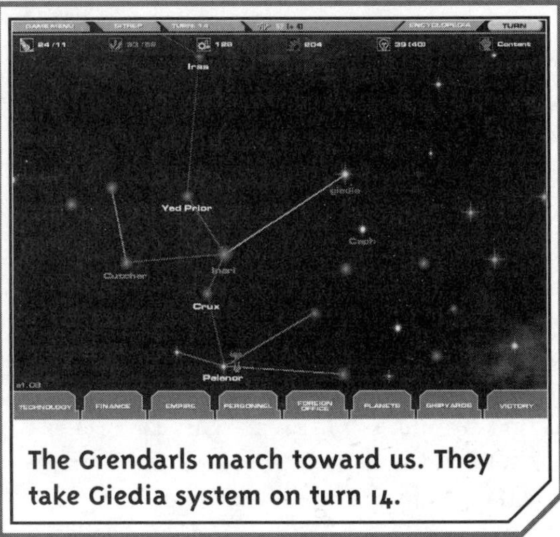

The Grendarls march toward us. They take Giedia system on turn 14.

To make matters worse, the Grendarls seize the Giedia system. Now they're only one jump away from our homeworld. Will they strike at us next? What is our next course of action? How much time do we have before extinction stares us in the face?

Taking Command

Like a harbinger of victory, the Ithkul leader Haunaukogrg brings scientific secrets with him and increases our Research by 10 percent per turn. Already our research teams have developed armor-penetrating lasers, hand blasters, and fighter armor for the war effort. Our technology has to outmatch the Grendarls'—it's our only hope.

The invasion strikes on turn 20. The Grendarls send two fleets to attack our homeworld. We're waiting for them. Two fleets can't win against our three and better armament. There are no survivors on the Grendarl side.

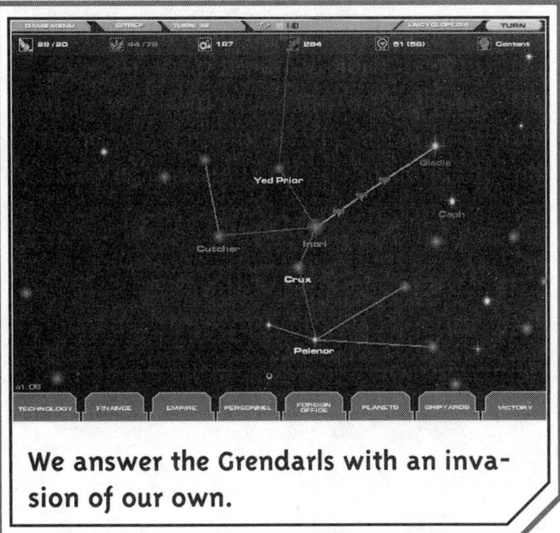

We answer the Grendarls with an invasion of our own.

As payback, we devote the next 12 turns to creating fleet task forces. One by one, they arrive in orbit, ready for a mission they might not come back from. If we are to survive, it's obvious that the Grendarls have to go. Our Research has been sizzling along, and with the setback the Grendarls faced in our home system, we think now is the time to press the attack. On turn 32, three long-range attack forces launch in a massive counterstrike against the Grendarl homeworld.

Once a peaceful people, the Trilarian are the most dangerous kind of fighters when forced to take up arms. Add scientific might to military force and you have a recipe for galactic destruction.

Playing the Nommo

Arakus III is the homeworld for the Nommo.

The Nommo military has no backbone—and they're not the bravest of groups either. They're in the basement when it comes to military confrontations. The other powers would walk all over the Nommo if they weren't so darn good at so many other things. Superior Bioharvesting and Diplomacy mean lots of food and bartering for the rest of its civilization needs. Top-of-the-line Research gives the Nommo a shot at fighting back. If they can supply enough high-tech weaponry to their limp grunts, the Nommo might, conceivably, possibly do some damage.

Your Homeworld

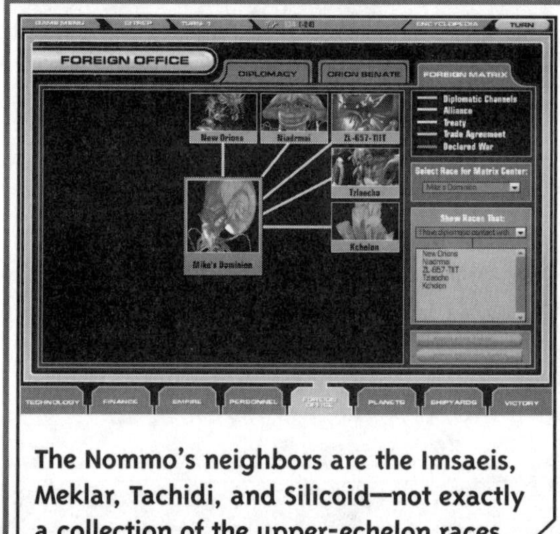

The Nommo's neighbors are the Imsaeis, Meklar, Tachidi, and Silicoid—not exactly a collection of the upper-echelon races.

Arakus III hosts the Nommo's first civilization. It's located in the middle of the galaxy but near one of the edges, so there should be room for expansion. It's got an average mineral rating and hard scrabble for soil—not the best of conditions to work with—so we'll have to nurse the planet's economy along in the early game.

Our immediate neighbors—the Imsaeis, Meklar, Tachidi, and Silicoid—are ranked near the bottom on our race depth chart (see Chapter 2). That gives us a little leeway; we don't have to work at the super speed we would to keep up with stronger races such as the Ithkul or the Cynoid.

First, we need to work on our food supply and take advantage of our superior Bioharvesting.

Bioharvesting and Research are our strong suits, so let's concentrate on them first. Under the planetary economics tab, let's drop military down to zero. We're not any good at it, so why waste money? If we have extra to spare later, we'll buy a fleet or two and see if we can win a fight. Crank economics up to 40 percent to increase funding for our Bioharvesting production. After we deal with a mineral deficiency and add another Mining DEA, we might consider plopping down another food DEA to have a huge surplus of goods.

It's a necessary evil to advance in energy and physical sciences. Although our military lacks power, there are too many problems with giving up on the military disciplines early. You might have that luxury later, once you've come up with an alternative game plan to military strength. Right now, we have to leave it as an option in case someone attacks us. In addition to the "necessary evils," we'll try economics and biological sciences to exploit our natural aptitude in Bioharvesting.

A minor annoyance shows up on turn five. A yellow unrest symbol pops up unexpectedly. We haven't really done anything too wacky. It turns out that our taxes are too high—the usual cause of unrest—so we click down taxes by two percentage points and that solves our dilemma.

We'll train our Nommo scientists in economics, energy, biological sciences, and physical sciences. Our Research abilities are second to none.

Galactic Expansion

Our empire is moving according to plan. By turn eight we discover a world for our next colony, invent some new technologies, and make friends with the Imsaeis.

What's wrong with this picture? We're on turn eight and no major disaster yet. It's quite the opposite. In the Wesen system, we discover a world to place our next colony. It's a green 2 with fertile soil—a suitable alternative world for our people. Once our population gets high enough, we'll set our migration policy to Wesen II, and people will begin to colonize it on their own. Technologies are appearing like clockwork. The Imsaeis take kindly to our words of economic trade, so a friendship is blossoming.

Our rate of expansion is far exceeding what you would normally expect. Three nearby worlds are ripe for colonization. One, Gomaki I, contains two specials: rare metals and erratic weather. To get the benefit from the rare metals—20 percent boost to Research and space port efficiency, when we get one—we'd have to live through erratic weather. The negative special hits Bioharvesting with a -25 to -75 percent penalty. For any society that relies on Bioharvesting, that's too devastating. Yes, you could terraform the erratic weather away, but it's such an investment that we'll have to pass on Gomaki I.

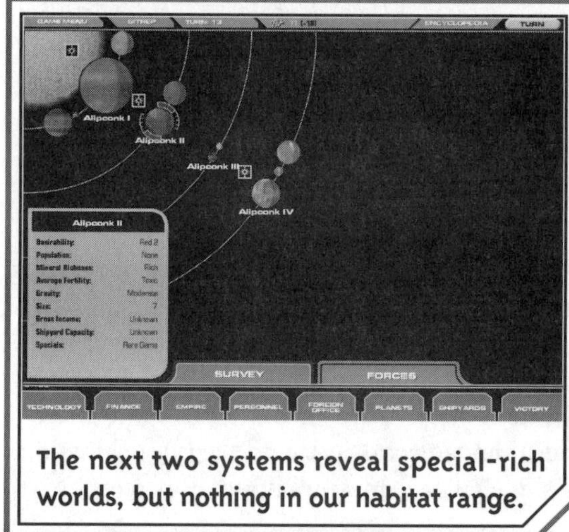

The next two systems reveal special-rich worlds, but nothing in our habitat range.

The next two systems we race to reveal specials galore, but no instantly habitable worlds. We don't want to spend time terraforming an environment just to live in it; there are plenty of worlds in the galaxy. Alipconk II is loaded with rare gems, but it's a red 2. Theta Reticuli V holds both archaeological ruins and rare metals; unfortunately, the environment's only a yellow 1 and can't sustain us without expense.

Our first military conflict ends in total annihilation—for us.

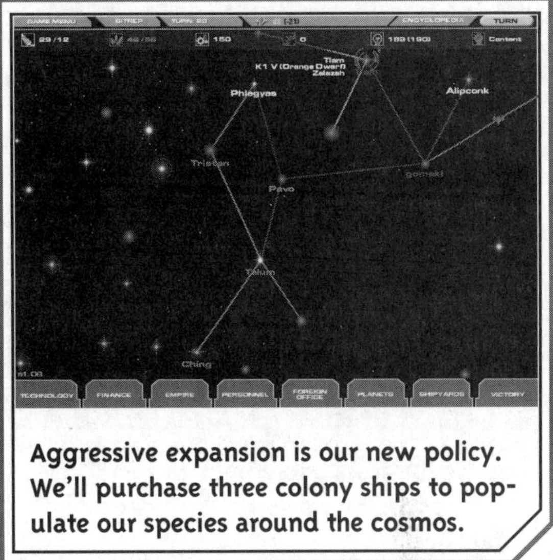

Aggressive expansion is our new policy. We'll purchase three colony ships to populate our species around the cosmos.

On turn 15, the Sakkra show up. We bump into them in the Ching system, and their fleet annihilates us. I don't think we even got a shot off. It's time to beat a hasty retreat and look for territory elsewhere. The Nommo shouldn't be above running away from a fight; they can win the game with their other resources.

Taking Command

Expansion continues to boom. Our new strategy is to take advantage of all the open systems we've discovered. We want colonies in as many of them as possible. We might not be able to defend them all, but if we're left alone long enough, the profit from those worlds will be staggering. The shift goes to "military spending," not for attack fleets but for colony ships. If we can build five or six ships and start that many new worlds, we can become the economic power in the region.

At this point, it's wise to switch your technology emphasis. We still don't want to give up energy or physical sciences. If our expansion plan works, we'll have ample military later on to augment with good advances. Instead, we lose economics and gain social sciences. We can dip into espionage to slow down our enemies. When we're ready to attack, the spies can supplement our military and make our attacks seem more effective.

The Nommo are far from done, even if our direction pushes us farther and farther away from our homeworld. We don't want to abandon it; Arakus III is too much of a prize for any race. We'll continue to support it defensively. However, there might come a time in the distant future when our homeworld won't actually be Arakus III.

Using our superior Diplomacy, we should stay in good favor with everyone in the region except the aggressive Sakkra. Maintaining alliances is crucial, as we can turn one against the other and weaken them all before we

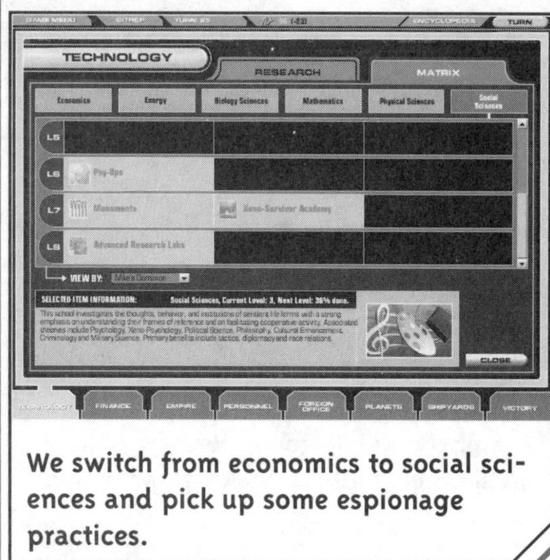

We switch from economics to social sciences and pick up some espionage practices.

make our ultimate move. Though we appear weak in strength, the Nommo are mighty in intelligence and savvy.

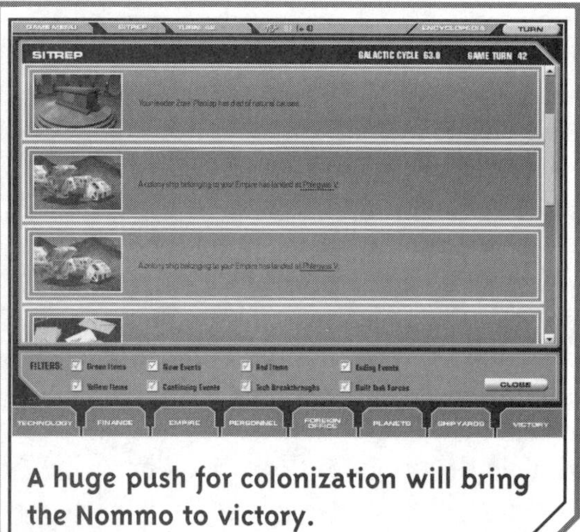

A huge push for colonization will bring the Nommo to victory.

Playing the Imsaeis

Floating around in gas giants can get tiresome if there's nothing to do. To avoid utter boredom, the Imsaeis like to tend their environment and sharpen their Bioharvesting skills. Not much for Research or Manufacturing, the Imsaeis enjoy speaking with other races and making deals to pick up the slack in their economy. Concentrate on the planet's ecology and avoid military confrontations unless you're not fond of your tentacles.

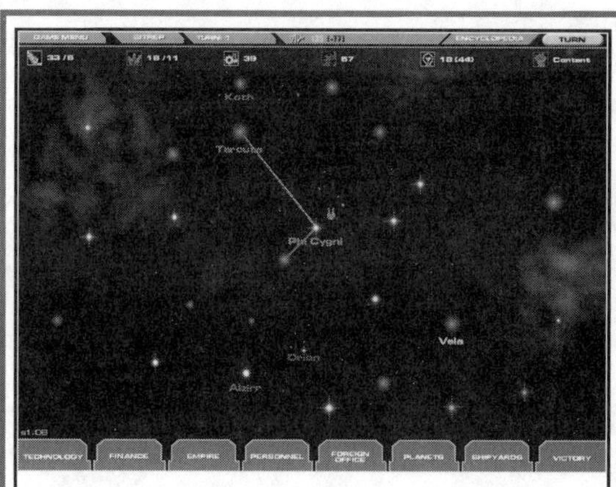

The Imsaeis and their turkey-like ships call the Phi Cygni system home.

Your Homeworld

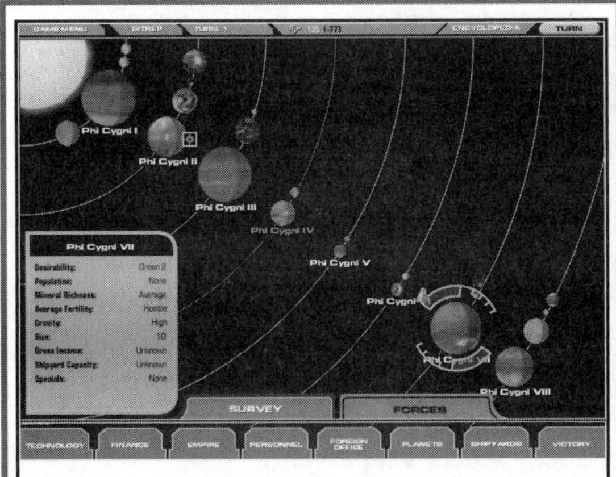

In our system, we'll try to make Phi Cygni VII work despite its hostile fertility conditions. It'll be a money pit at first.

Checking around our home system, as you should always do early in the game, we discover a lot of nothing. The best planet is Phi Cygni VII, which lies in the green but has hostile soil. Because the galaxy looks tight with a lot of neighbors, colonize at least one more world inside our home system. So, Phi Cygni VII it is. It'll take a lot of money to terraform it, but its size 10 will come in handy should we ever decide to design large ships.

Speaking of military, we'll keep it to a minimum. The Imsaeis rank at the bottom in military might, tied with the Nommo. Our superior Diplomacy will have to guide us through difficult times.

On the diplomatic front, we have six other races to speak with from the Orion Senate. The New Orions choose to ignore us. The Meklars, Klackons, and Humans seem frosty; we'll have to work on them. We need a big brother so we can gain access to defensive fleet power, and the Sakkra are the military powerhouse in the region. We'll start with a non-aggression treaty and work our way up to full alliance. If they don't listen to reason—or in the Sakkra's case, demands—we'll dip into the treasury and send gifts their way. Whatever it takes to get the Sakkra military on our side, we'll do.

Who knows if our neighbors in Tarcuta are friendly? Our scouts team up and head the opposite way.

On the second turn, the Meklars are already imposing trading restrictions on us. On the other hand, the Nommo send us an economic treaty. The Meklars look like a lost cause.

Galactic Expansion

On turn three, we discover a wormhole in the Remus system. It gives us quick access to other systems—good news, considering we haven't found a world that has fertile soil.

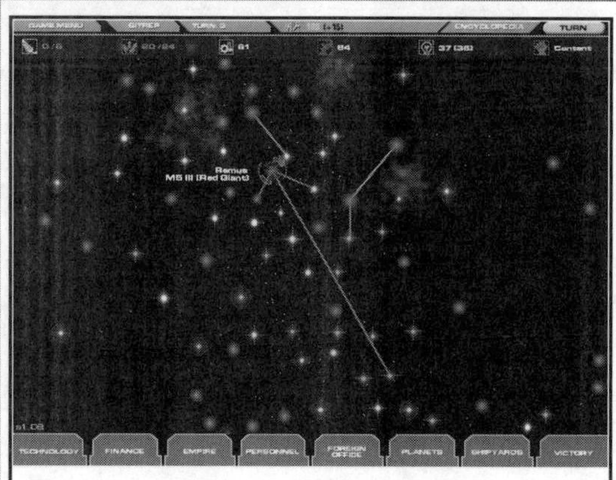
No luck with fertile planets. Hopefully, the wormhole in the Remus system will lead to greener pastures.

Problems creep in: On turn four, the Meklars declare war. We expected to deal with this hassle early. We'll step up our talks with the other powers and take disagreements with the Meklars to the Orion Senate and try to keep them shut down there.

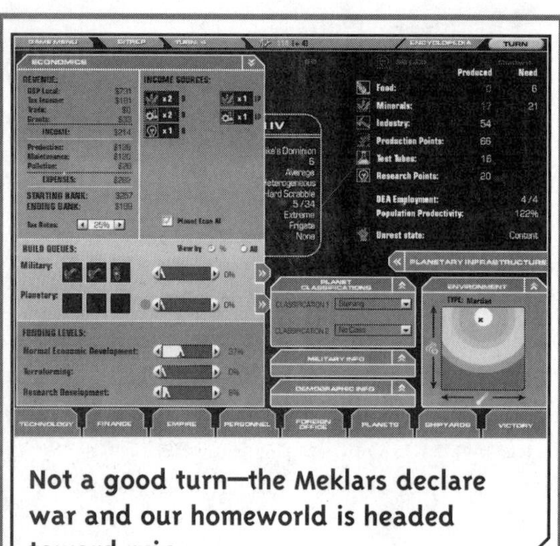
Not a good turn—the Meklars declare war and our homeworld is headed toward ruin.

More importantly, our homeworld is rapidly declining. Food and minerals are in shortages. If we don't do something immediately, it'll fall into ruins. We bump up economic development to 37 percent, still in the yellow and still effective spending.

On turn five, our negotiations bear fruit. The Sakkra and the Humans both wish to talk economic trade. The income we can generate from two trade partners puts us ahead of the growth curve. It seems the races do like us when even the warmongering Ithkul send a leader to us. Athezrulos increases factory output by 10 percent, but reduces taxes by 5 percent.

We can breathe easier on turns six and seven. The Nommo and Humans both accept non-aggression pacts. Usually, with committed Diplomacy, you can work a non-aggression pact into a defensive treaty of some sort. With the Nommo, Humans, and hopefully Sakkra on our side, the Meklars better watch their mechanical step. Our first colony forms on Phi Cygni VII; it's our first new world in a series of many.

The Nommo and Humans accept our non-aggression pacts. Our plan for strong allies is working.

Up to this point, we've been searching for worlds with fertile soil to take advantage of our Bioharvesting skills. Meanwhile, the Imsaeis homeworld continues to decline right under our noses. Our planetary viceroy had two problems to deal with—lack of food and lack of minerals. He chose to deal with the former by filling the planet full of new Mining DEAs. By the time we pay close attention, our population is dropping like flies. The viceroy was excommunicated, leaving us in charge.

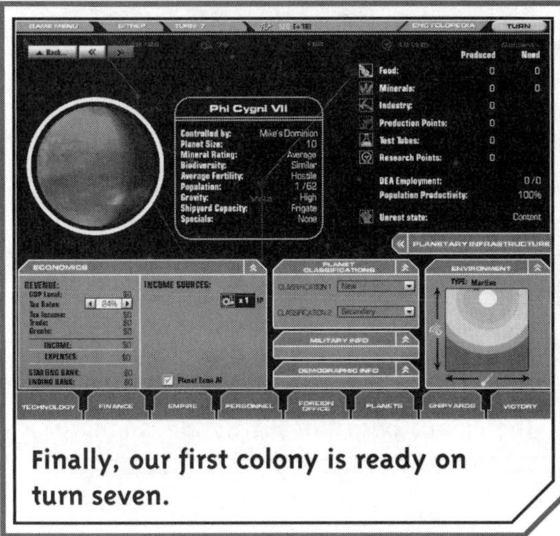

Finally, our first colony is ready on turn seven.

Taking Command

How to fix our homeworld's condition? First, we click on the Infrastructure screen and examine the regions one by one. Every region is full, and most of them with mines. Only one Bioharvesting DEA producing food exists—a serious mistake for a growing population. That'll teach us to trust our viceroys.

Events are part of the natural scheme of things. Deal with them when they come up or they can jeopardize your grand plans.

With our population cut in half, we build a second Bioharvesting DEA in the most fertile region. Accelerating economic growth to near 100 percent, we build the DEA in four turns. Our people go from starving to 18 units of food, more than nine times what

Our planetary viceroy steered us wrong. We had to correct our starvation problem by building a Bioharvesting DEA.

they need to survive. There shouldn't be any more worries about food shortages for a while. We'll fix our mineral situation by cultivating other worlds rich in ore.

Further exploration is crucial when you have a wormhole that can take you away from the congested inner galaxy. Fortune favors us with a second wormhole in the Poquannuc system. We have no military yet, so we can't guard these portals, but we can use the portals to conquer more new, ripe worlds.

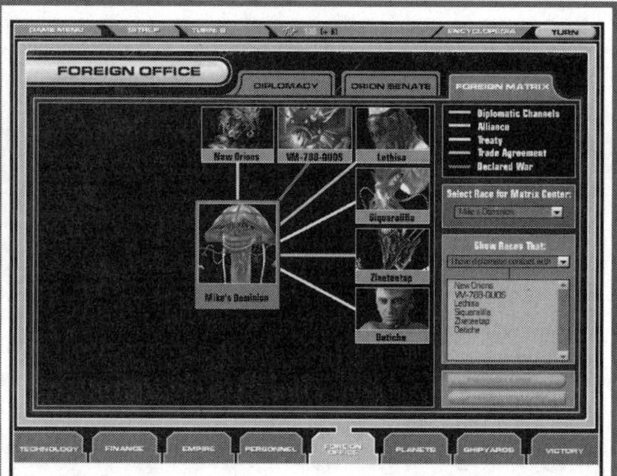

The door of opportunity is thrust open with our continued strides in diplomatic relations and the discovery of a second wormhole.

Our immediate safety relies on Diplomacy. Our next step is to convert the three friendly races to full alliances. Any race we meet on the other side of the wormholes can help if we bring them over to our side. With so many allies, we can interpose an ally's forces if they launch an attack. Of course, losing their military will anger our allies and they'll exact vengeance on the enemy without us lifting a tentacle. By keeping our allies content, we stay protected.

Playing the Eoladi

Like their Etherean brethren, the Imsaeis, the Eoladi are a peace-loving people in tune with nature. Given time, they can cultivate a garden out of a desert; they don't have the time in this galaxy, though. When taking them out for an excursion, don't worry about food and concentrate on minerals to keep your weakened industry running smoothly.

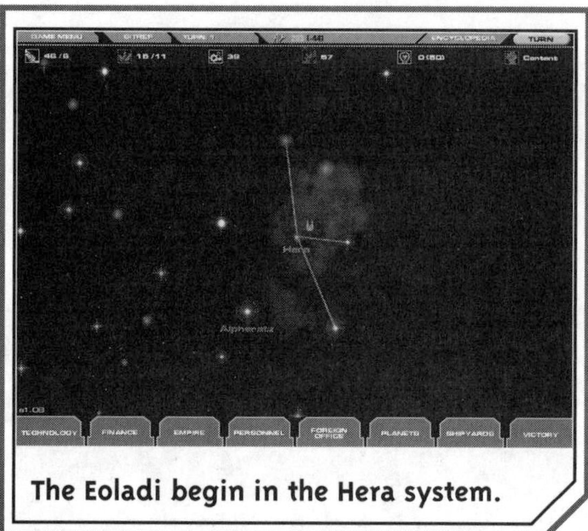

The Eoladi begin in the Hera system.

Your Homeworld

Our starting position is promising. One other race shows up on our galactic map, though when we check our Diplomacy screen later, there are actually two . . . and one of them isn't friendly. Even so, we have room to expand away from those empires, and if we don't bump into an enemy above us, we will have plenty of planets to subjugate.

The Hera system gives us a head start on our competition. Hera II and Hera IV contain rich minerals, and they're in the green, which means we can inhabit them without stiff

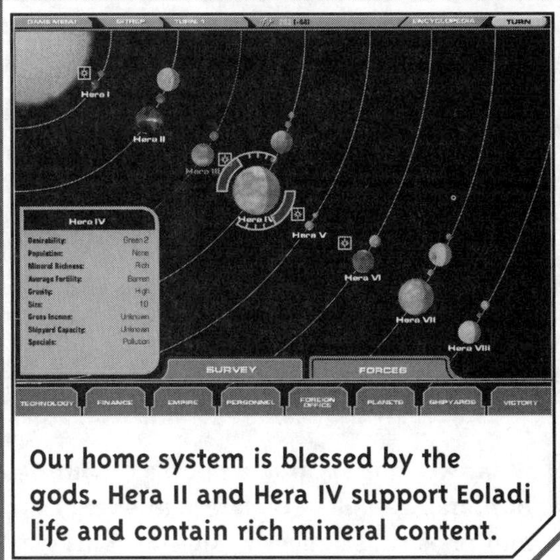

Our home system is blessed by the gods. Hera II and Hera IV support Eoladi life and contain rich mineral content.

penalties to our ecosystem. Because the Eoladi are excellent "farmers," we don't have to worry about food. However, getting minerals for our factories will cause problems. Where our surplus food situation is 40, our "surplus" minerals sit at 4. The sooner we gain a miner world or three, the better.

Check the Finance Menu to see that our income and expenses don't balance. They don't have to be a match, but you want to get off to a good start. Currently, we're spending 44 AUs more than we have. We can't afford to spend 192 AUs on planetary grants now. We can when we have more treasury built up. For now, we want to keep things on an even keel so we know what, if anything, causes problems in the turns to come.

Everyone else goes for military, political, and scientific spies first. Our espionage program recruits economic spies in the initial wave. We will embrace the traditional route later. Now, though, we're doing something different to throw off our opponents. They won't expect those types of saboteurs at their gates.

We have a hidden evil in our sector. The Ithkuls don't show up on our galactic map, but they do at the Diplomacy screen.

The Diplomacy screen throws us a curve. The Ithkuls are nearby. Bloodthirsty as they are, that's a serious threat that is hidden from our scouts. We couldn't ask for two tougher potential enemies than the Ithkul and Cynoid races. Following the Diplomacy manual, we offer non-aggression pacts to both in the hopes of slowing their hostilities.

Galactic Expansion

The Cynoids reject our non-aggression pact. We'll keep trying to make nice.

With two military powerhouses on our borders, we must accelerate in energy and physical sciences to support our military program.

Our first few efforts toward expansion haven't met with success. Other than the Hera worlds, nothing else met our needs. Persistence is a necessity in this game, so we press on.

Meanwhile, the Cynoids reject our peace proposal. The Cynoid diplomat politely declines, so they aren't out for blood. They don't want to be aligned with the Ithkul. We can't respect that, but we have to live with it.

Under the Technology section, we spend 40 percent on energy, 40 percent on physical sciences, and 20 percent on economics. The two potential military threats, the Ithkuls and the Cynoids, force us to spend in the military schools. If a war erupts, technological superiority might be the only thing that saves our butts. In other words, we want to outfit our warships with a mauler before they do.

Economics is a good partner to balance the military disciplines. With a poor Manufacturing skill, we'll need help with our economy, and advances like the automated mine and fiscal ubiquity will push us along.

On turn four, our first colony ship reaches Hera IV. Hopefully, the new economy will quickly pick up. Also on turn four, a new Nommo leader, Eleeil, joins us and claims to be a sweet-talker. If he can convince the Cynoids and Ithkuls to ally with us, he's hired for life.

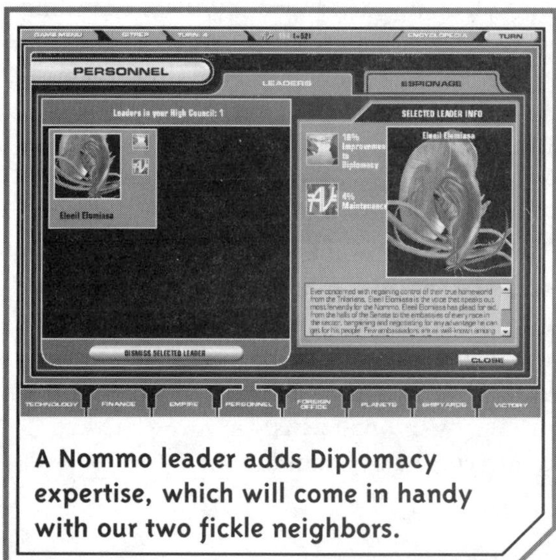

A Nommo leader adds Diplomacy expertise, which will come in handy with our two fickle neighbors.

Our scouts have an Ithkul sighting! While exploring the Pattaquonk system, we find space lanes to the Ithkul homeworld on Rigil-B. We want no part of those space lanes; however, it's good to know where they are. If an attack comes, we'll be prepared. Our first dozen defensive ships will head toward the Xioloti system. Conveniently, it serves as a "choke point" to defend against both the Cynoids and the Ithkuls. If we can bottle that system, we not only defend our territories, but we also force the Cynoids and the Ithkuls into each other if they want to navigate. Fighting between those two powers would not displease us.

Bingo! We find the Ithkul homeworld.

On turn five, the Ithkuls declare war. We have four spies ready to infiltrate, and we'll put four more in the pipeline. Even without a military ship ready for service, we can strike at our enemies with a hidden threat.

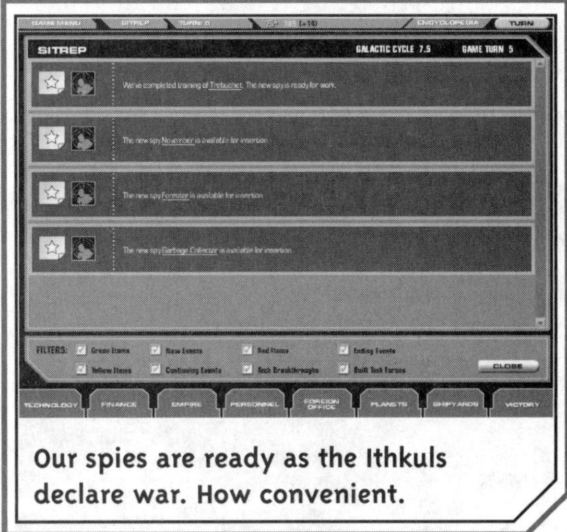

Our spies are ready as the Ithkuls declare war. How convenient.

Taking Command

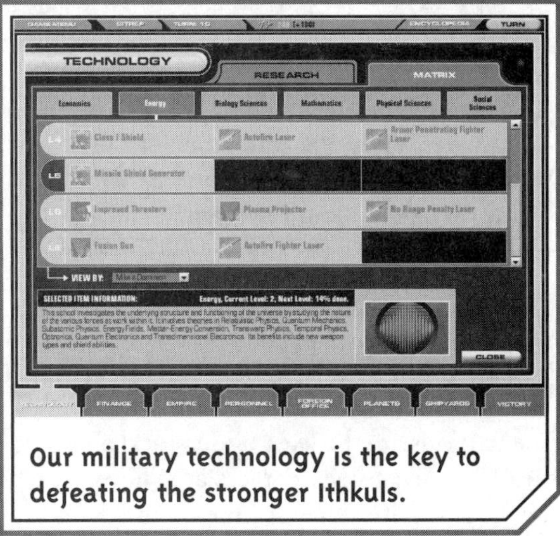

Our military technology is the key to defeating the stronger Ithkuls.

All our efforts focus on the Xioloti system. We want to set up there within a dozen turns. Exploring the system, we find the perfect military base in Xioloti I. It weighs in as a size 11 world, or 22 regions that we can fill with many ship-building advances and military

DEAs. From there, we can churn out giant ships and pack the system with fleets.

As early as turn 11, we send a fleet to safeguard the Xioloti system. We increase our homeworld's military spending to 50 percent and push our military-political policy to limited war. The Eoladi don't start as military favorites. That doesn't mean, though, that we can't beat the odds.

Until we defeat the Ithkuls, every task force we build from here on out will end up in the Xioloti system.

Playing the Silicoid

The Silicoids are the least understood aliens in the Orion Senate. Many races aren't even sure they're alive, since they seem to be made of inorganic crystal. Because they are so different, you'll have to adjust your thinking to play the Silicoids. They have no use for Bioharvesting. Instead, they eat minerals, so your Mining skill serves as both food production and economic profit. Don't count on your poor Diplomacy to get you out of any jams—nobody's going to help you but yourself.

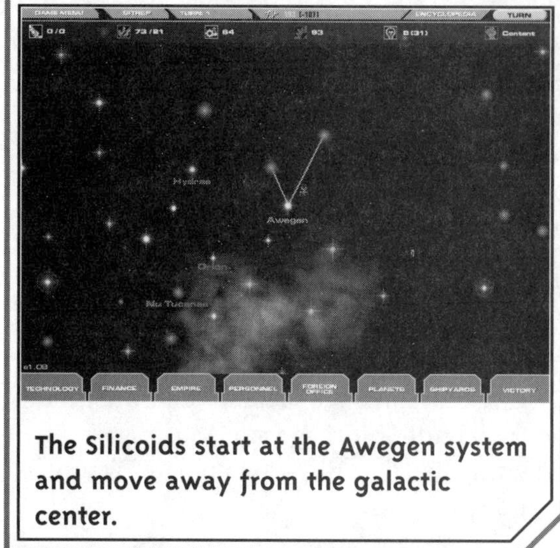

The Silicoids start at the Awegen system and move away from the galactic center.

Your Homeworld

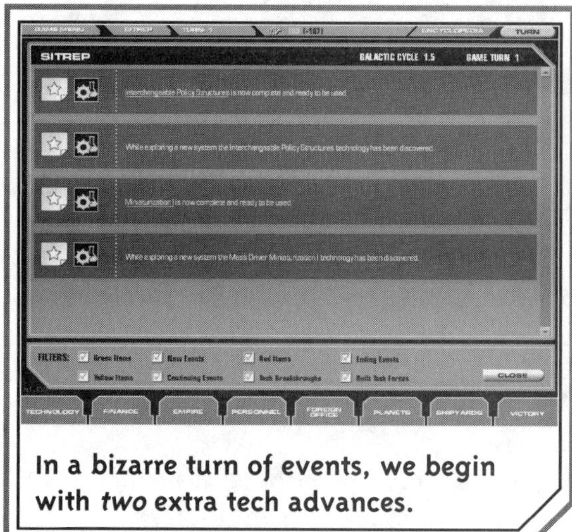

In a bizarre turn of events, we begin with *two* extra tech advances.

"Mine all mine," that's our slogan. We want to find and colonize as many rich or very rich mineral planets as we can. We don't need farms, so we'll build Mining DEAs for food and resources. We have the advantage of taking worlds that *only* have alluring mineral contents. Most races have to find planets that are high in both minerals and soil fertility.

We're blessed because we don't need the same nourishment as everyone else.

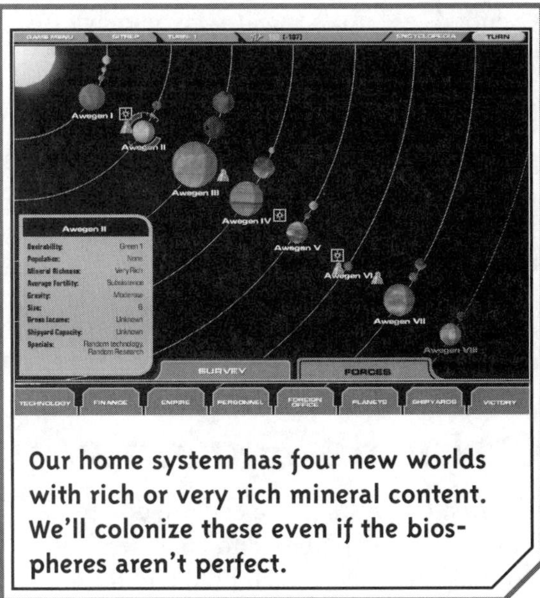

Our home system has four new worlds with rich or very rich mineral content. We'll colonize these even if the biospheres aren't perfect.

Our home system couldn't be better. Besides our homeworld on Awegen VIII, there are four other planets with rich or very rich minerals. Granted, most of these aren't in the green—actually only one of the worlds can support Silicoid life immediately—so it'll take some terraforming and economic development to swing the planets into line. The system's so ripe, we could exist only here and get along fine.

We won't stay in our home system, though. We want to see if we can find mineral-rich worlds in the green. While we're out and about, we meet up with the Grendarls and the Evons. The Grendarls fight well, and the Evons can pick you apart with espionage. We offer an economic partnership to both, more to find out where the races' loyalties lie than to make extra money.

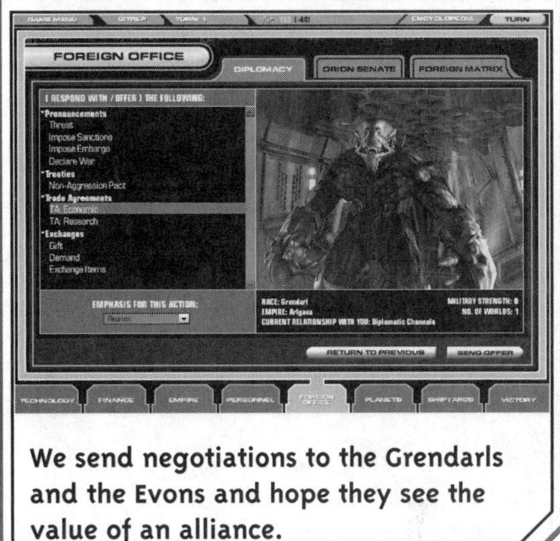

We send negotiations to the Grendarls and the Evons and hope they see the value of an alliance.

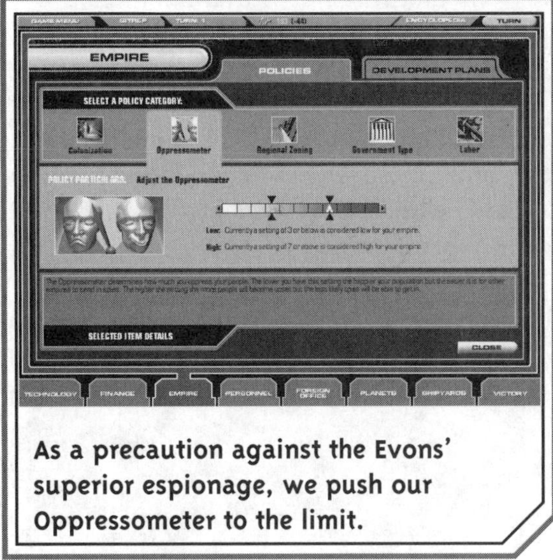

As a precaution against the Evons' superior espionage, we push our Oppressometer to the limit.

We don't outright trust the Evon. Under the Empire menu, we turn our Oppressometer up to maximum. If spies head our way, our new level of government security will catch them on our borders. At the least, we want to minimize the possible damage.

To take advantage of our Mining skill, we build another Mining DEA and an industry DEA on our homeworld's surface.

Still on turn one, we examine our homeworld's economy. Under planetary infrastructure, we notice that one of our regions doesn't have a plan yet for construction. We change that and indicate that another Mining DEA and industry DEAs should be built. Our world has become a giant mineral farm.

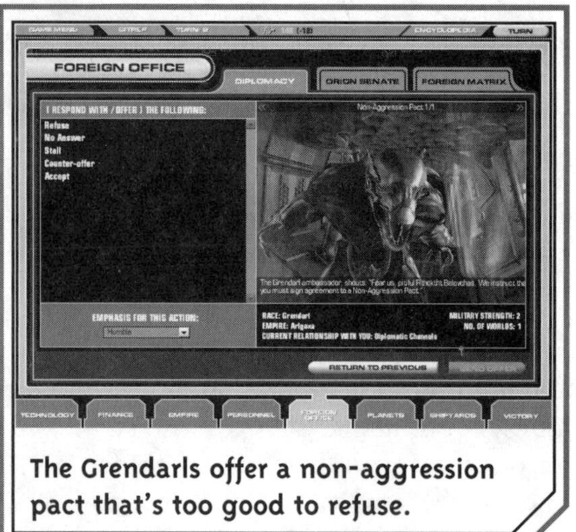

The Grendarls offer a non-aggression pact that's too good to refuse.

On turn two, the Grendarls come back with a non-aggression pact. It sounds great to us. Now we know, for the time being, the Grendarls are not a threat. Maybe they can become a full-fledged ally soon. No word from the Evons yet.

Over in the Orion Senate, the Evons propose diplomatic isolation against a race we haven't encountered. We immediately second the proposal so it goes through. Hopefully, this will solidify the Evons' hostility against this unknown race, keeping them away from us, and maybe earn us sympathy points with our neighbor.

Galactic Expansion

The first two systems we explore don't have enough mining potential to consider stopping long. They each hold a rich mineral world on an inhospitable world. With so many ripe home system worlds, we can afford to be picky.

A sudden splinter colony in the Zugamog system adds an extra world to our empire. It has a poor rating in mineral content but, because it was a freebie, we'll see if we can work with it.

On turn 10, an Evon fleet passes ours in the Zugamog system. They want to colonize in this system, too. We see no reason why we can't peacefully coexist, and let them plunk down on Zugamog III.

Over in the Fomalhaut system, we finally nab a very rich mineral planet. It's laced with ancient battle damage, which will seriously slow down the planet's development, but we're willing to try. In the Rhea system, another splinter colony opens for us. It has poor minerals and might be a liability in the long run. We'll hold on to it for now and see what happens.

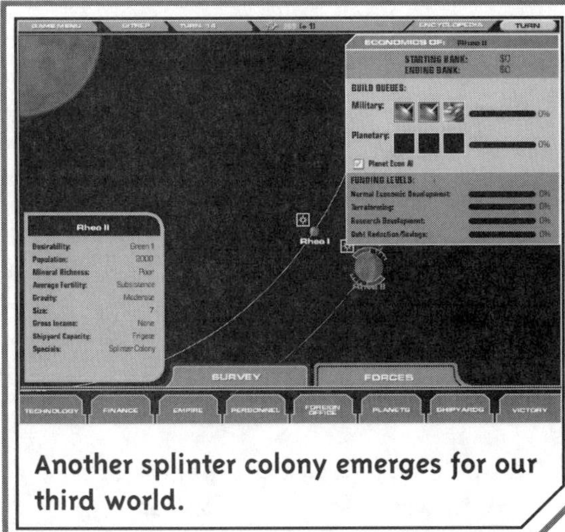

Another splinter colony emerges for our third world.

On turn 15, the Cynoids send a scout into our home system. We can't let it get away and reveal all our trade secrets; our system ships destroy it before it completes a single orbit around our homeworld. A Tachidi leader shows up, helping out in Research and espionage. It's time to make a change. We dismiss our first leader, who was starting to have a profound negative effect on unrest.

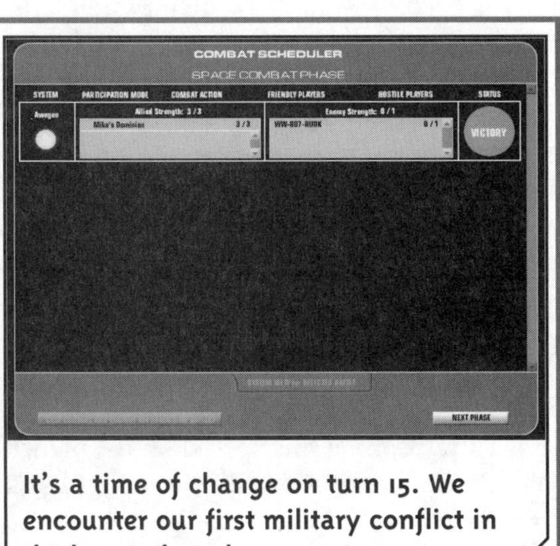

It's a time of change on turn 15. We encounter our first military conflict in the heart of our home system.

With the Cynoids angered, we need to plan our next step carefully. We don't want to go into heavy military. Instead, we'll try a balanced approach—a little bit of Research, a little bit of military, and a little bit of economy. We won't stop Mining; that will be a constant to drive our economy. Our progress looks steady.

Something does worry us, though. Our government agents captured spies on the border. No harm was done, but does that mean the Evons have changed their minds? Or did the Cynoids have an elaborate battle plan all worked out?

Taking Command

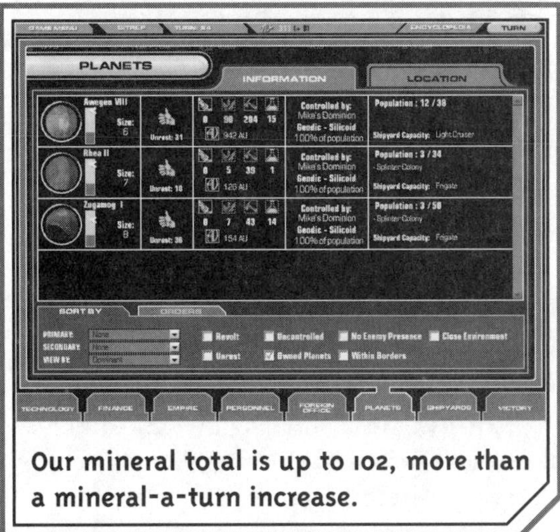

Our mineral total is up to 102, more than a mineral-a-turn increase.

Just comparing the mineral numbers from turn one to turn 24, we can see how far we've come. Our mineral total climbs to 102, up from 73 at the start. As long as we can gain more than a mineral a turn, we'll have the strength to go the distance.

Playing the Klackon

The Klackons have as much going for them as a slug in the desert. They can dig a little dirt and turn that into money. They can beat up on the weak races on the military front. Other than that, you're looking at the king weenies.

The Klackons fall into a sparse section of the galaxy. Only two other alien races surround the Klackons' Komi II.

Your Homeworld

The Klackons hunt for minerals. You have to . . .or else you're working in some other alien race's forced labor camps. If you can land early Mining colonies, you're in the money. Our homeworld, Komi II, has four mines, ample enough to support its industry. However, with the extra region space available, throw another Mining DEA in the mix. The extra profit from that Mining DEA will go to other needs in the empire.

It's not that the Klackons are pathetic in military strength; we're just plain average. We start with the standard three-ship fleet to guard our homeworld. We'll keep that there for security, but we need to expand our empire in other directions.

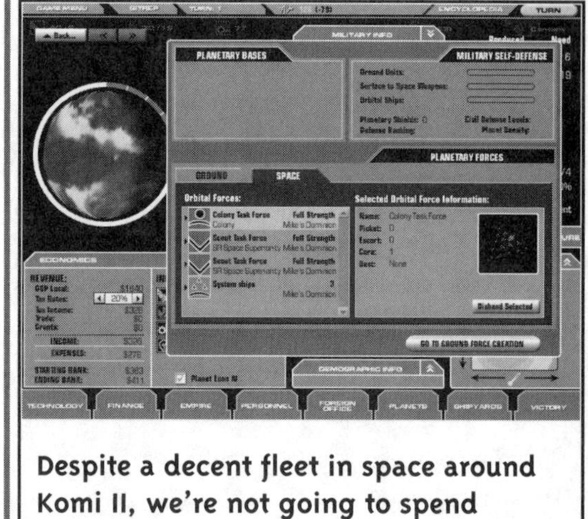

Despite a decent fleet in space around Komi II, we're not going to spend money on military. We need to eat, and to eat we need more food through planetary grants.

On turn four, the Grendarls offer a handshake. Well, they offer to take money off our hands, but they'll return the favor down the road. The economic treaty the Grendarls set up helps both races early on. Even more importantly, this one trade paves the way for stronger negotiations when it counts.

Our ships continue to explore *away* from the other owned stars. The longer we can avoid confrontation, the better. We'll fight only as a last resort.

Galactic Expansion

We have a decision in our first system. We find a stratosphere ring special on the planet Jabo IV. It increases your Bioharvesting DEA by +.75 and pumps up recreation by 15 percent. Jabo IV also hides a Sakkra labor

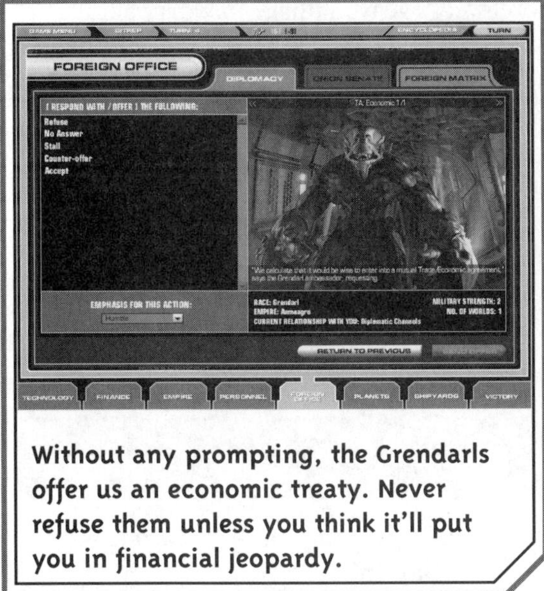

Without any prompting, the Grendarls offer us an economic treaty. Never refuse them unless you think it'll put you in financial jeopardy.

Hydroponic farms help with our ever-growing food supply needs.

The Eoladi attack us as our fleets pass in the Tegmen system.

camp. If we colonize, we get a boost to our Bioharvesting and more workers for our empire's industry push. Unfortunately, Jabo IV is a yellow world, so we'd have to sink money into terraforming to make it all worthwhile. We'll hold off for now, and come back to it if nothing better surfaces.

On turn six, we discover the Mirza system and a Trilarian warship. We give the order to shoot only if fired upon. The Trilarians are equally cautious and don't pose a threat at this time.

In Research, we split up our percentages. Economics gets 20 percent to help with the economy, mathematics nabs 20 percent as well in the hopes of reaching some of the higher advances, energy and physical sciences both score 15 percent to develop offensive potential. Social sciences is the only school not to get funds, while biological sciences absorb the most, with 30 percent going to helping our Bioharvesting weaknesses. In particular, the first advance, hydroponic farms, can help stimulate our planting and harvesting.

When we branch out into the Tegmen system, the Eoladi attack. It's a one-on-one, old-style dogfight, and we come out on top. Fortunately, this is only a scout vessel for the Eoladi, and their empire isn't anywhere close by. We won't have trouble from them for several turns at least, and we'll be preparing for them the whole time.

On turn nine, enemy spies blow up our government building on Komi II. Most likely it's the Eoladi, striking back for retaliation against their downed fleet. Regardless, we have to do something about it before it gets worse.

The Oppressometer's the answer. We click it up three notches to the maximum accepted oppression range for our race. We also immediately reduce the taxes from 22 percent to 19 percent, anticipating the public backlash that will occur with a sudden jump in government control. Even at 19 percent, the taxes are still above average.

Taking Command

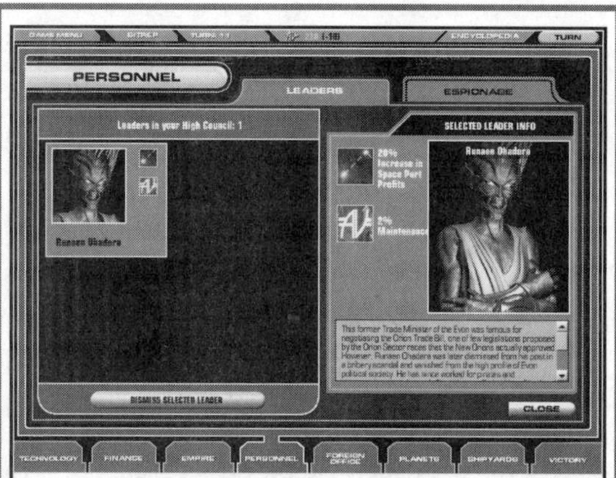

An Evon leader wants to join our cause, but we have to cut him loose. He only increases space port profits, and since we have none and won't for a while, we don't want to pay his two percent maintenance fee.

Our new crackdown tactics work. Government agents catch a few spies and begin an interrogation to reveal who sent them. The interrogation doesn't reveal much, but the attacks stop. We spent a little bit of effort on the Oppressometer, so let's not waste it. From here on out, we'll keep it at the top level—we won't have to worry about spies and just have to pay off the citizens.

Our anti-espionage task force catches the enemy spies.

Our next explored system, Draconis, looks similar to our homeworld and packs more diamonds. We set our colony ships to charge here. If all goes well, the Draconis system and several others untouched by other alien powers will be ours without a struggle.

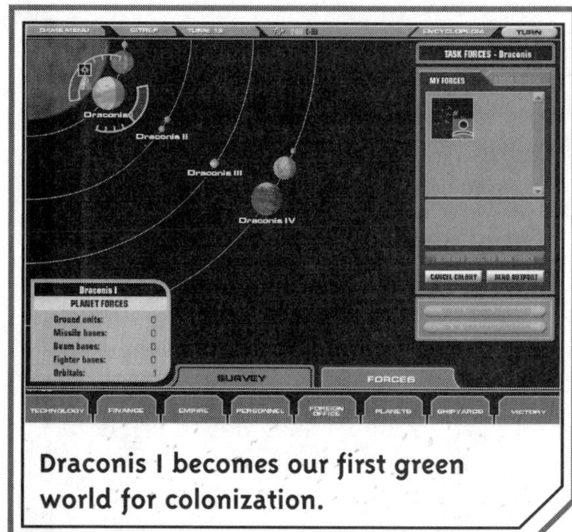

Draconis I becomes our first green world for colonization.

Of course, that's all wishful thinking. We're attacked on the next turn by two different races. One doesn't count—the Silicoids would attack us if they could, but they only have an abandoned colony here. Knowing that the Silicoids love minerals, odds are there's a ripe Mining world in the vicinity.

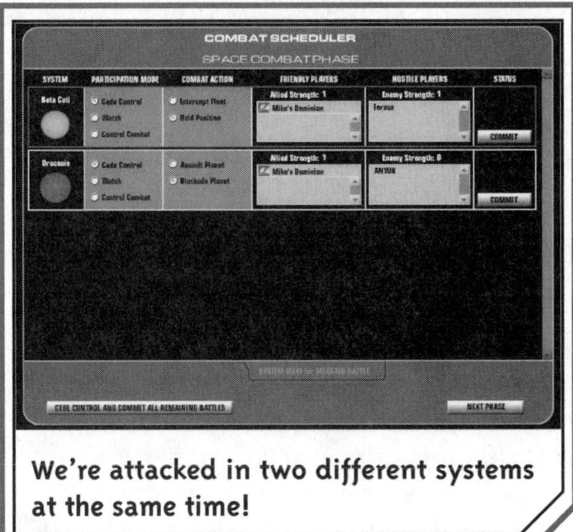

We're attacked in two different systems at the same time!

At this juncture or soon thereafter, we have to attack the Silicoids. They eat minerals for food, so they want all the mineral-rich planets in the area as snacks. We want them as resources. We could try to coexist, but our plans would be eating into each other. Best to get close and then strike at the Silicoids' most vulnerable colonies. So much the better if we figure out where their homeworld lies.

Surprisingly, we come out of this little arena the gladiator champion—and without having to cut other aliens to ribbons. If we can muscle out the local Silicoid competition and absorb their planets and resources, we won't be the laughingstock of the Orion Senate anymore. You know what they say about he who laughs last . . . .

A search for the local mineral-heavy worlds gives us a blueprint for where to go for the most wealth.

Playing the Tachidi

The imposing Tachidi aren't powerhouses. Actually, the big guys stand about average in military fortitude. They can bore holes in the earth and uncover priceless gems, but they

Tsukiyomi V rests in a quiet section of the universe—the Tachidi are the only occupants so far.

don't know how to pick up a hoe. Slightly better than their Insectoid brethren, the Klackon, the Tachidi still need assistance to control the galaxy.

Your Homeworld

Planetary grants and military are the only things we'll spend extra money on this time around.

Our game plan will be military. Being in a position where there are no alien powers within hailing distance, we can tend to our economy and stack up our fleets. Under Finance, we change the imperial sliders to reflect this new policy.

The Tsukiyomi system is one of the best you'll find. There are five planets, including our homeworld, that are green or in the sweet spot for Tachidi. Many of them have positive specials, and they're all rich or in minerals. It's the perfect setup for the Tachidi, who excel in Mining. Given time, we'll have the most profitable system of any alien power on the map.

On turn two, unrest creeps in. Our Imperial taxes are set too high, so we drop them down two points to calm everyone down. While we're on the Planets screen, we

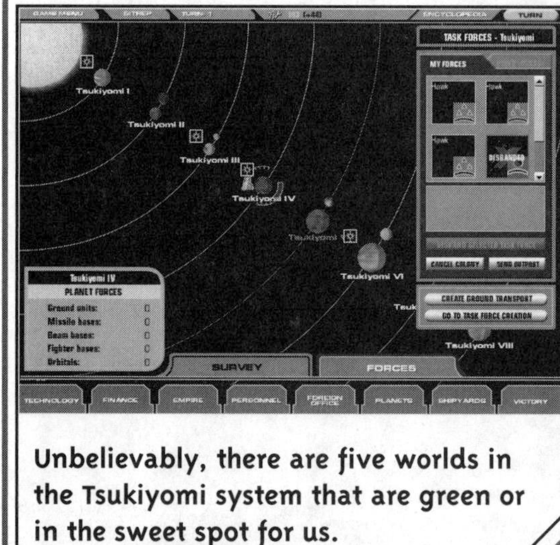

Unbelievably, there are five worlds in the Tsukiyomi system that are green or in the sweet spot for us.

tweak the numbers—economic development to 40 percent and Research to 6 percent. It starts out slowly and builds. We don't want to stockpile military units, we don't do so before the economic infrastructure is in place.

Under Research, we give 50 percent to energy and 50 percent to physical sciences. We'll need all the fleet and ground forces improvements as we climb the tech tree. If we keep Research flowing and our military production high, our offense will be formidable.

Galactic Expansion

Following the standard expansion blueprint, we send out scouts in opposite directions. The first one discovers the Kannghsaws system and a single world capable of supporting Tachidi life. Nothing special, so we leave the scout parked there and wait to see what our other scout brings.

The second scout does better. The Tarcuta system contains a planet with average minerals and barren fertility, but a random Research special. Not enough to get excited about. The true beauty of the system, however, is a wormhole across the galaxy to the Rigil-B system. Because the Tarcuta system has a wormhole and fans out to access three other systems, we label this system a chokepoint. Load as many fleets into this system as possible to safeguard the Tachidi border.

Our second scout finds a wormhole.

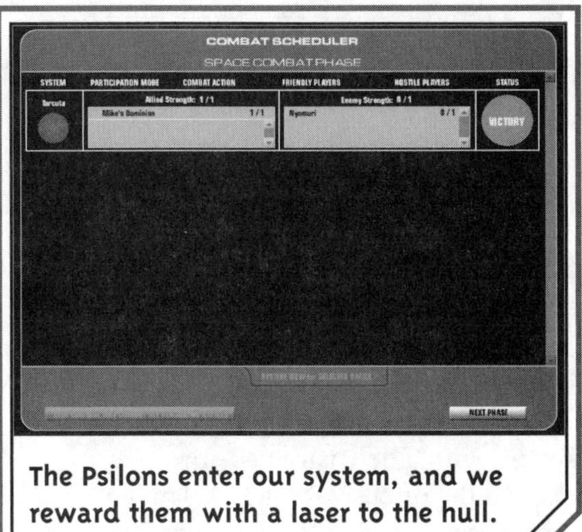

The Psilons enter our system, and we reward them with a laser to the hull.

The following turn, the Psilons enter the Tarcuta system. We could play nice and strike up a relationship with our new alien friends; unfortunately, they chose to park their ship in our newest choke point, so they've gotta go. We attack one to one and beat them. Maybe this will send a message not to mess with us.

On turn seven, our first colony springs up. There will be more as we colonize our home system from planet to planet. We'll let the planetary viceroy handle the new world, but we need to increase military production on our homeworld. Balancing economics and military, we pump 26 percent into each. In a few turns, we'll have another colony ship, followed by a second colony ship and a scout. The scout will be our last recon ship for a while; next, we switch to attack warships.

Our expeditions have been successful, and we keep racking up colony worlds. Counting the two on the far side of the wormhole we've just discovered and the four in our home system, our colony potential has reached six. We keep building colony ships, and our three current worlds are producing a surplus of minerals.

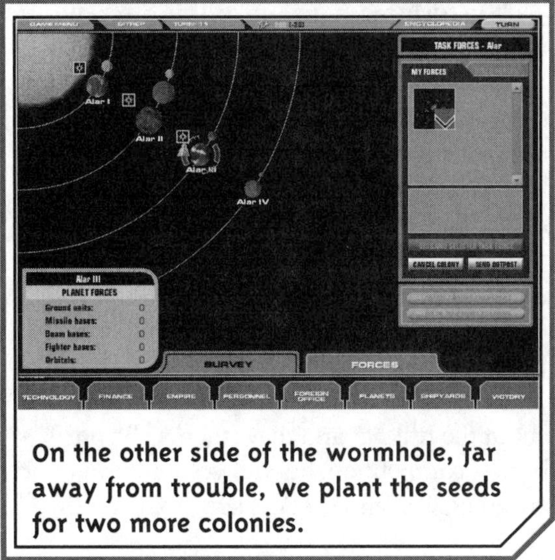

On the other side of the wormhole, far away from trouble, we plant the seeds for two more colonies.

On turn 11, we increase military spending. Check back at the planet level every few turns, at least in the beginning, to see if you're spending as much as you safely can.

This time we notch up military to 47 percent and economic development to 26 percent. The wheels are in motion for an assembly line of ships.

As military production increases, we can afford our first combat task force.

On turn 16, we finance our first serious task force. Instead of recon, we opt for long-range attack. We choose a squadron, which has two eagle mission ships in the core and one perimeter scout ship. Equipped with our best laser weapons, this squadron will hit the enemy before they launch a serious counterattack.

When we send our long-range task force out to the Tarcuta chokepoint, we notice a new neighbor. The Psilons were there, and now the Ithkul have started colonizing around the wormhole. Normally, you should be worried about the Ithkuls, and they still may be our biggest competition, but our colonization efforts are going well and the AUs keep rolling in.

Taking Command

By turn 23, we have eight worlds under our belt. Some of these came from splinter colonies and will take more time than the

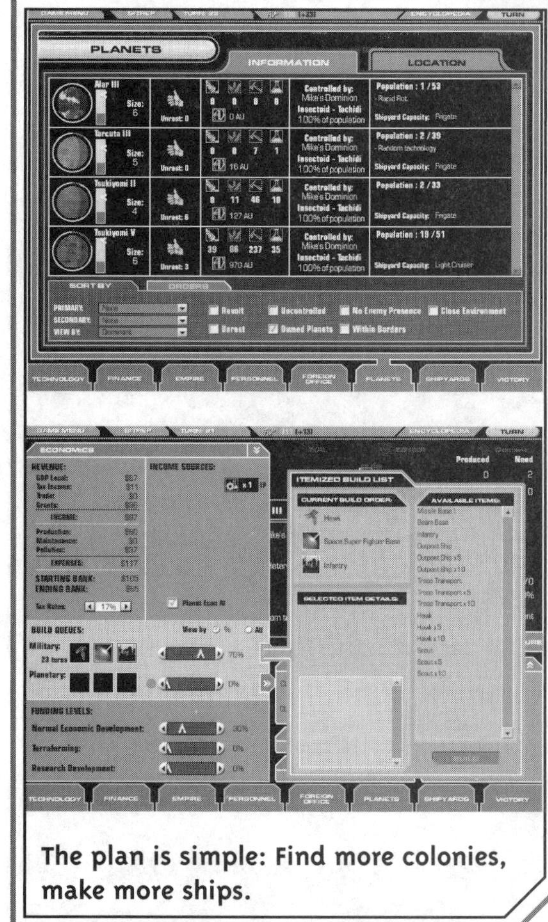

The plan is simple: Find more colonies, make more ships.

others to build. Most came from hard work building colony ships and sending them to green worlds. We might run into a bottleneck if we get surrounded by other races; for now, we want to expand slowly and back up each system with a defensive task force.

On the offensive front, we launch two long-range task forces into enemy space. We have more in orbit around our homeworld to reinforce the Tarcuta choke point. The two we send out against the Ithkuls are to test the waters and see if the new kids on the block can tread water in our war games.

The Ithkuls, tough as they are, don't stand a chance. We have better weaponry, nine ships to their five, and more coming.

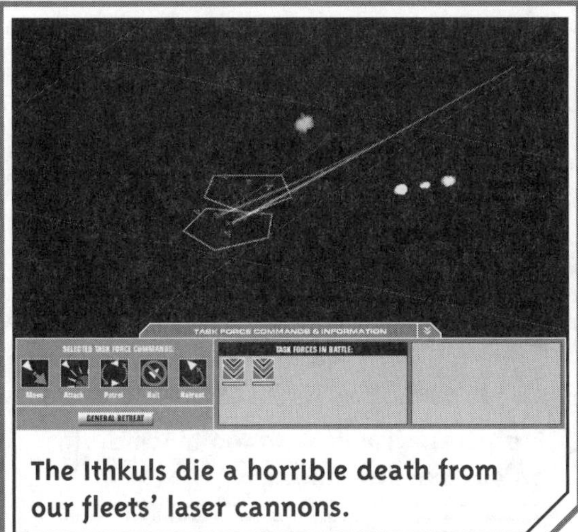

The Ithkuls die a horrible death from our fleets' laser cannons.

The Ithkuls start near the center of the galaxy in the home system of Knaa.

The first melee blows up three ships, and the second eliminates the remaining two before we lay siege to their homeworld. As we bombard the Harvesters, there's a grim satisfaction that the most powerful military race has been ground beneath our heels. If the Ithkuls fall so easily, can any other race hope to stand in our way?

Playing the Ithkul

You're on a mission of hate. No one likes you, and you would rather rip a race's throat out than serve it hors d'oeuvres. Even if you wanted to, you're not supplied with the tools to play with others nicely. Your Trade and Diplomacy scores are poor. On the flip side, your race is built to survive alone and has plenty of scores to succeed, like the superior Bioharvesting and Manufacturing.

Your Homeworld

With a severe handicap in Diplomacy, we start out in a tough spot near the center part of the galaxy. Usually that means a race or two will begin on top of us, and that could be touchy. We'll have to see what our neighbors have to say.

Starting with the leftmost menu, we'll set up our Technology first. With a military society like the Ithkul, choose the energy and physical sciences schools. Crank those babies up to 35 percent each so we develop weapon, armor, shields, and ships at a good clip. To team up with the military schools, we'll go with economics. Ithkuls are weak in Mining, and we don't want our production to slide. Economics can help us overcome some of our financial difficulties, considering that the rest of the races don't enjoy our company and we may be cut off early.

Next, we have two neighbors to deal with. The Nommo, have imposed economic sanctions on us. No trading in that direction. We'll make a deal with our other neighbors, the Raas, to see if we can mutually benefit with some economic trade. Even if everyone

We haven't made any action and already one of our neighbors, the Nommo, have imposed economic sanctions on us.

hates you, you need to talk with your alien friends each turn to prevent diplomatic tensions from getting out of hand.

Let's take a look at our homeworld, Knaa VII. Our viceroy would do a fine job, but he's decided to overspend on military (it's in the red). Much as we want to build a giant space armada on turn one, it's not happening. Rather than waste all that money pushing through military, we'll keep spending in the yellow—still twice as expensive as green spending, but we need help early on if our neighbors don't want to lend a hand. We'll increase economic development to help things run smoothly in the future.

A few turns later, we start to see the holes in our homeworld structure. We have no problems with Bioharvesting and are making decent money. However, we're short on Mining DEAs—the current ones just can't keep up with Manufacturing and it's costing us money. We'll have to build a couple more to balance out the deficiency. The production woes and our citizens' growing concern with our political future contribute to a rising unrest problem. We click down the tax rate by

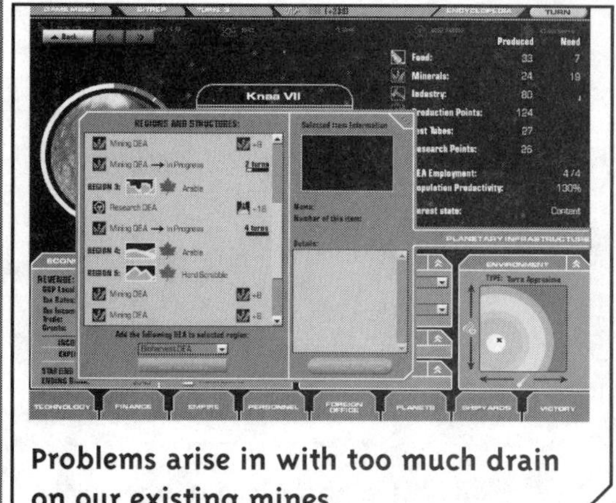

Problems arise in with too much drain on our existing mines.

two percent, from 20 percent to 18 percent. This reduction puts money in the citizens' pockets and makes them happy again.

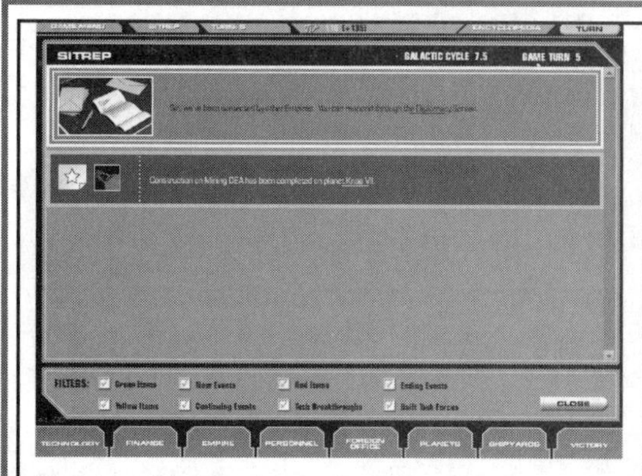

For every up, there's a down. We increase our Mining capacity, but our "friendly" neighbors reject our efforts at economic trade.

Good news arrives in the form of new mines on Knaa VII. These will increase our production and allow us to make more AUs through our superior Manufacturing. If we colonize more worlds and absorb those minerals, we'll be an economic dynamo.

On the other hand, the Raas reject our trade offer. They aren't fond of us, so we

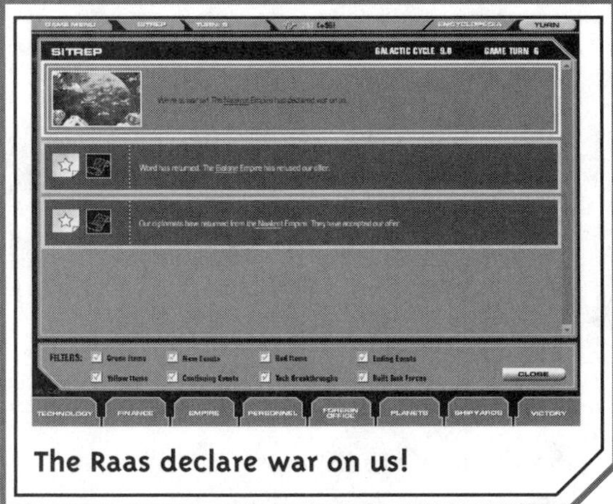
The Raas declare war on us!

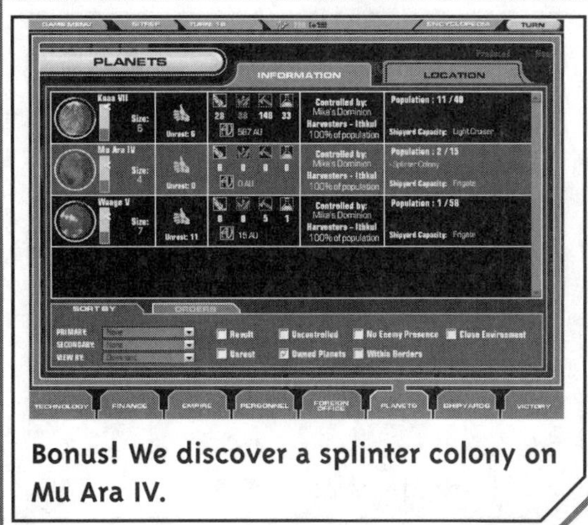
Bonus! We discover a splinter colony on Mu Ara IV.

might go solo soon.

Turn eight brings the inevitable news . . . one of our enemies has declared war on us. We would have expected the Nommo—remember, they imposed economic sanctions on us before we could say hi—instead, it's the Raas. We were hoping for a better relationship with them. It's time to set up our defenses.

Galactic Expansion

On turn nine, we finally find a world to colonize. It's the fifth planet in the Waage system. Nothing special about it, except that it's green 2, which means we don't have to do much terraforming to get it up and running quickly. We may need these extra resources soon if we starting fighting it out with the Raas.

Our universe is now defined for us. We may be able to get along with the Nommo. We'll set a scout in that direction to slip through and explore farther. Otherwise, we're expanding from the Waage system. We know another world will develop there, and we haven't met any nasty neighbors in that quadrant. No expedition will head toward the Raas; it'd just get shot down.

Our next explored system is a blessing. We discover an instant colony on Mu Ara IV, bringing our total up to three. If we cultivate these resources properly, we should outrace our slower-developing neighbors.

Our peaceful scout fleet arrives in the Nommo system of Chondote and promptly gets blasted to scrap metal. The next turn, they declare war on us—so there goes that expansion avenue without military support. Fortunately, the Nommo are combat wimps and won't pose a threat if we keep our military in scale with theirs.

Taking Command

Our first break comes in the form of an Eoladi leader. Aenuniee increases our tax revenue by 10 percent—a nice help. Who cares if he cuts trade incomes by five percent? No one trades with us anyway.

On turn 20, we switch our military into overdrive. We notch up the spending to 15 percent and give it a big boost through the imperial economic sliders. The imperial sliders also supply large grants to our planets so we can beat the Mining deficiency we still have.

Our first task force becomes an eagle long-range attack force. We'll send this toward the closest defensive chokepoint, the Lerion system,

Will our first break lead us to victory? A new leader joins our side.

The Humans aren't happy we blew up their ship.

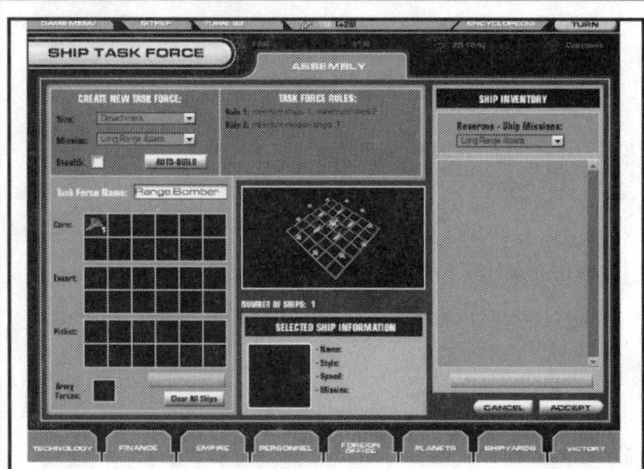

It's time to kick our military into high gear and put together task forces.

because it's near both the Nommo and the Raas. When we're ready, we can launch an attack against the Nommo from there.

Out of nowhere, the Humans send a stealth scout into our home system. We don't need that kind of surprise, so we unload with our three system ships protecting the homeworld. Needless to say, diplomatic discussions don't go well the following turn.

Despite the threats and diplomatic bashings from our alien neighbors, our early position is strong. We have defensive ships set all over the perimeter. With our superior combat strength and growing advances in energy and physical sciences, our military will be powerful.

The first phase of the Ithkul empire looks good. We have military command of the sector and technology excels at a rapid pace.

As we prepare to take control of the galaxy, we want to colonize a few more planets and stabilize our economies. At the same time, our fleets continue to fill our two key choke points near our homeworld and below Waage. In about 10 turns, we'll send a few fleets and hammer the Nommo homeworld. From there, the entire galaxy opens!